Presidential Power in Fifth Republic France

Presidential Power in Fifth Republic France

David S. Bell

Oxford • New York

First published in 2000 by
Berg
Editorial offices:
150 Cowley Road, Oxford, OX4 1JJ, UK
838 Broadway, Third Floor, New York, NY 10003-4812, USA

Berg is an imprint of Oxford International Publishers Ltd.

Library of Congress Cataloging-in-Publication Data
A catalogue record for this book is available from the Library of Congress.

British Library Cataloguing-in-Publication Data
A catalogue record for this book is available from the British Library.

ISBN 1 85973 371 9 (Cloth)
1 85973 376 X (Paper)

Typeset by JS Typesetting, Wellingborough, Northants
Printed and bound in Great Britain by Biddles Ltd,
www.biddles.co.uk

For Demeter

Contents

Abbreviations and French Political Groups

CAP	– Common Agricultural Policy
CD	– Centre démocrate (1966–74)
CDP	– Centre démocrate et progrès (1969–76)
CDS	– Centre des démocrates sociaux (1974–95)
CERES	– Centre d'Etudes, de Recherches et d'Education Socialistes
CFDT	– Confédération Française Democratique du Travail (Union confederation)
CGT	– Confédération général du travail (Communist run unions)
CIR	– Convention des institutions républicaines
CNCL	– Commission Nationale de la Communication et des Libertés
CNIP	– Centre national des indépendants et Paysans
CNPF	– Conseil National du Patronat Français
CSG	– cotisation sociale généralisée
DL	– Démocratie libérale
ECSC	– European Coal and Steel Community
EDC	– European Defence Community
EEC	– European Economic Community
EMS	– European Monetary System
EMU	– Economic and Monetary Union
ENA	– Ecole Nationale d'Administration
EU	– European Union
FD	– Force démocrate
FEN	– Fédération de l'Education Nationale
FGDS	– Fédération de la gauche démocrate et Socialiste
FLN	– Front de Libération Nationale (Algerian nationalists)
FN	– Front National (Le Pen's party 1972–)
FNSP	– Fondation nationale des sciences politiques
FO	– Force Ouvrière (Socialist unions)
GATT	– General Agreement on Tariffs and Trade
GDP	– Gross Domestic Product
GDR	– German Democratic Republic
HLM	– Habitation à Loyer modéré
IEP	– Institut d'Etudes Politiques
MDC	– Mouvement des citoyens
MPF	– Mouvement pour la France (de Villiers)

Abbreviations and French Political Groups

MRG – Mouvement des Radicaux de gauche (Left Radicals)
MRP – Mouvement républicain populaire (Christian democrats 1944–66)
NATO – North Atlantic Treaty Organisation
OAS – Organisation armée secrète
OAU – Organisation of African Unity
ORTF – Office de la Radiodiffusion Télévision Française
PCF – Parti communiste français
PDM – Progrès et démocratie moderne
PFLP – Popular Front for the Liberation of Palestine
PR – Parti républicain
PS – Parti socialiste
PSU – Parti socialiste unifié
(FN) RI – (Fédération nationale des) Républicains indépendants
RMI – Revenue minimum d'insertion
RPF – Rassemblement du peuple français (Gaullist Party 1947–55 and the 1999 breakaway from the RPR)
RPR – Rassemblement pour la République ('Neo-gaullist' Party 1976–)
SFIO – Section Française de l'Internationale Ouvrière
SGCI – Secrétariat général du comité interministériel pour les questions de coopération économique
SMIC – Salaire minimum interprofessional de croissance
SNCF – Société nationale des chemins de fer français
UDF – Union pour la démocratie française (Centre parties' alliance 1978–)
UDSR – Union Démocratique et Socialiste de la Résistance
UDR – Union pour la défense de la République (Gaullist Party in June 1968)
UDR – Union des démocrats pour la République (Gaullist Party 1971–6)
UDT – Union démocratique du travail – Left-wing Gaullists joined with UNR for elections in 1962
UDVe – Union des démocrates pour la Ve République (Gaullist Party after January 1968)
UNR – Union pour la nouvelle République (Gaullist Party created in October 1958)
URP – Union des Républicains de Progrès pour le soutien au Président de la République (1973)
USSR – Union of Soviet Socialist Republics
WEU – Western European Union

Preface

Many people have given their advice and have read through part or all of the drafts of this book. I am grateful to them as I am to those politicians and party workers who gave their time to help me with my research. Many politicians generously allowed me their time in giving interviews and that material has been incorporated. I also owe Prof. E. C. Hargrove, Prof. J. Gaffney, Prof. B. D. Graham, Prof Morris, Prof. Colliard and Jean-Marcel, who read drafts, a considerable debt for their help. In addition I must thank the archivists of the OURS and the Institut Charles de Gaulle in Paris, and the librarians of the FNSP and their friendly help in the Salle des dossiers. Our publisher has been unusually patient and without the Nuffield Foundation's support the many visits to archives and to interview people would not have been possible. I owe particular thanks to David Goldey of Lincoln College (Orfèvre dans la matière). The faults and deficiencies are, of course, my own.

D. S. Bell

Introduction

Nothing, observed Machiavelli, is more difficult or dangerous than to initiate a new order of things (Machiavelli 1961, Ch.2). Setting a new order, based on a simple patriotic idea, was de Gaulle's contribution to the Fifth Republic. In one of the many paradoxes of de Gaulle's politics it was not the Constitution, although he focussed on it: the Constitution did not 'fix' the order of things, but the politics set in motion by de Gaulle did. It was the change wrought in the party system that best explains the political system of the Fifth Republic. In that way the Republic became de Gaulle's Republic. It is, therefore, to the foundation of the system and the politics set in motion that attention must first be directed. De Gaulle's work is political but not ephemeral and has constrained subsequent leaders who have all, to some extent, reacted against it (see, for example, A. Duhamel 1991).

When viewed through a political lens, then, Fifth Republic politics have remained de Gaulle's politics. This observation is sometimes taken to mean that contemporary French politics is shaped by the Constitution and the institution of the Presidency, but it can be 'unpacked' to reveal the constraints that de Gaulle imposed on the new Republic. In other words the impetus which de Gaulle gave to the Republic was neither constitutional nor institutional, but primarily political. De Gaulle was a 'political artist', of such power that he gave French political life a momentum which it was easier to adapt to than to turn (S. and I. Hoffmann 1968). In this way the course on which de Gaulle set modern France made the Fifth Republic 'de Gaulle's Republic', in a way which subsequent politicians (by no means minor figures themselves) were forced to recognise. All four succeeding Presidents close to adapt de Gaulle's heritage rather than change it.

If this perception is correct, then de Gaulle's achievement was in certain ways comparable with Mrs Thatcher and Clement Attlee in the United Kingdom or Franklin Roosevelt in the United States or, perhaps, Konrad Adenauer in Germany. That is not through the creation of an 'ism' (for example, 'Thatcherism' or 'Reaganism') but the development of a political outlook with institutional consequences very difficult to counter and supported by a coalition of forces which proved highly durable and subsisted long after the leader's departure. De Gaulle had, intentionally or not, a long political reach. This political reach was extended because of the political stance de Gaulle employed, because the first President set out positions which were very difficult to counter directly. De Gaulle's political ideas, though vague, have had a very long half-life (Bouthillon 1993 and 1994). De Gaulle deployed rhetoric, myth, manoeuvre and manipulation. These are essential, but rare, political talents, which were used by the General to the extent that he was effective as few of his Republican predecessors had been.

Seeing de Gaulle as a 'politician' and asking how he accomplished what he did is a legitimate question although it may appear disrespectful to his acolytes. It involves peering at the underside of the embroidery, which is never aesthetically uplifting. However, there are many studies of the finer side and they do not detract from the approach employed here. None of the politicians discussed need any defence from academics and all are big enough to warrant critical study. In 1958 de Gaulle did, after all, save the Republic from civil war or a military coup and perhaps from both. De Gaulle was a great political figure, but the emphasis here is firmly on the 'political'.

It is the theme of this book that Fifth Republic politics is 'pure politics', that is the building and maintenance of authority and not the exercise of a command relationship. As Richard Neustadt has shown in the American Presidency, politics is the power to persuade backed up by the status of the institution (Neustadt 1964, p.43). 'Do this' and 'do that' are, of course, instructions issued by the Presidents, but the argument here is that it is only possible because of the backing from the political position built up and acquired by the political astuteness of the politicians at the top. In de Gaulle's case he both created the political focus on the Presidency and set the broad policy for the ensuing two decades. Only Franklin Roosevelt could claim as much in a developed society and it bears examination. In the first instance it requires a study of the Constitution to determine the legal background (or lack of it) to the Fifth Republic Presidency and then an analysis of the politics of the Presidency.

There are two parts to the following investigation. In the first part the main lines of the politics of de Gaulle will be examined along with the failures. De Gaulle's Presidency will not be subject to a blow-by-blow analysis, but certain themes will be drawn from the General's years in supreme power to show how they channel subsequent politics. These include a review of the referendum as an illustration of de Gaulle's 'heresthetic' both abilities to manipulate the political world and his determination to use the instrument to establish the new institution at the same time as bolstering his own authority (Riker 1986). There will then be an overview of the Presidential 'reserved sector' of foreign and defence policy and how this was to influence the Republic's policies. There is the chapter on the 'events' of May '68 as an example of the weakness of the Fifth Republic style as exemplified by de Gaulle. These themes will be carried through in the second part with an examination of the four subsequent Presidents of the Republic: Georges Pompidou, Valéry Giscard d'Estaing, François Mitterrand and Jacques Chirac. This section is in chronological order and case by case.

De Gaulle as the 'Solon' of the New Republic

There are numerous biographies of de Gaulle ranging from hagiographies to condemnations. There is no need to rehearse these here, but some points about the political career and approach of the General are worth repeating. In this brief introduction, attention will be drawn to the political background of de Gaulle's Presidency and the establishment of the General's powerful political position. De Gaulle created a political persona (which he, himself, referred to in the third person) and it is that 'ideal' figure, an artefact of a political mind, which had political impact. Without 'de Gaulle' the mythical figure, de Gaulle the politician could not have been so effective. Thus it is worth a detour to look at how de Gaulle of 'Gaullism' came into being and how the myth was used.

Political Artistry

De Gaulle's Sorelean 'pouvoir moteur' was founded on 'l'Appel', his 'call to Resistance' of 18 June 1940. This, accompanied by subtle politics, was the foundation of the persona 'de Gaulle' as well as of the simplifying 'myth' of France. It was this founding call that became the basis for later claims. At the Liberation, de Gaulle's claim to represent the Republic was based on his refusal to capitulate, as were later claims to know where the French interest lay. De Gaulle's vision presented in his books curiously air-brushes out the ideological battles that raged across twentieth-century Europe. This is not just an observation about de Gaulle's subsequent attempt to dissolve the blocs and return to the 'real' Europe of nation-states underneath the 'camouflage' of ideology, but it seems also to hold for the war as well. De Gaulle was, of course, no admirer of the Nazi regime, and the war was an epic struggle, but it was between the 'eternal' nation-states in his view: de Gaulle referred to 'Russia' not to the 'Soviet Union'. In other words, de Gaulle turned marxism – which held that the clashes between nations or ideologies were distractions from the under-lying class struggle – upside down. On the contrary, de Gaulle appears to believe that the class struggle hid the clash between nation-states – the rest were epiphenomena (Aron 1990, Ch. XVI).

However, de Gaulle, in developing this view and by asserting that the Republic had continued (in London) where the Free French were based, both side-stepped old cleavages and the problems posed by collaboration and the Vichy régime (Conan and Russo 1994). In taking this view de Gaulle ignored, or overrode, the factors of division in French society. Hence de Gaulle in a way enabled the French nation to turn its back on the Occupation and forget (to some extent) the divisions and to unite behind a new leadership. De Gaulle's return to power in 1958 was equally ambiguous. Gaullist myth has it that the General predicted, Cassandra-like, the fall of the Fourth Republic; the 1958 coup of that year was thus a vindication (Gaïti 1998). As Gaullist ideas these have been powerful and have been repeated endlessly down to and including the present day, but they are myths. Their significance as ideas is political and not historiographical (though they are real events) and they are part of rhetorical Gaullism's interpretation of events which has proved useful to later politicians.

It was de Gaulle's Resistance record of hyper-patriotism which enabled him to lay claim to the moral high ground ('All my life I have had a certain idea of France . . .') in the unforgettable first page of *Mémoires de Guerre* (de Gaulle 1994). Without having first established himself as a Resistance leader and the incarnation of the 'real' France, undefeated and defiant, the claim (and the first page) would have been ignored or ridiculed. It was an amalgam of patriotism and persona which had an immediate plausibility coming from de Gaulle, an army officer with only a brief participation (in the Reynaud Cabinet) in the politics of competing interests in the bear pit of the Third Republic. No other political figures would have been able to make such a claim let alone sustain it, yet de Gaulle does so and both reinforces and uses the persona to political effect. It is not, of course, naïve; as an autobiography it is an enormously interesting variation within the genre. These war memoirs are neither simply a self-justification (although they are that) nor a self-revelation (entirely absent) but instead establish the identity of the subject with France and French interests. In this, his own version, the central figure has no individuality apart from the nation and de Gaulle's remit was therefore established as unlimited. For all its patriotism it is a 'Great Man' view of history: people do not make events but heroic actors do. But it is also Republican in that the heroic actor profoundly represents France.

Betrayal

What de Gaulle implies, to the reader who accepts the Gaullist line of thought, is that the French nation is something above and beyond the people themselves and with a destiny of its own. But France has been betrayed, in some unspecified way, by individual politicians. In his own works de Gaulle also establishes himself as above politics. Many politicians would like to claim that they are unlike their colleagues, but not many succeed. De Gaulle's claim that he was unlike the other 'players' came to be widely accepted. One of the sources of the Presidentialism of the Fifth Republic is the distinction between the President (in this case de Gaulle) who is a statesman and above the ruck of politicians and the politician. De Gaulle, in the memoirs, acts for a purpose higher than the sectional interests of mere politicians and has a historic role to perform. In contrast to most memoirs, de Gaulle's childhood is abolished and he emerges as the immaculate conception of the nation with no precursors and no contemporaries. De Gaulle's dismissal of his pygmy-statured contemporaries has often been remarked: what is noticed less is that he also disappeared from public life after his defeat in 1969 and anointed no successor. He presents himself as an army officer joining up from the highest of motives and with no desire other than to serve in times of trial; his 'compagnons' are those who share the motivation and inspiration set out on the first page of the *War Memoirs*.

De Gaulle had no need to establish his patriotic credentials after the war; what he did was to set out a magnificent fairy tale France embracing all sections of opinion, overcoming the 'ferments of dispersion'. This is done mainly through a parade of images which would be meaningful to different sections of opinion, but which would not be combined by any partisan politician. That de Gaulle was wide ranging in his choice of images only underlines the all-embracing vocation of Gaullism. There was the royal allusion to Versailles, the Napoleonic reference (Invalides) and to the Army's exploits remembered on the Arc de Triomph as well as the Church's great Notre Dame de Paris. This eclecticism was not open to other leaders (Clemenceau, for example) and de Gaulle makes good use of it.

De Gaulle's placing of the state (by implication) on the same level as religion does not look typically Catholic, nor is his exaltation of state 'sacro egoismo' consistent with the religious outlook. Whatever de Gaulle's beliefs were in private, they were unorthodox in their public expression of the primacy of France and accompanying political ethic ('soyons donc fourbes', as he might have said). De Gaulle's is not, however, a social vision. The Dreyfus Affair is mentioned only to regret its effects on French society, dividing a people which needed instead a healing unity for the trials ahead. In this view the divisions which made modern France what it is, and which evolved the compromises of Church and state, for example, are deplorable examples of the national taste for contention. Unity, through leadership, is what matters. But de Gaulle did not advocate a fascistoid authoritarian peace of repression: de Gaulle restored the Republic twice. De Gaulle had more insight than to believe that repression could make him the genuine representative of the people.

All the same, the principal agent of division, Clemenceau, is the only Republican hero named and the Republican icons cited are all battle honours won by the Army. Gambetta, a Republican 'great' who saved the country's honour by raising irregular armies against the Prussians in 1870, is an obvious precedent for de Gaulle's action, but goes unmentioned. In sum, the imagery is not all things to all people (it is too contradictory for that) but it lays out a non-partisan commitment to an ideal 'France'. It is a claim which is established by regretting the defeats of the French Army of the Napoleonic Second Empire by the Prussians as well as the climbdown by the Republic to the British at Fachoda.

By calling up the image of the crowds at Longchamp and the greeting of the Russian Czar (an unpopular despot at that time) de Gaulle conjures up the prospect of a foreign policy of 'raison d'état' supported by the public. In this view the *salus populi*, the state ego is linked by the leader who can express it without interference. France, following the dictates of *Staatsraeson*, the book seems to say, will be united and strong; it is the public which, appropriately enlightened, understands and the elite, which does not. It is not a 'liberal' vision of the 'national interest' (Aron 1994–5). In the liberal view national interest emerges from the inter-play of competing forces in the political arena and nothing is definite or predetermined. In the event de Gaulle seemed to regard conflict (even of a lower order than May '68) and unrest as a regrettable evidence of a falling off from greatness. For liberals the question of which interest is the national one can only be settled through politics. By contrast de Gaulle offered a Presidency run by a figure above and beyond politics determining the national interest and expressing the profound sentiment of the nation.

A figure above politics (like Hitler or Stalin), even though claiming to represent the 'real will' of the people, is not democratic. What distinguishes de Gaulle from the many pretenders to incarnate the nation is that he insisted on the special bond between himself and the people as continually put to the test in free elections and referendums. When his appeal failed in 1969 he resigned. Although he claimed that all authority in the Fifth Republic should ultimately emanate from him, de Gaulle did not practice a dictatorial assimilation of power in his person because it was subject to ratification by the voter (de Gaulle 1971, p.30). All the same, an uncertainty remained through the life of his Presidency not least because of the initial extravagant claim (and the lack of any check on supreme power in the Constitution where that power was exercised by the President).

'Gaullism', thus established, is both sufficiently domineering and at the same time unspecific enough to justify action and to permit a useful latitude of interpretation. In the first paragraph of the memoirs de Gaulle views France as a 'Madonna' of the frescoes and a Princess of the fairy tales. This bold image, carried by sheer style, does not commit the politician-author to any particular course of action. A politician wrapping himself in the flag is not exceptional; all politicians claim to act from uniquely patriotic motives. The real problem is invariably one of means: not of whether the country should be strong or weak, but how it is to be done. It is a measure of de Gaulle's position that his own self-evaluation was accepted: he was allowed to portray himself as the singular patriot. De Gaulle in this way was not just the best of the politicians, but in another category altogether. To an English language audience it becomes even more bizarre when de Gaulle writes of himself as the embodiment of France. (As it was to some French people – see J.-F. Revel 1959) Other politicians would like to claim such a stance, placing themselves above the mêlée, speaking for the united and essential nation and casting doubt on their opponents' motives; it is difficult to think of any modern example which has been quite so successful for so long.

De Gaulle took the view that France ought to be great because France, unlike other powers, had a universal mission, and was called to make exemplary actions (and suffer equivalent misfortunes). This claim was based, not on the principles of the Revolution, Liberty, Equality and Fraternity, or on the declaration of Human Rights, nor yet on Republican government, but on a romantic *machtpolitik*. If the images de Gaulle uses are to be taken at face value, then the first President harks back to a Napoleonic France (or perhaps) the France of Louis XIV, which was the dominant European power. De Gaulle's France was a state which would give the lead into a kind of reactionary utopia of 'necessity of state'. Leaving aside the extent to which de Gaulle was motivated by this view, as distinct from using it as a covering justification (and on this there are many views), its practical effect was overconfidence. It enabled de Gaulle to act as if France were a superior to other 'great powers'. At its most extreme it placed France on a level with the United States and the USSR, so clearly impossible that it is difficult to take seriously. But it also moved France, in its own view, out of the generality of middle-rank European powers into a new status.

It was this new status which de Gaulle established that proved difficult to manage subsequently. De Gaulle created a rhetorical position which was very difficult to contest and which proved tempting to future Presidents who quickly occupied this high ground of 'national interest'. As importantly, however, de Gaulle allocated to himself the authority to identify and promote the 'national interest' which he did from the vantage of the Presidency. This status was vital during the Algerian crisis and served de Gaulle well in domestic as well as foreign policy (where he had a weight beyond what was warranted). But the weakness of his vision was revealed in the 'events' of May 1968 and in the invasion of Czechoslovakia, the bloc politics, of August 1968. As well as de Gaulle the politician the institution of the Presidency itself gained from de Gaulle's politics. How this was accomplished, the manoeuvres, and the consequences will be followed through in the subsequent chapters.

The Constitution

Formal constitutions do not locate the real sources of power in a state. Without going as far as Loewenstein who asserted that 'if no constitution existed at all, the prevailing power monopoly . . . would not be altered at all', it remains that the Fifth Republic Constitution does not explain why and how a presidential system evolved in the Fifth Republic nor what the pressures on it are nor what its capacities might be (in J. Blondel 1970, pp. 145–60). It is in order to answer these questions that this book reviews the political development and genesis of the contemporary Fifth Republic presidency and that means that an excursion through constitutional theory is unavoidable. First, therefore, a clearing of the constitutional ground.

In keeping with the view that in constitutions the least is best, and that the best is flexible (the English virtue), the Fifth Republic has been better served on the latter than the former (Rémond 1989; Wolf-Phillips 1972, p. 27). For, constitutions try to fight the last battle: they look back to solving the problems which preoccupied a society; their drafters cannot see into the future, 'nous entrons dans l'avenir à reculons'. But the future contains too many unknowns and the nature of society is too protean to permit the framers to do more than to restrict excesses or contain abuse. In the last analysis a constitution is only as good as its political personnel and the attempt to restrict forces in society can only lead to destructive clashes. Hence the evolution of the Fifth Republic Constitution away from the intentions of its framers should not be regarded as something untoward even if the emergence of the Presidency as the primary institution was faster and more dynamic than was foreseen. This development bears out the view that the force of constitutional rigidity should not be overdone.

The Executive in the Fifth Republic

Paradoxically, the Constitution of the Fifth Republic, and especially where it concerns the President, is not ambiguous. In a legal contest to head the executive between the President in the Elysée and the Prime Minister in the Matignon, the Premier would win. In the Fifth Republic Constitution, a prime ministerial regime is set out analogous to the many in Western Europe and the Presidency was something of a grace note on the constitutional keyboard. In this reading of the 1958 Constitution the regime is well inside the 'Republican' tradition: the President has few formal powers; such executive power as the President has had is entirely and intensely 'political' (Mollet 1973, pp. 228–31).

In the Constitution the President, if not the executive head, is of course an important figure. But of course the working of Fifth Republic France's political institutions has been 180 degrees at odds with the legalistic reading of the Fifth Republic as a prime ministerial régime with the government responsible to the parliament rather than a presidential régime (Andrews 1982, p. 29). It therefore has to be determined how the spirit and the letter of the 'Prime Ministerial' Constitution (usually called 'parliamentary' because of the responsibility of the government to the Assembly) have been so fundamentally turned away from their original purpose. In the Fifth Republic the President became one of the most powerful of Western executives (more so, in fact, than the President of the United States) and the question to be explored is how this power has been marshalled. It is a history which is at odds with many of the founding and sustaining myths of the Presidency; not the least of these is the belief in the 'non-political' nature and non-political source of Fifth Republic authority stabilised, so it is said, on the foundations laid by de Gaulle in 1958 but mapped out by him in 1946. De Gaulle's view of the Presidency as the sovereign was stated in the famous press conference of 31 January 1964 (Maus 1985, p.p 16–18).

Accordingly, from a political perspective and as an explanation of presidential authority, the emphasis has to move from the Constitutional and institutional in the explanation of the Presidency to the leadership style of the Republic and the astuteness of its office holders and the social and political support they have been able to muster. It is the Fifth Republic's presidential leadership which has been the creative force and which has built – by political artistry – a 'latent' constitution of a new type; one which has been wrested from the weak legal constraints of the manifest constitution. In other words, the Fifth Republic Presidency, precisely because it has no substantive constitutional backing, is an act of political self-levitation with few parallels in modern Western Europe – exceptional events of catastrophe and world war apart.

Power and Authority

It is useful, as a start, to turn to the research on the Presidency of the United States for the elaboration of a key distinction. Stephan Skowronek, a historian of the American Presidency, distinguishes between institutional power and authority. Power is the resource that the Presidents have at their disposal to get things done: authority stems from the warrants that can be drawn to justify action and secure the legitimacy of changes (Skowronek 1993, p. 17ff.). A president will first 'situate himself in public discourse' and construct a narrative to claim authority by virtue of who he is. However, in the case of the French Presidency, there is very little power. There are very few constitutional formalities on which the Head of State can rely, and even the small margin built up by the increment of tradition was itself crafted too recently to be accepted as a 'given' circumstance.

The Fifth Republic Presidency is new while the United States is, in many ways, one of the oldest continuous political societies. Authority in the Fifth Republic has been generated to some extent through the use of constitutional prerogatives, but it has chiefly resulted from making the Presidency the point of reference in French politics. The Presidency has been made the executive focus and its potentially high visibility has been used to legitimise the exercise of personal power; the institution, as a result, has both gained in stature and consolidated its coalition of support. In sum, the Fifth Republic Presidency is about as near to a purely political institution as any chief executive in a Western society today.

French 'Republican' Presidents

Although French Republican Presidents were not usually mere cyphers, their power was limited. Republican Heads of State have been slightly more than symbolic, having duties of promulgation and presentation, nomination, signature and registration. Republican Presidents have chaired the Council of Ministers ('Cabinet') and had a role in political and diplomatic life, which was more than purely representative. However, for Republicans, traditional distrust of the Presidency was set when President Louis Napoleon in a coup d'état on 2 December 1851, abolished the Second Republic and proclaimed himself Napoleon III, installing an authoritarian régime with the ruthless use of state power. Napoleon's Second Empire dissolved in the rout after the Franco-Prussian war, and was succeeded by the Third Republic. The Third Republic might have become a Constitutional Monarchy with a non-executive Head of State but the restoration foundered and the Republicans gained a majority and held it despite the attempts of the President to hold it back.

Because of the Napoleonic precedent, the Presidency was distrusted by Republicans who were thus impelled to support a French form of 'parliamentary sovereignty' with its major and minor premises. Major premise: the Parliament represents the sovereign people. Minor premise: the Parliament takes decisions in the name of the people. Conclusion: no other institution had or could have that vocation (and certainly not the Presidency). After the struggle in 1877 between the Republicans and the royalist President Marshal Mac-Mahon, the Presidency of the Third Republic settled (mostly) into the pattern of the regular election by the two houses of Parliament to the Presidential Palace, the Elysée, of dignitaries who would pose no threat to Parliament. Hence, after a trial of strength, the 1875 Constitution became fixedly Republican, having taken a parliamentary turn from the May 1877 crisis. After the Mac-Mahon crisis, the President was reduced to a dignified non-executive role, his position became untenable and he resigned in 1879 (Pisani-Ferry 1965).

Few personalities stand out in the list of Heads of State of the Third Republic. Jules Grévy who succeeded Mac-Mahon in 1879, promised on his inauguration, 'je n'entrais jamais en lutte contre la volonté nationale' (a national will expressed in the Assembly – that is). It was remarked of President Faure who died in office in '*rocambolesque*' circumstances in 1899 that 'en entrant dans le néant, il a dû sentir chez lui'. Clemenceau dismissed the office saying that there are 'two useless organs the prostate and the presidency' and advised his colleagues to 'vote for the most stupid'. Hence, after President Mac-Mahon lost a conclusive political struggle, the regime became a republic with a non-executive President.

In the Third Republic after 1875 there were periodic attempts to assert presidential power, but these ran into the entrenched resistance of the Assembly. In the best remembered or these instances, President Millerand tried to oppose the left-wing coalition of the 'Cartel des gauches' after it had won the 1924 elections and, his position having become untenable, he was forced to resign (Dansette 1960, p. 256). Seven years before that President Poincaré, at the crucial point in the First World War, had been kept 'out of the decision making loop' by Prime Minister Clemenceau (1917-20) although the former President subsequently went on to become a forceful Prime Minister in 1922 and again in 1926 and 1928 (Amson 1985, pp. 139–59; Duroselle 1988, pp. 651–5). Clemenceau himself, on the other hand, was a victim when the elegant but empty Paul Deschanel was elected President in preference to himself (Deschanel had to resign through illness). Albert Lebrun, the last President of the Third Republic and with Grévy one of the two re-elected, made no impact during the Fall of France, which led de Gaulle to comment that 'comme chef d'état, deux choses lui avaient manqué: qu'il fût un chef, qu'il y eût un Etat'. Others, like Raymond Poincaré and the conservative André Tardieu, came to believe that a radical reform of the Third Republic Presidency was needed (Derfler 1983, Ch 5).

To a large extent the Fourth Republic codified later Third Republic practice to the extent that Vincent Auriol (its first of only two Presidents) remarked, somewhat understating his own role, that the President was only 'un greffier et un facteur'. Vincent Auriol, elected in 1947, had had a distinguished ministerial career and had been one of the eighty deputies who refused to vote full powers to Pétain in July 1940. At the beginning of the Cold War Auriol made full use of his considerable moral authority, his parliamentary experience and his talents as a mediator to find prime ministers in unstable and conflictual conditions (during his septennate there were twelve cabinet crises). Auriol also played an important part in bolstering the Fourth Republic against the quasi-insurrectional challenge from the Communists which started in November 1947 and against the gaullist tidal wave which threatened to engulf the 'Third Force' parties in the following year. As President, Auriol was outspoken and took a distinctive 'Atlanticist' and activist line of foreign policies (negotiating treaties) and on the French Union (which he supported). He also used his powers to call for the reconsideration of legislation and to change the direction of events by the choice of Prime Minister and by persuasion (Auriol 1970).

René Coty, the last President of the Fourth Republic, was an obscure senator, a conservative, and a constitutional lawyer who was uncomfortable with the Fourth Republic's institutions and a protagonist of reform. President Coty returned to a much more passive role and made few public pronouncements; those that he did make were subordinate to the prevailing consensus and a contrast to Auriol's frankness. However, Coty's view was that he was 'President of the French' and he took a much less hostile attitude to the Communists than did Auriol (for example, often consulting them during reshuffles). Although Coty was unadventurous in finding prime ministers, he did try to seek out the person who could survive in an increasingly divided and riven Assembly. Nevertheless, under Coty, the crises became worse and more intense, several lasted for weeks and at one point France was without government for 127 days. If he was less active in foreign affairs than Auriol, he made suggestions for constitutional reform (Fauvet 1971). Coty is remembered chiefly for the thirteen ballots (over seven days) required to elect him and for his intervention in 1958 to bring de Gaulle back to power: he threatened, faced by the reluctance of senior politicians, to resign unless 'le plus illustre des Français' were made prime minister (Amson 1985, p.p 173–87). In the Third and Fourth Republics, then, Presidents played a modest role in keeping with what Republicans expected. It was not simply a failure of personality or of interest (though it was in some cases) but the lack of political backing which limited their ambitions. When confronted by momentous events, Presidents did not have the authority they needed.

Fifth Republic Politics

But the Fifth Republic, as its framers saw it, did not stand in the context of previous presidencies (Debré, pp. 44–6 in Harrison 1969). Liberal Constitutions use power to check power ('checks and balances') and set institutions to control each other unless, that is, they have mainly or exclusively ceremonial functions. A ceremonial President could be absolved of 'responsibility' to other institutions but an active President should not; putting the 'fox in charge of the hen coop' is not a sensible practice. Fifth Republic Presidents were not expected to exercise the executive role, the Prime Minister is; constitutionally the government is responsible to the Parliament not the President. Article 68 states that the Presidents are responsible for actions taken in carrying out their duties 'only in the case of High Treason' and in that case they will be tried by the High Court of Justice (impeached). Such lack of daily accountability (impeachment or nothing) is not consistent with the leading executive role the Fifth Republic Presidency has assumed. With the emergence of the Presidency as the real power in the Fifth Republic Article 68 stands as anomalous.

Framers of the Fifth Republic Constitution, who came from most points of the political compass, thought they had strengthened the executive against an Assembly that was widely held to be domineering and irresponsible in the Fourth Republic (P. M. Williams 1968, Ch 1). Yet the map of the politics of the 'Gaullist' Republic magnifies the Presidency much as Mercator's projection enlarges the island of Greenland. Under Title II of the Constitution the President receives early and quite substantial attention, but the institution is mentioned in a quite specific and delimited context. Reference is made to the President in the following Articles: 5, 6, 7, 8, 9, 10, 11, 12, 13, 14, 15, 16, 18, 19, 52, 54, 56, 58, 61, 64, 65, 67,

68, 88, 89 and under Title XV which is a temporary disposition. It is worth noting that, although the list of Articles citing the President is, at first blush, impressive, Article 19 reduces their import by stating that all the President's acts (other than 8/i, 11, 12, 16, 18, 54, 56 and 61) are countersigned by the Prime Minister and by the relevant minister. When no countersignature is needed it is where the President 'arbitrates' to ensure respect for the Constitution (Articles 54, 56, 61), intervenes in other bodies (Articles 8, 11, 12, 18) or acts in a crisis (Article 16). Other articles allow the President not power to issue commands but to deliver the ability to appeal to countervailing powers: the Prime Minister in Article 8, the electorate in Articles 11, 12 and 18; the Constitutional Council in Articles 54, 56 and 61. On the other hand the President has little power to block and the President is not (constitutionally) much more than the adviser and 'porte-parole' whose signature is formal and not discretionary.

In the Fifth Republic Constitution there is none of the schizophrenia of the American Constitution in which the President is enjoined (in Article 2) to simultaneously exercise 'expansive powers for independent action' and 'affirm the fundamental order of things' (Skowronek 1993, p. 20). In any 'conservative' or restrictive reading of the Fifth Republic Constitution the President is very much like the Third Republic's. Under the Third Republic the ministers were 'held to account', took decisions, the President 'presided' but did not govern, could take no decisions 'save in agreement with the Ministers' and the responsibility was the government's (or in some cases that of individual ministers) (Mollet 1973, pp. 28–9). It was a Presidency which presided over 'national solemnities' and the President 'headed' military forces and appointed officers (a Third Republic remit) (Poincaré 1919, pp. 172–3).

The Presidential 'Referee'

This interpretation of the Fifth Republic's Constitution is buttressed by Article 5 which states that the President 'Provides by their arbitration for the regular functioning of the public authorities and the continuity of the State'. Article 5, which implicitly restricts the Presidency, has been a subject of controversy (see Massot 1987, pp. 220–1). Although not explicitly mentioned in the Constitutions of the Third and Fourth Republics, the idea of 'arbitrage' was a familiar attribute of the Head of State. President Gaston Doumergue (1924–31) referred to his role as that of 'l'arbitre impartial' and Auriol commented in his diary that 'Présider [was to . . .] 'diriger sans décider . . . c'est arbitrer' (Auriol 1970). If the concept is followed through it leads to a Presidency more like Auriol's than Coty's (or most Third Republic Presidents), but it is dependent on circumstance, moral authority and influence. De Gaulle did not propose much more in the famous Bayeux speech of 1946 laying out the gaullist conception of the presidency where the word was used to mean advice or, in a crisis, dissolution (Harrison 1969, pp. 24–7).

Later Articles of the Constitution dealing with the President confirm this disinterested and non-political role. In Article 64 the Higher Council of the Judiciary is established. This continued a Fourth Republic innovation and was intended to enable the President to protect the judiciary from the vagaries of political interference. However, in the Fifth Republic, until 1993, it was composed entirely of the President's nominees, and the judges' representatives regularly called for a reform. Thus in the Fifth Republic Article 64 makes the President the 'defender of the independence of the judicial authority' and Article 65 has the President preside over the Higher Council of the Judiciary. French Republicans have always been suspicious of 'government by judges' but the separation of powers is a venerable democratic principle even if governments find it highly inconvenient.

Hence, the President of the Fifth Republic who emerges from the Constitution is a neutral 'umpire' who has three principal tasks: i) to see that the Constitution is respected; ii) to 'arbitrate' to ensure the continuity of the state; iii) to be vigilant on the issues of national independence, territorial integrity and the respect for treaties. Constitutional means are then provided to enable this 'arbitration' (J. Fournier 1987). To ensure the respect for the Constitution, Articles 54 and 61 can be invoked to enable treaties and laws to be placed before the Constitutional Council; Article 56 allows the President to nominate three of the nine members of the Constitutional Council (including its President); and, under Article 89, on the proposal of the Prime Minister a revision of the Constitution can be endorsed. As 'Arbitrator' the President nominates the Prime Minister (as in the Third and Fourth Republics); accepts or rejects a proposal for a referendum (by the Parliament or Government); calls for the reconsideration of a law (Article 10); dissolves the Assembly and sends a message to the Assembly. To ensure the continuity of the state the President has the powers of nomination (Article 13) and accredits Ambassadors (Article 14), chairs Higher Councils and Committees of Defence and can use the draconian powers of Article 16 when there is a threat to the State.

Article 5 of the Fifth Republic Constitution depicting a regulator above the battle, a President/arbitrator, seems to foreclose a dynamic leadership role for the President and the reinterpretation of the Article, turning a referee into a team captain, cannot be rationally defended although many have risen to the challenge (including de Gaulle who, when taxed, invoked the Latin roots of the word: see Mollet 1973, pp. 68–9). But of course, legal arguments cut no ice with public opinion and in the Algerian war, with authority collapsing, the French people were disinclined to contest the growth of Presidential power, all that stood between them and civil war. All the same, Presidents from 1958 have pushed their authority to its limits, ignoring constitutional problems believed to be too nice for human solution (Carcassonne 1996, pp. 51–3). Although they have found it useful to invoke 'arbitration' as a justification ('rôti je te baptise carpe'), successive Presidents have used powers beyond even a very elastic extension of the concept. Such questions have led jurisprudentialists to ask whether an article so constantly violated should be amended or abolished: there is no effective direct juridical control on the President and it does little for the rule of law to manhandle the Fifth Republic Constitution (Ardant 1987).

Presidential Power Reviewed

However, the perception remains that presidential executive power does indeed emanate from the Constitution and a review of that argument will be necessary before proceeding to the discussion of Fifth Republic political development. Here the starting point is the election of the President as set out in Articles 6 and 7. These, in their original form in 1958, widened the traditional electoral college for the President (in keeping with de Gaulle's Bayeux speech) from the two houses of Parliament to the number of 81,764. These include local elected representatives mainly from the small rural communes of metropolitan France although France was industrial and the Head of State was also the head of an Empire. This led Professor Georges Vedel to remark that the President was the representative 'du seigel et de la betterave', but the direct election of the President by universal suffrage was thought impossible in 1958. Direct election would, for one thing, have led to the domination of metropolitan France by the Empire (*Spectacle du monde* No. 7 1962 and *Paris Match* No. 704 1962).

Once decolonisation had been accomplished one obstacle to direct elections was removed. In 1962 the Constitution was amended to provide for the direct election of the President by universal suffrage. There were to be two ballots. If no candidate had an absolute majority on the first then in the second ballot, held two weeks later, only the two leading candidates (after withdrawal) could stand. De Gaulle's victory seemed to confirm the presidential practice that had emerged during the Algerian war and enabled it to be extended into normal times where the President has a majority in the National Assembly. Direct election thus legitimised presidentialism after 1965, although de Gaulle, elected by notables in 1958, established a politically dominant position for himself and exercised supreme power for seven years before he became the first directly elected President of the Fifth Republic.

In the 'cohabitations' of 1986–8, 1993–5, and 1997, where the prime ministers have come into their own as chief executives, it was evident that the amendment of 1962 did not confer additional powers on the President although it enabled some expansion of presidential authority. It did this because election created a new and competing legitimacy enabling the Presidents to shift the margins of the Constitution to a presidential interpretation enabling them (for example) to refuse to sign ordinances (or refuse a referendum) but not to dominate them (see below). After 1965, the 'will of the people' was exercised through two separate and potentially antagonistic institutions: the Assembly and the Presidency, both elected by universal suffrage. Had there been no amendment in 1962 it is difficult to see, in the absence of de Gaulle's extra-constitutional legitimacy, how ordinary politicians could subsequently have played the same role, or been able to be the leading political figure in France. Direct elections also created another arena for political competition and set in train a system reshaping process, which has not yet run its course. As Giscard d'Estaing noted in 1962, the institution of direct elections almost certainly meant that future candidates would have to have party backing and that elections would further accentuate the party political nature of the Republic (against professed gaullist inclinations).

The President in the Articles

With Article 8 we return to more familiar constitutional territory: 'The President of the Republic appoints the Prime Minister. Their period of office is terminated by the Prime Minister's presentation of their resignation along with that of the government. On the proposal of the Prime Minister, [the President] appoints and promotes other members of the government.' That means that the President nominates Prime Ministers (as is the custom in Republican France and elsewhere) but cannot dismiss them. This was confirmed by de Gaulle himself who, when asked by the *Comité Consultatif Constitutional* whether the Prime Minister could be dismissed by the President replied with a forthright 'no' (Actes, p. 118).

Of course, in 'normal' times the Prime Minister has been a political moon reflecting the light from elsewhere, implementing a presidential programme and liable to the sack ('put in the reserve of the Republic') when their usefulness has run out (Maus 1985, pp. 38–40). Presidential dismissal of Prime Ministers in the Fifth Republic is a political fact if not a constitutional right and demonstrating political authority, but where the majority in the Assembly changes during the septennate (as it does in 'cohabitations') this power evaporates. A President cannot thwart the majority in the Assembly to impose a Prime Minister the winning coalition does not want. There was a Third Republic precedent when, after the victory by the left 'Cartel de gauches' in 1924, the conservative President Millerand tried to nominate (the right wing) Frédéric François-Marsal. This 'presidential' nominee was refused by the Assembly (Dansette 1960, p. 253). A solid left-wing coalition made any other choice impossible and Millerand departed after François-Marsal was censured in a motion by 327 votes to 217.

With the institution of a universal franchise for the Presidency a competing of legitimacies became possible even though it cannot be resolved in the Constitution. If there is a solution, it will come from the 'fait majoritaire' characteristic of the Fifth Republic. A determined hostile majority (as it did in 1924) reduces the President's margin for manoeuvre to almost nothing. On the other hand a confused and fragmented Assembly might leave the President (like the Fourth Republic's President Auriol) searching the Parliament for potential Prime Ministers and 'variable geometry' majorities. In the Third and Fourth Republics the surprise solutions to governmental crisis resulted from the turmoil in partisan alignments and the shifting kaleidoscope of majorities and potential majorities. In those circumstances the President could be a 'René Coty' and look for consensus, or an Auriol and take creative chances. After 1958 what Presidents could not legally do was dismiss a Prime Minister once appointed: under the Fifth Republic Constitution only the Assembly can do that.

The Cabinet and the President

In most Western European systems the Head of State is kept informed of Cabinet decisions without sitting in on them. It is one curious stipulation of the French Constitution's Article 9 that the 'President of the Republic presides over the Council of Ministers [Cabinet]'. This was the recognition of the regular meeting of all the Cabinet Ministers on Wednesday mornings introduced at the Restoration. Under the Third and Fourth

Republics the Prime Minister drew up the agenda; in the Fifth Republic the Prime Minister continues to set it on Friday and sends it to the Elysée on Monday for Wednesday Cabinets. But in the Fifth Republic the Cabinet is 'une institution seconde' and its deliberations are not decisions in the legal sense except in a limited number of cases. In both the Third and Fourth Republics, some Presidents did chair Cabinets actively: Auriol was particularly able to exert influence in this respect (Auriol 1970, p. 87). However, the Cabinet does not have the same significance in France as in the United Kingdom and there is a long tradition of 'Cabinet' meetings without the Head of State. Strong premiers short-circuited presidential meddling by holding 'conseils du cabinet', Cabinet meetings without the President, chaired by the Prime Minister, to reach agreements before the formal Council of Ministers.

However, the Cabinet does have constitutional power: it issues 'ordinances' (Cabinet decrees), nominates civil servants and hears policy statements from ministers and the President. Hence a limited number of decisons have to be taken by the Cabinet in the presence of the President. If a Cabinet of one political persuasion is chaired by a President of another (as it is in 'cohabitations') then a collective solidarity is reinforced against the political 'enemy' in their midst. Cabinet collective decision making gains as an attempt to prevent the President from exploiting splits in the coalition. But if there were an highly antagonistic 'cohabitation' the government could get round the restrictions by extending the Prime Minister's powers of nomination and where the Parliament agrees the President's prerogatives could be eroded. It is also possible for the Prime Minister to call government meetings in the President's absence; and the collective 'conseil interministériel' performs the same function. After 1997 Prime Minister Lionel Jospin called regular government 'seminars' to agree policies and thrash out differences between coalition partners out of the President's sight.

This practice of calling 'pseudo Cabinets' has distinguished precedents and was used by de Gaulle himself in the last months of the Fourth Republic to cut President Coty out of the decision-making process (de Baeque). In 1969, when the anti-Gaullist Senator Alain Poher became interim President after de Gaulle's resignation, the Couve de Murville governments met without the President. In other words, where the majority remains solid the disputes can be settled beforehand and few loose ends will be left for the President to pull at. Hence, under successive 'cohabitations' Cabinet meetings have been perfunctory and sometimes glacial, but the Cabinet is not the only institution of collective deliberation and joint decision making. Article 9 is a strait through which important issues must pass under presidential scrutiny, but it can be navigated.

Intervention at Other Points

Article 10 provides no ostensible base for presidential power; it states: 'The President of the Republic promulgates laws within the fortnight following their final adoption [. . . the President] may ask Parliament to reconsider the whole law or specified articles.' This Article confers no veto power nor does it permit latitude over the period of delay before promulgation. Under Article 10 this demand has to be countersigned by the Prime Minister who can refuse (Goguel in *le Monde* 1/1/87). But the interpretation of Article 11, on the other hand, provides one of the few comedies in constitutional literature. It states that 'The President of the Republic, on the proposal of the Government during Parliamentary sessions, or on the joint motion of the two Assemblies [. . .] may submit to a referendum any bill dealing with the organization of the public authorities, entailing approval of a Community agreement, or authorising the ratification of a treaty that, without being contrary to the Constitution, might affect the functioning of the institutions.'

Republicans have distrusted the referendum since its ruthless use in the mid-nineteenth century by Louis-Napoleon as a tool of dictatorship; its use in the twentieth century by fascist leaders has discredited it almost totally with the left (Conac and Luchaire 1987, p. 252). There were safeguards in the Fifth Republic Constitution, which did not allow it to be called on presidential initiative, despite the widening of the remit for action from the narrow confines of constitutional amendment under Article 90 of the Fourth Republic. It is clear that the procedure for the referendum for the amendment of the Constitution is quite separate. Chapter XIV 'On Revision' contains only one article: Article 89. Under that procedure the referendum comes only as a possibility (not an obligation) at the end of a long line process of deliberation and ratification by the Assembly and Senate. Article 89 does not constitute a bolstering to presidential power, except insofar as the President is free to decide to submit the amendment to the referendum or not after the two houses have approved it by qualified majorities.

By the same token the term 'public powers' used in Article 11 is not an elegant variation on 'Constitution'. Referendums under Article 11 could only be used for three things: organisation of public authorities, approval of an agreement with the 'Community' (that is the former French 'Commonwealth') and the ratification of a treaty. In August 1995, President

Chirac's revision of the Constitution added 'réforms rélatives à la politique économique et sociale de la nation et aux services publics qui y concurent'. As with the rest of the Presidential domain in the Fifth Republic, the use of the referendum is ultimately a matter of adroit exploitation of political opportunity (originally by the General) more than a legal power used officiously.

Presidents may 'after consultation with the Prime Minister and the Speakers of the Assemblies, declare the dissolution of the National Assembly' – so says Article 12. Apart from Mac-Mahon's dissolution of the Chamber of Deputies at the beginning of the Third Republic (the '16 May crisis 1877') the President's right of dissolution (with the concurrence of the Senate) in the Third Republic went unused. In the Fourth Republic the Prime Minister could request a dissolution and it was used once (on 2 December 1955). By contrast the Fifth Republic places few constraints to dissolution on the President who has to 'consult' – unwelcome advice has been rejected out of hand; but another dissolution cannot take place for a year after a presidential dissolution.

This right of dissolution was seen by the framers of the Constitution in the light of what Michel Debré called the 'real power' of the President: to call in other authorities. This is not a 'power' to order the voters to do their sums again to get the right answer (what the President wants) and it does not guarantee a presidential majority. In 1988 President Mitterrand's government was a minority government (without the Communists, then outside the presidential coalition) after the June general elections which followed the clear presidential victory of the previous month. As the conservative President Chirac discovered in 1997 when the left returned to government, the voters can inflict a damaging defeat on the President's supporters. On the other hand, Article 12 is an essential element in the armoury of a President who can guarantee a majority at the polls; but that is dependent on circumstances and the exercise of the political arts.

With Article 13 the Constitution moves the Presidency from the responsibility for giving observations and advice (Massot 1987, p. 294). Here it is stipulated that the 'President . . . signs such ordinances and decrees as have been considered by the Cabinet [and . . .] appoints to the civil and military posts of the state'. Some, for whom the Constitutional 'indicative is an imperative', took this article to meaning that the President had to sign ordinances and that, as with a constitutional monarch, this could not be refused (*Le Monde* 18/5/86). Others, notably former Prime Minister Barre, felt otherwise and this in practice was the case (see *L'Express* 31/5/85).

Similarly, Article 38 allows the government to fast track its programme by legislating through ordinances (these have to be ratified by Parliament later). However, in July 1986 in one of the first shocks of the first 'cohabitation', President Mitterrand refused to sign the ordinances denationalising sixty-five industries. Decrees cover an area where direct election has given the Presidency the authority to determine not to sign and this renders the legal argument superfluous (Carcassonne 1996, p. 97). It is, notwithstanding, a limited power as Article 13 (and Article 38 – see below) only covers that small number of decrees having to go through the Cabinet, and although the ordinances enable governments to move rapidly they are not vital. In 1986 the government was not so much inconvenienced as annoyed and, backed by a solid majority, put the measures through the National Assembly. In 1986 it was the slight slippage in the timetable and the highlighting of the policy which enabled political damage to be inflicted.

Nominations are, as a source of patronage, highly political but the numbers referred to in Article 13 are very small and the nominations which do not have to pass through the portals of Article 13 are extensive – sufficient for a spoils system for the greediest of political parties. In fact the 'cohabitation' governments have placed nominees into key positions to carry out their policy and the President's ability to prevent a 'witch hunt' was determined by politics rather than the law. President Mitterrand chose, as a strategy, to give the government a free hand in the 1986–8 'cohabitation' and preferred to take a stand only on a few important posts (not always with success). In 1986 48 of the 153 ambassadors, 67 of the 118 prefects, and 81 of the 188 high civil servants were moved as were rectors, those in the state media and the nationalised industries, though with no noise (*Le Monde* 19/3/87).

The 'Reserved Domain'

Although the powers in question are purely formal, with Article 14 the Constitution enters the so called presidential 'reserved domain' – not that previous Presidents were inactive in foreign affairs (Auriol 1970, p. 467). This term was coined by Jacques Chaban-Delmas to explain the new Presidency at the Gaullist Party conference of November 1959. According to Chaban, de Gaulle's foreign and defence policy (including Algeria) was supposedly in the presidential 'reserved domain' where the President was sovereign. Chaban's turn of phrase seemed to encapsulate the situation, quickly became a widespread one and was often assumed to be constitutional doctrine. If France had an unwritten Constitution the 'reserved domain' could have been on the way to becoming a principle of the Constitution and foreign affairs were readily accepted by the public as a presidential domain (Chantebout 1992, pp. 634–5). The popular expectation that the President will play a determining role in foreign policy has become a support for the executive Presidency. One of the most vigorous opponents of the 'improper interpretation' of the 'reserved domain' was the youthful François Mitterrand, but as President it was a case of 'Moi, je ne suis pas de mon avis' (Mitterrand 1996, p. 88 and p. 105). It came to be one of the expectations of the Fifth Republic that the President would take the lead and prime ministerial activism here can be regarded as faintly disruptive. Because of the public view the presidential 'reserved domain' became the 'nerve centre' and the key object of struggle in 'cohabitation' politics. In its original formulation the 'reserved domain' referred to defence and foreign affairs, but it is not part of the Fifth Republic Constitution and was not accepted by the first four Presidents themselves (who saw their responsibilities as being total) (Conac and Luchaire 1987, p. 334).

Article 14 presents a similar situation to Article 15, however, as it states that the President of the Republic 'accredits Ambassadors . . .' and that '. . . Ambassadors are accredited to . . .' the President. This is a description of high diplomatic protocol and is not a key power either in policy formulation or execution within the supposed 'Presidential domain'. This constitutional hole was, in a backhanded way, confirmed by President de Gaulle (*Memoirs d'Espoir,* p. 345), and by Georges Pompidou (*Le Monde* 26/4/64). Both 'Gaullists' repudiated the notion of 'reserved domain' as did President Mitterrand (*Le Monde* 23/10/86). Yet the Fifth Republic Presidency had by 1981 become synonymous with active and solitary policy making by the Elysée in the 'reserved domain'. If presidentialism has any constitutional basis then it is here in the area of 'high politics' that the status of the Fifth Republic has to be tested. The articles, which the presidentialist interpretation of the Constitution relies on, are few in number: Articles 52 and 53 for foreign policy and Article 15 for defence.

Article 15 says that: 'The President of the Republic is Head of the armed forces. They preside over the Higher Councils and Committees of National Defence.' President Giscard d'Estaing noted that the President alone takes decisions on nuclear 'dissuasion' and President Mitterrand stated (*avec superb*): 'La pièce maitresse de la stratégie de dissuasion en France, c'est le chef d'état, c'est moi' (Grosser 1984, p. 301). Against this must be set Articles 20 and 21, which make the Prime Minister responsible for national defence. This paradox disappears if Article 15 is read as conferring a ceremonial title and if the committees and councils which the President chairs ratify, but have no decision-making power (Conac and Luchaire 1987, p. 529). Had the drafters intended a 'reserved domain' they would not have made it subject to a countersignature.

Article 15 can thus be construed as the dignified – formal and ceremonial – part of the Constitution: the President, it states, '. . . is Head of the Armed forces [and] . . . presides over the Higher Councils and Committees of National Defence'. This is a traditional function of a French Head of State and confirms civilian predominance. Under the Fourth Republic's Article 98 the President 'disposed of the Armed Forces'. 'Head of the Armed Forces' was a title bestowed on the Head of State and the President was Chair of the Higher Council and Committee of National Defence. It is clear that in the Fifth Republic this is in direct line of descent from the Third and Fourth Republics under which action was taken *in the name of* the President but the attributions are ceremonial rather than real (ibid., p. 577).

Practice has, of course, been different and even under 'cohabitation' the Defence and Foreign Ministers had to be negotiated with the President in a way the other Cabinet appointments were not (*Le Monde* 20/3/86). The negotiation was to save appearances. In 'normal' times, however, the authority of the presidential 'monarchie nucléaire' has been very evident in defence and, for example, the President created a 'conseil d'état-major quotidien' during the Gulf crisis and intervened in the detailed operations as well as setting out the grand strategy (Cohen 1997). This exercise of supreme power should not detract from the constitutional need to read the Article in conjunction with other stipulations (like Article 21) and the necessary countersignature by the Prime Minister and other relevant ministers. Military power is, in any case, dependent on other materiel support and has so many ramifications that it can hardly be used in isolation from civilian ministries and still less against the government.

The decree giving the President the power over the nuclear trigger is one dating from 14 January 1964 (and a government could revoke a decree) (Pac 1989). Moreover it might be taken to be unconstitutional as it could conflict with Article 34 giving Parliament the power to make laws concerning national defence (Chantebout 1986). In practice the Parliament has to set the all-important budget for defence and the armies and that means that a determined government can over time deprive the Elysée of effective oversight of the 'reserved domain' (as in others). There is also President Lyndon Johnson's *boutade* which, taken at face value, would seem to put nuclear power in perspective: 'the only power I've got is nuclear . . . and I can't use that' (Sidey 1968, p. 260).

The Presidential 'reserved domain' in which the President is the determining power in foreign affairs is supposedly mapped out in Articles 14 and 15 and is often said to be confirmed in Article 52 which states that: 'The President of the Republic negotiates and ratifies treaties.' However, in foreign policy making the Emperor is similarly clothed: Article 52 states that the President, as in the Third Republic, 'negotiates and ratifies' treaties. Against this must be set the need for a Prime Minister's countersignature (Article 19) and the stipulation in Article 53 that the main types of treaty (which are enumerated) are matters of law. For this reason the constitutionalist Bernard Chantebout stated that 'curiously the constitution only envisaged presidential intervention for the formal ratification of treaties and allowed the government to conduct the main part of diplomatic questions through simple "international agreements" which are not submitted for ratification' (Chantebout 1989). It is evident that in modern conditions the negotiation of treaties requires very close collaboration with the government and that the Constitution provides no basis for the solitary exercise of power in the so-called 'reserved domain' (Zorgbibe 1986).

Although the President's predominance cannot be openly challenged because of the public's expectations, the three 'cohabitations' do show that the substance can be removed. In fact the formulaic statement that the 'President signs and ratifies treaties' is similar to the Third Republic's constitutional law of 1875 (and the Fourth Republic's Article 97) and that was in practice to mean that foreign policy was conducted in the President's name by diplomatic staff at the Quai d'Orsay (Carcassonne 1996, .p 219). Under the Third and Fourth Republics the President worked to promote the government's foreign policy (whatever it happened to be) something that is the opposite of Fifth Republic 'normal' practice in which the Cabinet applies the President's programme. Hence, to continue Article 52, the President is 'informed of the negotiation of any international agreement not subject to ratification' but is not given power over them. These inter-governmental agreements form the main part of international interactions in Western Europe and they are not subject to the presidential control, for they are not given the control of the ministries needed to make such authority real. This is confirmed by Article 35 which makes clear that only Parliament can declare war and by Article 53 which declares that the ratification of the most important treaties (peace, commerce and anything involving state finance) comes into the domain of Parliament. As regards foreign and defence policy, therefore, the President's powers in the Constitution need the agreement and active cooperation of the government and the attempt by the President to negotiate a treaty which would be repudiated by Parliament (that is against the majority) would be a singular blunder or a high risk political gamble.

Emergency Powers

Doubts about Article 16 giving 'Emergency powers' to the President have never been entirely assuaged even though it was deployed only once from 23 April to 30 September 1961 following the abortive 'Generals' putsch' in Algeria. Because it has only been used once, and because de Gaulle was in commanding position, the precedent is not helpful but there has been a perpetuation of the notion that it permits a 'Draconian' executive to emerge. It is an innovation in French Constitutional law as it delegates potentially unlimited powers in a 'crisis' and it does make the beneficiary, the President, the sole judge of 'crisis' and the immediacy of the threat. Constitutional imperatives on 'consultation' are not real safeguards and although Parliament sits as of right there is no need for the President to be bound by any advice and the only control is after the event, for example the possibility of the President being arraigned for High Treason.

De Gaulle invoked Article 16 in a 'clear and present danger', a 'crisis', as had been understood by the framers, but then extended the period well beyond the ten days of the army mutiny and told the Parliament that it was not empowered to censure the government or to debate in extraordinary sessions. De Gaulle stated in April that the Parliament could not discuss matters relating to the emergency and in August – when the emergency was over, but when the debate on the budget was looming – that that was all they could discuss. A farming problem had erupted after the Algerian mutiny and the Assembly was not allowed to debate a bill on the issue. This interpretation was never challenged, but only because the General had public support and the 'crisis' meant that few were prepared to push their reservations to the point of conflict (Williams and Harrison 1971, pp. 189–92). Most importantly, and contrary to some suggestions, Article 16 cannot be used to resolve the conflict between a sitting President and an incoming but opposed majority. That would amount to a coup d'état (Duverger 1996, p. 507). It is, of course, for use in national 'crisis', not mundane political scrapes.

The Presidential Sector

There follow two articles where presidential acts do not require any countersignature. These are Articles 17 and 18 and are the symbolic exercise of decision. Since the ancien régime, and perpetuated by the

Revolution, the Republics have provided for a Presidential right of pardon. This is an important human rights provision but not a significant power in the political armoury. Under Article 18, the President has the right to send messages to Parliament, but there is no debate on the message and it is not a means for presidential intrusion into the legislative domain. These 'messages' can, however, where well handled constitute a 'Bully Pulpit' and they have been used to underline that the source of authority is presidential as well as to dramatise the President's role (for example, in the Gulf crisis). But once again, although such messages can bolster an existing authority, they do not establish or create power.

In Article 19 it is stipulated that the acts of the President to be effective have to be countersigned with the exception of: Article 8 (1), 11, 12 16, 18, 54, 56, and 61. Those presidential acts, which do not require countersignature, are not, *stricto sensu*, presidential 'powers' despite claims to the contrary. This article, although it innovated in allowing for presidential action without countersignature, lays the foundation for prime ministerial power and limits the presidential domain – if, that is, it is read in a purely legalistic manner. Thus the President's domain is limited to: Article 8 (the nomination of the Prime Minister) depends on a majority in the Assembly; Article 11 (the referendum) requires a proposal to come from the government; Article 12 (dissolution) turns the decision over to the electorate; and Article 18 (messages to Parliament) which does not confer the right to make American-style 'State of the Union' addresses. Whereas Article 61 enables the President to refer bills to the Constitutional Council, the outcome depends on the Council, as does the reference of a treaty to them (Article 54). That leaves Article 54 which gives the President the right to nominate three members of the nine-strong Constitutional Council, but as the other members are nominated by the Speakers of the Assembly and Senate it is a 'normally' a minority interest. Only under Article 16 (Emergency Powers) can the President act alone; nonetheless acts under this Article are subject to post-facto control, endorsement and validation or they lapse.

Conceived as a way to patrol the legislative/executive divide, the Constitutional Council is a Fifth Republic innovation (Bell 1992, pp. 22ff.). It is highly political like the United States Supreme Court, but unlike its American counterpart its activity is modest and it is not a Supreme Court. It has, under Article 61, the authority to review legislation before promulgation to determine the constitutionality of provisions and it can examine treaties in the same light (Articles 54, 56 and 61) but it cannot pronounce on the interpretation of laws after they have been promulgated and applied. Presidents nominate three members (one of them takes the Chair); the nominees can be anyone (not necessarily people with a legal competence), serve for nine years and may not be reappointed. However, the Constitutional Council is not necessarily at the President's call and has asserted its independence at times in an unspectacular manner (Harrison 1990). Once nominated members are not revocable, and were often older figures with nothing to prove and hence have not been afraid – sometimes – to render judgements which are politically disruptive for the authorities as it did when it ruled against a government-sponsored bill in 1971.

Prime Ministerial Power

Under the Third Republic the authority of the Prime Minister ('président du conseil') had been growing and in the Fourth Republic it had become a key institution (Anderson 1970, pp. 66–9). Prime ministerial power, although limited by the instability of coalitions in the Fourth Republic, was confirmed by the conservative Antoine Pinay in 1952 and reached its apogee under the Pierre Mendès France Premiership of June 1954 to February 1955 (Lacouture 1981, Part III). If the Mendès France premiership was without immediate sequel, the Fifth Republic did continue the evolution of the office for a brief time (before the Algerian crisis caused de Gaulle to step in) and the new Republic gave it a bigger staff and wider interests (Ardant 1991).

On the frictionless plain of hypothesis the Prime Minister dominates the Fifth Republic and, from this viewpoint, the 'cohabitations' were more 'normal' than the periods of presidential domination. In 1958 the Fifth Republic tried to rebalance powers in the executive's favour to enable stable governments to take firm and effective action. It was the solution to France's endemic instability to bolster the Prime Minister and, through the premier, the government.

Because the Fourth Republic had already started trying to correct the deficiencies of 'régime d'Assemblée', by constraining the Chamber of Deputies, the enshrining of these provisions in the Constitution had wide support in the political elite (P.M. Williams 1968). In French Republican Constitutions the novelty was the bounding of the Assembly's sovereignty by, for example, restricting the area of legislative activity (under Article 34) and giving the agenda setting powers (under Article 48) to the government. But in politics, and in the Fifth Republic, there is no need to muzzle a sheep. However that was not foreseen and the drafters of the 1958 Constitution intended to reinforce the Prime Ministerial executive and to back it with other institutions including the Presidency.

Prime Ministerial pre-eminence is set out in Articles 20 and 21 as follows: 'The Government shall determine and direct the policy of the nation. It shall have at its disposal the administration and the armed forces . . . it shall be responsible to Parliament' and 'The Prime Minister shall direct the operation of the Government . . . shall be responsible for national defence . . . shall ensure the execution of laws . . . shall have regulatory powers and shall make appointments to civil and military posts.' These are not qualified. But this spectacular suit of clothes has no Emperor. In 'normal' times the government is responsible to the President, not the Parliament, and it is the President who has usurped the role to 'determine and direct' the nation's politics. Hence Duverger's famous question about de Gaulle's first spanielling Prime Minister makes political ('M. Debré, existe-t-il?'), but not constitutional sense. Debré, one of the main drafters of the Constitution, was able to organise his principles as the General required.

But the Prime Minister is pervasive in the Fifth Republic Constitution and even when not mentioned is a *Geist* who can be evoked at many points. Because the Prime Minister is at the nodal point of powers, a hostile majority during 'cohabitation' can imprison the President but not the Head of Government (who, unlike in the Fourth Republic, can deputise for the Head of State). Specific powers are given to the Prime Minister: a Premier proposes ministerial appointments (Article 8), proposes referendums (Article 12), can call special sessions of Parliament and can request new sessions (Article 29), can demand secret sessions of Parliament (Article 33), has the initiative in legislation (Article 39) and can submit a bill to a joint committee of the two Houses to resolve disagreements (Article 45). In addition only the Prime Minister can pledge a government's responsibility or make a bill a matter of confidence (Article 49 – i and iii). Under Article 54 the Prime Minister can refer treaties and (under Article 61) laws to the Constitutional Council or can propose amendments to the Constitution (Article 89). Whereas Article 19 makes most presidential acts subject to prime ministerial countersignature, and under Articles 12 and 16 consultation of the Premier is obligatory, the Premier's proposal is necessary before the President can call a referendum (Article 11) and revise the Constitution (Article 89). In the Constitution the Prime Minister is a *primus inter pares* in the function of the government under Articles 11, 36, 38, 41, 43, 44 and so on and so on. This Constitution depicts a Prime Minister who is the motive force and the leader of the governmental team who answers to Parliament as well as ensuring Cabinet solidarity through bi-lateral and multi-lateral meetings and developing strategy.

Hence the Prime Minister is the responsible executive power under the Constitution apart from the wholly exceptional conditions of 'national crisis'. To ensure the execution of laws the administration of the Republic is at the Prime Minister's bidding (prefects and others are under the Prime Minister's direct control) and to that is added the armed forces and regulatory powers as well as the stopping at Matignon of the gravy train of nominations. In the Parliament itself, albeit much reduced in the Fifth Republic, the Prime Minister has a legislative function and has several weapons to deal with obstruction from the Assembly. In addition to those already mentioned, these include the power to set the Parliamentary agenda (Article 48), the use of the 'package vote' to pass (or have rejected) a whole bill on a single vote, to restrict private members bills and to legislate by decree (Rials 1985, p. 113 ff.).

Within the so-called 'reserved domain' the Prime Minister is 'responsible for national defence', a power which was confirmed in a decree of 7 January 1959 (by de Gaulle). However, although a decree of 14 January 1964 later stated that the President commands the strategic air force (Force aérienne stratigique), there is perhaps a judicial vacuum in this area and possibly a violation of the Constitution (Cohen 1986; Giscard 1985). If defence politics is taken as an ensemble, and not simply power over the button (including the all-important budget for defence), the President is in a position of potential political weakness vis-à-vis the Prime Minister. Given the interconnections of budget, trade, and foreign and defence policy with government strategy and practice and with diplomacy the position is clear: the idea that the 'high politics' of diplomacy and the 'low politics' of domestic wrangles can be separated is a throwback to the eighteenth century. During the 'cohabitation' of 1986–8 foreign policy was one of the principal stakes in the struggle between President Mitterrand and Prime Minister Chirac. This Montague-Capulet relationship had its absurd aspects, but was mainly fought out behind closed doors. Even though foreign policy was presented as a Presidential domain, and care was taken not to humble the Presidency, the memoirs of the Foreign Minister leave no doubt that it was the Prime Minister's policy (Raimond 1989, p. 222; Balladur 1989).

When the Presidents of the Fifth Republic have majorities, the Prime Minister is the President's manager. Under 'cohabitation' the worm turns and the Prime Ministers reclaim their constitutional prerogatives to become the principal motive force. After 'cohabitations' lasting two years each the elections of 1988 and 1995 returned the situation to the 'normal' one of presidential domination before the elections of 1997 introduced a new 'cohabitation', this time potentially for five years. Prior to the 'cohabitation' of 1986, the Leader of the Opposition, Jacques Chirac, argued that the coexistence of two opposed political outlooks at the summit of the State was perfectly possible as long as a 'parliamentary reading' of the Constitution was made. Mitterrand's more portentous comment was that the 'cohabitation' would be about the 'Constitution, the whole Constitution and nothing but the Constitution'. However, in keeping with the argument here, the struggle was about political advantage, authority in Skowronek's sense, but not about the Constitution as such (which was not amended).

Conclusion

Constitutions, as Martin Harrison observes, have a way of confounding their authors and their critics (Harrison 1969). Future evolution of the Fifth Republic Constitution, which has not ceased to grow, depends on political developments and not on the legal wrangling over the 'true' meaning of various articles (Duverger 1996, pp. 556–68). However, the Fifth Republic Constitution still surfaces as an issue in political debate as, for example, does the question of the creation of a 'real' presidential régime. Up to 1999, all that can be said is that the two 'readings' of the Constitution, one prime ministerial and the other presidential, both have their partisans and both remain latent possibilities for future use. There are other possible 'readings' as yet untried and the *pons asinorum* of the lack of stable majorities, which the Fourth Republic could not pass, has yet to be negotiated and a 'no holds barred' conflictual 'cohabitation', if unlikely, cannot be excluded. For the interim the lesson seems to be that the Presidency of the Fifth Republic is a political institution grafted onto the Constitution and which was created by a supreme effort of political will working with popular consent. This is the work of politicians and of political statecraft but neither predetermined nor set for the future. Thus the next stage is to examine that achievement.

Part I
Setting up the Politics

–2–

De Gaulle's Republic

De Gaulle is often regarded as a 'charismatic' or 'heroic' leader and, although the concept of 'charisma' is contested, the Weberian idea does give us some insight into the problems of the nascent Fifth Republic (S. and I. Hoffmann 1968). Charismatic leadership is crisis leadership, responding to what Weber calls 'charismatic hunger' in which people impute extraordinary qualities to leaders and expect political miracles of them (Gerth and Wright Mills 1947, p. 295). De Gaulle's success in returning to power in 1958 stands in contrast to his loss of it in 1946 when he quit – expecting to return – but was kept out of office by the tenants of the régime (Hartley 1972, p. 91). But the essential component in 1958 was the Algerian war. Fourth Republic authority had evaporated in May 1958 when the military uprising in Algeria threatened to overthrow the régime.

In 1958 de Gaulle had two problems: to get into power and, once there, his main task would be to restore authority; his second problem, was to maintain authority. In the first instance de Gaulle was like the typical 'charismatic' leader whose writ was personal and whose legitimacy over-rode the established process. De Gaulle reflected this personal 'charismatic' authority to the point of caricature (J.-F. Revel 1959) and the legitimacy incarnated by de Gaulle's person was, initially, the principal characteristic of the new Republic. This personal authority was continually reinforced by other events, some like the referendum, manipulated by de Gaulle but others, like the 1962 assassination attempt, used for his own purposes, as he also did with the momentous Algerian crisis (Rudelle 1980, p. 254).

This personal ascendancy had to be maintained, in Weberian terms 'routinized', by some means other than through the Gaullist network of associates and by direct command from the General. This was where de Gaulle turned to the Presidency as an institution on which to found a new legitimacy. De Gaulle chose to reinforce the authority of the institution of the Presidency as the source of power and transmitted a new governmental architectural structure to successors. However, as will be demonstrated, the politics of this authority were not straightforward and proved increasingly difficult to manage. But, for the purposes of analysis here, the principal focus is the Presidency and the building of institutional authority. Its strengths and weaknesses will be examined, but first a look at the situation at the end of the Fourth Republic.

Algeria

Algeria was the immediate cause of de Gaulle's return to power. Algeria was in fact a colony but constitutionally was a part of France and not thought of in the 1950s (even by many on the left) as a colony. It was a society of nine million or so 'Muslim' Algerians who were dominated by the million settlers of diverse origins (but fiercely French) who maintained a quasi-apartheid regime. Little attempt had been made to make the Muslim population full citizens and such moves as there were to better their conditions or give them equal rights were usually sabotaged or prevented. This division, as some (like Raymond Aron) saw, was unsustainable but so was the full political equality of all in a French Algeria (Aron 1958). These 'defeatists' were not taken seriously and even on the left the 'progressive' solution was taken to be the 'levelling up' of the Muslim majority who would then be full French citizens like the *colons* (Grimal 1965, Ch 13).

Most people and politicians reacted to Muslim discontent as a problem of law and order and tried to repress the insurgent movement of the Front de Libération Nationale, which had started in November 1954. Politicians reacted by increasing the Army presence and an infernal dialectic of violence started. In 1956 the independence movement began urban terrorism in earnest and soon a recognisable guerrilla war was in progress between the Army and the FLN insurgents. This was an insurgency which had started under the left-wing (and admired) government of Mendès France and the 1956 Socialist government had scrapped a reform programme when confronted by the settlers. Two years before, in Indochina at Dien Bien Phu, in 1954, the French Army had been defeated in humiliating circumstances by insurgents and it was determined not to lose another 'war of the flea' (Taber 1970, p. 103). Its methods were neither orthodox nor scrupulous. Army pride and moral authority were at stake, but then it was backed by the *'colons'* (the so-called *'pieds noirs'*) while and the metropolitan public was not, before 1958, disposed to support the dismantling of the Empire. *Algérie française* partisans, in other words, had the upper hand even while they were not 'winning the war' against the FLN. In 1958 the 'war' had been in progress for two years but the settlers were dissatisfied with its progress and the Muslim population was being progressively but surely alienated. None of the Fourth Republic's figures had the support to find a solution, discontent mounted in Algeria and the Republic's authority was fatally undermined (Horne 1977, Ch. 5).

This was the position when de Gaulle was returned to power on the back of a military coup. A 'pronunciamento' of 9 May 1958 by General Salan, the Commander in Algeria, and the setting up of Committees of Public Safety was turned by the gaullists to support the General (Droz and Lever 1982, p. 170). This coup was for some the 'original sin' of the Fifth Republic and its military beginnings had to be dissipated over the seven years until the direct election of the President. Leaving aside the exact involvement of Gaullists in the uprising in Algeria, and they were on-hand to use the discontent to say the least, de Gaulle was faced with the problem in 1958 of having at the same time to use the military's pressure and to disassociate himself from it in order to reassure the political elite (Rudelle 1988, p. 103). De Gaulle, who maintained a stance of loyal sedition, on several occasions refused to condemn the plotters or call on the Army to obey the Republic, acts which, in lesser figures, would have been close to treason. Meanwhile his supporters assured the Algerian settlers and the diehard colonialists of the commitment of the General to the French Empire. Michel Debré, for example, had promoted the argument that the Fourth Republic was too spineless to defend French interests and, in particular, incapable of defending French Algeria. To retain Algeria, asserted the voluble, aggressive and excitable Michel Debré (a stranger to verbal nuance), de Gaulle had to be returned to power and the Fourth Republic dissolved (Williams 1970, p. 168).

In May 1958 there was no Gaullist Party to speak of and the dominant forces in metropolitan politics were the Communist Party and the weaker Fourth Republic parties of the centre and conservative right. Moreover, in Algeria authority had been devolved onto the Army by Fourth Republic politicians who hoped to see the 'disorder' in Algeria ended by military means. Incapable of finding a political solution to the Algerian crisis the Fourth Republic political elite made it a military problem. By 1958 the Army itself was able to escape civilian control; for two years it had been increasing its ability to determine its own course of action. Because the Army had been made responsible for the Algerian problem (it had developed its own counter-insurgency warfare) it had much at stake and had given guarantees not just to the settlers but to the many Muslim supporters of French Algeria (like the Army's 'harkis'). Army 'honour' was involved, but it was not just an abstract military virtue. Officers and others feared that the abandonment of its supporters by France would lead as it had in Indochina (and as it later did in Algeria) to reprisals (O'Ballance 1967).

By 1958 the internal governance of the 'colony' had also been largely devolved to people sympathetic to the maintenance of French dominion. De Gaulle could have decided to gain support from one or other of the competing groups but decided, consistently with his outlook, to bring France together behind him: the colonisers and decolonisers, the last-ditchers and temporisers, the constitutionalists and refounders, the left and the right and the centre. In 1958 it worked and avoided having France tear itself to pieces. De Gaulle had, it could be argued, to bring back the Army and administration under political control (and that by 1958 could only mean his own personal rule) before progress could be made.

De Gaulle's Position

De Gaulle had retained the support of Gaullist networks which he was able to call on; close associates like Debré and Roger Frey who could speak with – it was assumed – the General's authority. These supporters could also plot on de Gaulle's behalf and some, like Léon Delbecque used the Republic's commission and confidence to intrigue against it. Jacques Soustelle, who was (before he fell out with the General) one of de Gaulle's most effective supporters, intervened in Algeria at a crucial time in May 1958 to divert the flow of events to the General and away from the Republic's government. De Gaulle could appear to be the Cassandra, but in effect his supporters were helping fulfil the predictions. De Gaulle was able to maintain an ambiguity about his own intentions through his famously delphic pronouncements while his supporters reassured different (often antagonistic) communities. This use of lieu-tenants as go-betweens to speak on behalf of the leader but (and crucially) not bindingly was also employed by Mitterrand (as was the technique of the personal network). It 'became known' that those closest to de Gaulle spoke the General's mind and this enabled the ambiguity to be carefully maintained at crucial points. De Gaulle was more artful, however. Such was de Gaulle's calculated vagueness that everybody who visited him at Colombey-les-Deux-Eglises during his 'retirement' and on the eve of his take-over in May 1958 got the impression that the General was in personal agreement with them.

De Gaulle in 1958 remained, therefore, more or less uncommitted in public and Gaullism was a blank space onto which people wrote their own manifesto. De Gaulle would find a 'solution' to the Algerian war, but what the 'solution' would be was not made manifest and in 1958 (before decolonisation of European African Empires had got underway) it was easy to assume that it would be the continuation of French sovereignty over the area in some form. This ambiguity was a political achievement celebrated by the Gaullists themselves as statesmanship of a high order. De Gaulle they argue, avoided the 'lie direct' but by misdirection conveyed the impression of his support to incompatible groups who, of course, wanted to believe in de Gaulle as 'theirs'. His supporters like Debré were not ambiguous at all. Subsequently, as Prime Minister, Debré had to conduct the most agonising U-turn but others (like Jacques Soustelle) could not renege on deeply held positions.

But in May 1958 there was near anarchy in France. It is argued that a scrupulous regard for the niceties of political convention and choirboy morality at a time of near civil war would not have been responsible. In this academy's view had de Gaulle descended from the heights a 'solution' of the 'sale guerre' would not have been possible. This might well be true; nonetheless, the highly political misdirection of saying one thing and doing another was an essential part of the Fifth Republic's very foundation. The attempt to both contain and utilise the Army coup and to keep universal support could only last while the circumstances were exceptional, that is as long as the Algerian crisis continued and the nature of the 'solution' was unclear. In May 1958 de Gaulle was in Colombey-les-Deux-Eglises carefully maintaining a good distance from the developing crisis when General Salan's *pronunciamento* was issued in Algeria. On 15 May de Gaulle forced the pace and rallied those who hesitated or contemplated drawing back: he released a statement that he was 'ready to assume the powers of the Republic'.

In the Assembly, Fourth Republic politicians had tried to retain control by supporting the centrist Pierre Pflimlin's government. Settlers in Algeria had interpreted Pflimlin's appointment as a step towards the FLN (which it was not) and this precipitated the 13 May coup in Algiers. Republicans hoped to see the authority of the state restored but it was already too late for that and the Fourth Republic had run out of credit with its citizens. The politicians had the General forced onto them by the forces (especially the Army) threatening something worse gathering outside the Assembly's 'House without Windows'. Pflimlin's declaration of a state of emergency on 16 May was formulaic without the Army and police willing to enforce it and the government when it tried to discipline the insurrectionists only demonstrated its impotence. Pflimlin, who could not bring to heel the rebel Army, had to try to bring them back under his authority in which manoeuvre he was hindered by de Gaulle and the Gaullists. Corsica fell to an Army takeover on 24 May and Committees of Public Safety supporting the rebels were set up. An attack on metropolitan France was in fact planned (Droz and Lever 1982, pp. 162–8).

De Gaulle Takes Over

De Gaulle met the Prime Minister on the 26th and then let it be known (falsely) that the process of transfer of powers had begun. On the 29th President Coty put his thumb on the scales to tilt them in de Gaulle's direction. Coty, threatening to resign if de Gaulle was rejected by the Assembly, called on the 'most illustrious of Frenchmen' to take over. That threat, with the assurances the General had given to the centre politicians in a press conference of 19 May that he was not going to seize power, was enough to ease him into the Premiership of the Republic. On 1 June de Gaulle got the approval of the political class, more or less, and full powers. Apart from the Communists, numbers in most groups voted de Gaulle to power (by 329 to 224) and few politicians of the first rank voted against the General – Mendès France and Mitterrand were exceptions. It was not a large margin for the General, for deputies supported him only under duress. But in politics, as in cards, when nothing else is turned up clubs are trumps. De Gaulle had, however, managed both to disguise the element of force and coercion and yet kept faith with the putschists by not ordering them back to barracks. His legitimacy needed confirmation, a problem reflected in the Cabinet drawn from all shades of opinion (though not the PCF), and the search for public support in metropolitan France and Algeria (on 4 June). Jacques Soustelle, the enthusiast for *Algérie française* who later turned against de Gaulle, was kept away from policy making but as Minister for Information his presence reassured the settlers as did the nomination of Michel Debré as Minister of Justice.

De Gaulle took over an empty shell. Whatever de Gaulle's private convictions – and he likely thought at first of a federal solution for retaining Algeria and the African colonies – he was obliged to comfort the settlers' illusions as a stage on the way to restoring Paris' authority. De Gaulle started on a course of action that could be understood to be the reinforcement of *Algérie française*. These actions included the promotion of the putsch leader General Salan, the Plan Constantine (involving enormous expenditures intended to raise living standards) and reassuring visits to Algeria. At the same time de Gaulle reinforced his personal authority, loyalists were promoted and the possibility of another coalition of extremes coming together was avoided. In Algeria, most of the Army and the settlers had different priorities and once they were separated the threat to metropolitan governments diminished. In particular the '*colons*' were progressively but systematically deprived of the military and police backing that gave them their power in Algeria (and in other settler colonies like Rhodesia and South Africa).

De Gaulle's Direction

Organisations of the extreme right and the settlers, however, were not so easily deceived and soon began to distrust de Gaulle – the beginning of what they saw as the 'betrayal'. De Gaulle had, however, deprived them of the political means to make that disillusion effective. Public opinion in France itself was also changing – in the opposite direction, with revelations about torture employed by the Army and the unpopularity of a conscript war for a cause increasingly less seen as France's own (Vidal-Nacquet 1958). In between 1956, when first deployments were made, and 1960 the world had changed from being a colonial one to a decolonising one in which Algeria was an oddity. This anomalous status was made clear in the United Nations where new post-colonial states were beginning to outnumber the old states and were putting France in the pillory (Jacobson 1962).

In September 1959 de Gaulle announced the policy of 'self-determination' for Algeria (de Gaulle 1970, Vol. III, p. 120). Empire loyalists were enraged. This statement of the direction of de Gaulle's policy caused the extreme *Algérie française* diehards to break with the Gaullists (it was followed by a change in colonial policy which, in effect, enabled the decolonisation of Francophone Africa). In January 1960 barricades were erected by extreme *Algérie française* partisans but, unlike 1958, the Army remained (mainly) loyal to the Republic and de Gaulle then removed ministers who had been unreliable. Succeeding where the Fourth Republic had failed, with a solid public backing, but a still not totally reliable Army, de Gaulle thus tried to reassure the Army that it would not be defeated in the war against the insurgents. Army pride, it was implied, would not be damaged but at the same time negotiations with the FLN were revealed. De Gaulle, in this as in other discussions, was prepared to negotiate only from strength. De Gaulle may not have seen the need to bargain with the FLN. He relied on reforms and on the Army to eliminate the insurgents from Algeria itself as a prerequisite to any settlement. In the course of 1960, however, it became even clearer that a 'self-determined' Algeria would be run by the FLN which had eliminated any competition for Muslim support. In November 1960 de Gaulle alluded for the first time to a future 'Algerian Republic' (de Gaulle 1970, Vol. III, pp. 258–9).

OAS Tactics

On 8 January 1961 de Gaulle held a referendum on Algerian policy, offering three alternatives: integration, association or independence to be decided by referendum. Predictably, and despite left-wing and extreme right opposition there was a massive 'Yes' vote giving de Gaulle the leeway to pursue a policy independent of the Army or the settlers. *Algérie française* extremists recognised that they were blocked politically in France and turned to violence as the only way to reverse this policy, founding the terrorist OAS in February. Shortly after the beginning of talks with the FLN the General announced on 11 April that a 'sovereign' Algeria should be envisaged: on 22 April a putsch was attempted by some professional units and led by four officers (three of whom had been retired and one had been transferred out by de Gaulle). Their putsch failed to gain support for the conscript Army was reluctant to follow, and the country rallied behind its President, demonstrating that 'clubs are not trumps' when something else is agreed upon. Under de Gaulle, in contrast to the Fourth Republic, the state's institutions were supported, and only de Gaulle had popular confidence for resolving the Algerian conflict; his writ ran even into the officer corps. After the 'putsch' the military became de Gaulle's resource. Opposition to French withdrawal came from the OAS which hoped to remove de Gaulle (in the hope that policy would then change) and to terrorise the population in France and in Algeria itself into supporting *Algérie française*. By 19 March 1962 an agreement had been reached with the FLN and without obstructive attention to the details once thought all-important (Buron 1975, p. 187). De Gaulle's ability to cut the Gordian knot was a sign of political strength and the 'Evian Agreements' were massively approved in a referendum in April (Williams 1970, Ch 12). This agreement did have some intricate mechanisms for protecting some settler and French interests but it gave way on most of the points (like the oil reserves in the Sahara) previously regarded as essential (Pearce 1993).

De Gaulle was backed by French public opinion which had turned against the settler cause (appalled by OAS bombings) and had full control of the state – as the Fourth Republic had not. He decided not to retain French sovereignty in any part of what became Algeria and not to demand guarantees for settlers. Most of the settler population and the Muslims who had supported France fled and created a refugee problem in southern

France where the dispossessed *pieds noirs* arrived. They returned with their grudge against the Gaullists which were not expressed at the time, but remained simmering, and found expression in votes for the extreme right Front national in the 1980s. Le Pen's movement continued this combat in some ways and promoted the ideas of *Algérie française* in a new context adapted for the 1980s.

De Gaulle's idea of a 'clean break' (if such it was) did not materialise. De Gaulle turned his back on the Algerian crisis but it remained a factor in French politics. With the two countries culturally and economically intertwined the relations could not be severed as they were with (for example) Vietnam and 'Algeria' remained in the background of the Fifth Republic. Revelations about the horrors of the 'sale guerre' surfaced in the following decades and problems associated with Algerian migrant workers and the second generation of Muslim French (*'beurs'*) remained to remind France of the Algerian tragedy. It left a legacy of anti-Arab racism and posed severe problems for the integration of second-generation immigrants. People remembered the war: veterans, immigrants, *harkis* and *pieds noirs*. Some 24,000 French soldiers had been killed and perhaps as many as one million civilians (mostly Muslim) died in Algeria; one million refugees fled to France in 1962; the scale of the repression in Paris in 1961 was only fully acknowledged for the first time by President Chirac in 1999.

Conclusion

De Gaulle had returned to power to end the Algerian crisis. The essential prelude to that was the re-establishment of the authority of the French state and the central civilian control of the Algerian departments. De Gaulle decolonised after the Army had ostensibly won a victory (unlike Indochina) and then provided it with other vocations and nuclear weapons. De Gaulle's authority was such that decolonisation was possible in 1962 and was effected. It had, however, taken four years of devastating war in Algeria to reach that stage. In 1962 it was a political solution to the war that was imposed, not an economic, humane or balanced one. There was a political solution in the restricted sense that metropolitan authority was unimpaired and the Presidency was by that time, and as a result of its role in the crisis, the lead institution. De Gaulle was confirmed as the dominant figure in 1962 and the botched assassination attempt at Petit-Clamart only served to make clear what France owed to the President. De Gaulle capitalised on his popularity as the peace maker with two referendums and a snap election which assured his power until 1965.

–3–

Referendums

Referendums are not a new subject of research. However, the usual approach has been to examine the democratic nature of the Fifth Republic referendum because of de Gaulle's claim that it exemplified a special relationship between the President and the French people. These are important questions, but the intention here is to illustrate the use of the referendum as a presidential weapon in particular circumstances in a modern society: the 'heresthetics' of the Fifth Republic referendum and its use to build the legitimacy of a new institution. It is a question of the use of the referendum and the conditions for its success or failure as a device. Most of the referendums bear – in one way or another – on presidential power and in the first years of the Fifth Republic they were essential in establishing the presidential system (Wright in Butler 1978).

The Constitutional Position

Successive Presidents have used the referendum although the referendum is not, under the Fifth Republic Constitution, a presidential power. It is available on the proposition of the government for strictly limited purposes under Article 11, Article 53 and Article 89. A President can call a referendum only at the request of the government – the Constitution is unambiguous on this point. Article 53 states that 'no cession, exchange or addition of territory is possible without the consent of the populations concerned' and was invoked to justify the Algerian settlement in July 1962 as well as in Djibouti (1966 and 1977) and the Comoros Islands (1974). In Article 89, which makes provision for amendment of the Constitution, the referendum is the last step in a procedure which stipulates that any amendment must be passed first by the Assembly and Senate in identical terms. But the seven metropolitan referendums of the Fifth Republic held under Article 11 are more problematic. This Article, although amended on 4 August 1995, refers to the laws on 'public powers', economic and social policy and the ratification of treaties which affect the functioning of institutions. De Gaulle used the referendum to amend the Constitution, but subsequent Presidents, lacking the General's authority, have not.

In 1958 there was a referendum to ratify the new Fifth Republic Constitution and there were seven after that. Those in 1958, 1961 and in April and October 1962 were part of the consolidation of de Gaulle's power, with the Algerian war and with de Gaulle's solution to the crisis. These four referendums were also all 'plebiscites' on de Gaulle's Presidency (as was that of 1962) and the main issue was the confirmation and continuation of President de Gaulle's leadership. All the same the General only put his position as President explicitly at stake on two occasions (in October 1962 and 1969) but the effect was the same – a popularity poll for the President (Williams 1970a).

The Fifth Republic

In 1958 a referendum was necessary to launch the Fifth Republic on a solid basis and to avoid the mistake at the foundation Fourth Republic. In 1946 the Constitution of the 'Mal aimée' had been approved by a grudging 53 per cent which amounted to only 36 per cent of registered voters. A constituent referendum was necessary and it helped disguise the Fifth Republic's origins in a military coup. In the contemporary world the installation of a new Constitution and its subsequent amendment are invariably conducted through the referendum. In 1958 de Gaulle's referendum had the additional advantage of swinging the political elite behind him and isolating his opponents (composed of some individuals and the PCF), and in 1961–2, of isolating the Fourth Republic politicians in fruitless opposition to him.

As few people read the new Constitution and even fewer voted with the constitutional consideration uppermost, the referendum demonstrated the stature of the General in French politics to all but the most blinkered. It showed that de Gaulle was picking up support from hitherto staunchly Communist areas and making inroads into the electorates of the 'Fourth Republic' parties. De Gaulle, in short, was given a resounding vote of confidence such that no domestic group could contest the legitimacy of either de Gaulle or the new Constitution. This public backing was essential if de Gaulle was to face down the Army and the Fourth Republic parties and politicians (Williams 1970a, Ch. 10).

De Gaulle could not depend on a majority in the Assembly and had no arsenal of powers to look to in 1959 when he moved from the Matignon as the last Prime Minister of the Fourth Republic to the Elysée as the first President of the Fifth. In the 1958 general elections the political class in general claimed to be Gaullist but the Gaullist Party itself took 199 seats. This was a good result for the General's supporters but the other parties, who (as the vote of censure in 1962 showed) could not be counted on, also polled strongly. In addition to the 77 Algerian deputies, there were 86 on the left (PCF, SFIO, Radicals), 133 conservatives and right-wingers and 57 MRP. Through the referendum of 1958, de Gaulle dramatised the full support that he then had through the referendum of 1958 and showed the wide basis of his leadership. It is also possible that the 1958 referendum had been intended to have an international impact: it showed who had the power and the basis on which it was held (public confidence); this aspect, for de Gaulle, was a major force, just as his leadership of the Resistance had been in 1943–4.

In May 1958 de Gaulle had gained the confidence of politicians across the political spectrum and the referendum of September had maintained that support with both the last ditch colonialists and the liberals. In this instance the assertion 'me or chaos' carried real weight. Although de Gaulle could rely on the crisis to keep the deputies behind him for the main part), the Assembly elected in November 1958 was not loyal to him. De Gaulle's intentions were, of course, uncertain and different impressions were conveyed (some diametrically opposite). This ability to speak with many voices and to reassure antagonistic groups at the same time this uncertainty could not be maintained for long and the fault lines with which the coalition was riven would reopen sooner or later. At some point large parts of de Gaulle's coalition would have to be disappointed and their expectations dashed. For some, whose emotional and lifetime investment was immense, this would be devastating. As the war ground on it became evident that those who had supported de Gaulle in order to retain Algeria would be 'sold out'. De Gaulle was, however, by then strengthened by a first success.

Algeria

Although there is no way of knowing, de Gaulle probably had some notion of what to do about the Algerian crisis on his return to power. All that can be said is that de Gaulle had not previously shown any clairvoyance about the fate of the French Empire. He had supported the maintenance of the Empire and the principal Gaullist argument appeared to be that only de Gaulle's return to power could prevent the collapse of the state and with it the abandonment of the colonies. Until 1954, Gaullists in the Assembly opposed all concessions and negotiation as a 'sell-out' and had no solutions (other than de Gaulle's return) to offer. After 1954, de Gaulle tried various solutions; each associated with a referendum. He started, in 1958, with the integration of the Muslim population into French citizenship, then the 'paix des braves', followed by self-determination and then independence. It is possible that de Gaulle was, like other politicians, seeking an outcome but was uncertain what this would be. His success was to give himself the leeway to search without hindrance, and to turn a settlement, which would have been regarded as a historic defeat for any Fourth Republic government into a political success for himself.

However, unless there were metropolitan political stability nothing could be accomplished in Algeria; but it was precisely the Algerian imbroglio that prevented any domestic stability. De Gaulle began the process of taking the government 180 degrees way from where the 1958 *Algérie française* coup had hoped to confine it. De Gaulle's policy was to both continue and intensify the war against the insurgents while constructing support which would enable the government to do as it wished. Debré, the Prime Minister, had no such authority and de Gaulle was drawn *nolens volens* into the detailed policy making. De Gaulle's strategy was not widely understood (and it may not have been altogether coherent) and the government, the negotiators and the FLN were all in the dark as to the real objectives. In this sinuous progress towards a peace the referendums showed that de Gaulle had overwhelming backing at each stage, and were also useful as a battering-ram to shake their supporters lose from the old parties, particularly on the right.

De Gaulle's carefully crafted ambiguity had survived after the proclamation of 'self-determination' in September 1959; what had been made clear was that it was the President's policy. This unwelcome declaration for the settler right was met with an abortive putsch in October and then by the 'week of the barricades' in January 1960. De Gaulle's visit to Algeria in December 1960 provoked massive settler demonstrations and then counter demonstrations from the previously quiescent Muslim population. During these demonstrations the Army remained crucially loyal to the government in Paris, but the idea of Algeria remaining as part of the French Republic with the consent of the Muslim population was no longer credible. De Gaulle made artful use of the worst crisis for the Republic since 1947. It was the crisis that enabled de Gaulle to make himself the point of reference for politics and the master of the agenda. Moreover, by 1960–1, the direction of the General's foreign policy was also causing dissent in the Assembly and altering the support for his coalition.

Self-determination

In January 1961 de Gaulle's referendum asked: 'Do you approve the bill submitted to the French people by the President of the Republic concerning the self-determination of the populations of Algeria and the organisation of the public authorities in Algeria prior to self-determination'. This was two questions, the second of which contradicted the first (Williams and Harrison 1971, p. 31). Although the Gaullist Party supported the President, the SFIO and MRP were increasingly unsettled and the Radicals and CNIP were both split and factionlised. The Gaullist 'Yes' campaign was by far the best organised, it benefiting from flagitious partiality in the state-controlled broadcasting media and was well funded. Long interventions by the President, frequent government interference in TV and radio and a broadcast message calling for a vote to show confidence two days before polling completed the barrage (Williams 1970a, p. 126).

De Gaulle could not assume support of this nature, but in 1961 the contrast between the two was the difference between a pantomime horse and a Derby winner. At that time no permanent, alternative or credible coalition could be put together in opposition to de Gaulle. There were opponents in plenty, and the line-up included (by 1961) many prominent personalities, but no consensus consolidated on any question, let alone the central one (Goguel 1983, Vol. II, Ch 2). Although the 'progressives' had for a long time been uncertain or even ambivalent about de Gaulle's increasingly high-handed manner, the referendum caught the left in decolonisation mode; conservatives were caught between their dislike of decolonisation and fear that their electorate would rally to de Gaulle regardless; the extreme right and *Algérie française* bitterly attacked de Gaulle. Colonial 'imperialists' were led by the former Gaullist star Jacques Soustelle, an old 'compagnon' who had been secretary general of the RPF and a 'desert crosser'. Now distrusted by de Gaulle, he was in the process of moving to extreme, quasi-insurrectionary, conflict with the President over the decolonisation of Algeria. Defence of *Algerie française* led to strange bedfellows and Soustelle settled in with unappetizing extreme right-wingers and proto-fascists but there were also Christian Democrats, Independents as well as some Radicals and Socialists. The PCF's tortuous evolution on the Algerian question also brought it alongside the extreme right (not for the first time), the PCF promoted a rejection of the President on the pretext of demanding immediate, direct negotiation with the rebels (Joly 1991). Its complicated counsel went unheeded by much of its electorate. There was also a call for a 'No' from the small leftist Parti socialiste unifié, a 'No' which underscored that, not even in this referendum, was 'No' a 'Yes' to *Algérie française.*

This cacophonic 'No' campaign only reinforced the message that there was no alternative to the President and the government's campaign was able to play up the vague hint at resignation made by the General if the referendum did not deliver the 'frank and massive Yes' (whatever that might be). Gaullists described the departure of the General in Transylvanian terms. In metropolitan France the vote was 17,447,669 'Yes' (75 per cent of voters) and 5,817,775 'No' (25 per cent) and abstentions of 8,533,320 (26 per cent of the electorate). In the PCF's bastions (like the Paris 'red belt') many Communists voted 'No' and the *Algérie française* supporters were not a majority of the 'No' (Williams 1970a, p. 125). There was clearly no public support for the continuation of what was now becoming a purposeless colonial war. This had not been the perception in 1958 when Algeria, even on the left, had been seen as an integral part of France.

But the referendum legitimised the new policy of 'self-determination' and, of course, the President's action. De Gaulle was given a carte blanche to terminate the war in whatever way and by whatever means he chose. De Gaulle reacted by shelving the bill approved by the referendum (Ibid., p. 127ff.). After the referendum the *Algérie française* supporters were a small and isolated group and the massive personal endorsement of de Gaulle by the January 1961 referendum seemed to eliminate any possibility of a repeat of the coup of May 1958, a military insurrection followed by a collapse of civilian authority. No Sixth Republic would rise from the streets.

Yet de Gaulle's referendum triumph indeed provided the impulse for another insurrection led by Generals Challe, Zeller, Salan and Jouhaud in April of 1961. This was in fact a measure not of strength but of desperation. Its failure led, not to the abandonment of the cause of *Algérie française,* but to the creation of the Organisation de l'Armée secrète (OAS) terrorist movement. It was not a rational campaign; it was intended in some way to intimidate Algeria back into the French fold and to assassinate the author of the policy of 'dismantling the Empire'. A leaderless France would then, so the conspirators thought, be led back into the colonial campaign. It was a recognition of the towering status of the President.

In Algeria, the vote which would seal the fate of the settler and *Algérie française* aspiration to keep the colony as a part of France (while retaining their privileged position) was difficult. Even as the FLN were maintaining a public stance of refusing to negotiate, the Muslim population was becoming more openly nationalist and less inhibited about anti-settler and anti-French sentiments. It was the Army, however, which was thrown into the balance and instructed to bring out the Muslim vote to ensure a 'Yes' vote for de Gaulle. In bringing the voters to the polls the French Army could demonstrate its control of the country and give de Gaulle a stronger hand vis-à-vis the FLN. In the Algeria departments the referendum was won with 1,748,000 'Yes' to 782,000 'No' and 1,800,000 non-voters. It was a 'No' which came mainly from the settlers and the 'Yes' included a large number of Muslims many of whom had been coerced to the polls. Negotiations, nevertheless, restarted in the Swiss Spa town of Evian in May 1961 (Droz and Lever 1982, p. 313).

OAS violence, terrorism and bombing in Algeria and the mainland, starting in 1961, were designed to intimidate but instead provoked a backlash in France. The Algerian crisis moved into its final stage with the power of the settlers broken, the opposition routed and the FLN in no position to impose its own solution, but capable of foreclosing others, given de Gaulle's determination now to end the war. In the final series of talks with the FLN, de Gaulle had imposed his authority through his negotiator, Louis Joxe (Buron 1975, p. 187). Joxe had attempted to secure safeguards (notably) for the 'pieds noirs' while the FLN played for time (Williams 1970a, p. 34). An outline agreement was reached in February 1962 and on 18 March a detailed document was agreed. Criticism came from many quarters, for Joxe had given way on the touchiest points of disagreement: protection for settlers and Muslim supporters of France, French rights and bases; Debré, a vociferous supporter of *Algérie française* in the 1950s, handed in his resignation – which was refused. The chances of an orderly handover – leaving in place the settlers, crucial to sustaining the most modern sectors of the Algerian economy – were sabotaged by the scorched earth tactics of the OAS. It was a tragic end as the settlers fled leaving everything behind as Algeria descended into chaos. But metropolitan opinion was weary of a war which had lasted twice as long in the Fifth Republic as in the Fourth and were unwilling to continue to fight, hostile to the extremists of *Algérie française* and unsympathetic to the plight of the settlers and the 'harkis' who fought for the French in Algeria. De Gaulle was no miracle worker, but rather a political 'surgeon'; the legacy of bitterness, torture, assassination and refugees has been long lasting and helped feed support for the anti-immigrant rhetoric of the Front National. But the solution confirmed confidence in the President, in the short term and in the presidentialised institutions of the Fifth Republic.

The 'Evian Accords'

A third referendum was held, this time in April 1962 to ratify the Evian agreements and give the President the power to implement them (Ibid., p. 129). De Gaulle, however, played a more subtle game. He faced a problem similar to that which had felled Mendès France at a similar juncture in 1955, Mendès France negotiated a settlement to the Indochina war which brought popularity to his government and to himself. His success in ending the war removed the centripetal force which kept the incompatible coalition partners together. Mendès France was thus unable to retain parliamentary support in the move from crisis to normality. De Gaulle needed to turn his public popularity and the relief at the settlement into an extension of his tenure as the determining authority in the Republic. His opponents in the Assembly were waiting for an opportunity to defeat him and end his domination of the political scene. De Gaulle had to force his opponents into declaring themselves on an issue on which he held the Ace. In April 1962 the referendum approved the Evian agreement by a massive 91 per cent of the vote and Prime Minister Debré urged the President to capitalise on the government's popularity and dissolve the Assembly. It was yet another vote of confidence in de Gaulle and the government's record was again in the balance. This referendum was probably *ultra vires*: Algeria was not then a state, nor a member of the 'Community' and the changes did not come under 'the organisation of public powers'. (Further, although the government can legislate by ordinance, the President cannot).

By holding a referendum on the Evian agreement, de Gaulle had constrained his opponents to support both him and his settlement or, in extremis, to abstain (not easy for political parties). In this referendum the parties, most of which supported the 'Yes' side, expended little effort in what was seen as a predetermined outcome: given that an agreement had been concluded and that the public was eager for a settlement there was a groundswell support for 'Yes'. Communists, Socialists, Radicals and Christian Democrats supported the settlement but tried to prevent the General being handed a blank cheque by salting their recommendations with criticisms. De Gaulle's government used the media to the full, the General appeared twice on the state television service and the Gaullist Party supported the 'Yes' side without reservations. On the other hand the opposition was disorganised and mainly featured a few individuals campaigning to reject the agreement. An enfeebled extreme right was anachronistically defending the *Algérie de papa* but some of those who opposed the agreement advocated abstention rather than getting out of step with their constituents (Goguel 1965).

On 8 April there was a substantial victory for 'Yes' and de Gaulle. Turnout was lower than in 1961, perhaps because the 'Yes' vote was widely anticipated, but little could be concluded from the higher abstention rate of 23.02 per cent (6,779,303). With 17,866,423 votes, some 66.77 per cent of the electorate (Algeria did not participate) and 91 per cent of the vote it was a landslide which buried a 'No' of 9.19 per cent of votes (1,809,074). Quite unexpectedly, de Gaulle celebrated this triumph not by dissolving the Assembly, but by sacking the Prime Minister, Michel Debré, on 14 April and nominating the unknown non-parliamentary figure of Georges Pompidou. Debré, who fought for governmental authority over the Assembly, was not a popular figure with the deputies, but this nomination showed that de Gaulle believed the Prime Minister to be the presidential 'right hand' and not the Parliament's choice. Then, shortly after the new government was installed, the MRP ministers resigned in protest at de Gaulle's European policy and the government's majority began to look shaky in an increasingly assertive Assembly. But de Gaulle was not ready. He needed the situation to be more clearly defined and to divide the Gaullists from the Opposition. Everybody in the mainstream supported the peace deal and the decolonisation; de Gaulle needed to force the question to his own advantage.

The Peace Dividend

Outside of the Soviet bloc, the support for the President in the referendums of 1958, 1961 and 1962 had no parallels; de Gaulle's problem had been to mobilise support for the Presidency against the Parliament while retaining support there. But the crisis wound on through the last stages of French retreat in 1962. OAS assassins provided a further occasion with an almost successful attempt on de Gaulle's life at Petit-Clamart in August 1962, reminding the country how fragile the new institution and stability were without the General. De Gaulle had his excuse, and went on the offensive, arguing that his successor (not to be elected until 1969) would need the backing of universal suffrage to maintain their authority. Most of de Gaulle's opponents did hope that the Presidency would diminish as a force and rejected direct election, which could reinforce the institution.

In holding a second referendum in 1962 on direct election of the President de Gaulle revealed himself as the Michaelangelo of the main chance, realising that he had to force a show down with the Opposition but on his terms and in his time. An issue was needed which would have popular support and which would place adversaries in an indefensible position. De Gaulle decided on a referendum to introduce the direct election of the President. Metropolitan France could no longer be outvoted by an Empire which had been decolonised and de Gaulle's prestige was at its highest. Because of the OAS assassination attempt, de Gaulle was able to capitalise on the *peur du vide* and raised the stakes by threatening to resign if the vote was other than wholehearted. Indeed the choice between a vacuum and continuity seemed to be exemplified by the Opposition. On the one side was the united Gaullist Party (and its allies) and on the other were the 'Old Guard' of the Fourth Republic and extremes from Thorez (the Communists) to Le Pen (of the colonial right). The 'No' camp was an incoherent collection of 'Christian democrat, social democrat, liberal, European, independent and peasant, marxist Leninist, reactionary, progressive, existentialist and nihilo-merovingian'. It had no programme and was in no sense an alternative to de Gaulle.

Prime Minister Pompidou's government, to all appearances, anticipated that the Opposition in the Assembly would condemn de Gaulle's proposed referendum as unconstitutional (which it was) and contrary to Republican principles (Roussel 1984, p. 149). Opposition politicians fell into the elephant trap and on 5 October a censure motion was carried with the Gaullists making only a ritual show of rejecting it. This was the excuse – provided by the Opposition – that de Gaulle needed and the Assembly was dissolved. That meant a general election in the wake of a referendum, revealing the deficiencies of the 'No' camp. Thus Opposition parties were caught in the position of refusing the public the right to vote for their own President, campaigning that the public should vote against having a vote. Under de Gaulle the Presidency had become the keystone of the constitutional structure and the General's supremacy was clear. To refuse to extend the franchise for the presidential elections appeared to be perverse; to confirm the Gaullist accusation that the political class conspired against the public to the detriment of the national interest and of natural justice. The fact that the referendum was unconstitutional further provoked the opposition to the General, but the Fifth Republic had been introduced by referendum and although the learnèd doctors were correct in legal terms, de Gaulle had got the politics right. While stopping short of being another landslide victory, the result at the end of October was a striking personal success for de Gaulle. Although it was the lowest 'Yes' vote to date de Gaulle, for the first time in the Fifth Republic, had been opposed by the entire political Establishment, which had campaigned against de Gaulle. On a high turnout (only 23 per cent abstention), 62 per cent voted 'Yes' (13,150,516 or 46.7 per cent of the register) and 28 per cent voted 'No' (7,974,538 or 37.7 per cent of electors).

Régime Transition

In 1962 de Gaulle had engineered a transition to his advantage from the exceptional condition of internal insurrection to 'normal politics', through the use of the referendums. The victory in the October referendum was followed up fast by general elections in November. Opposition politicians had no time and not yet sufficient incentive to attempt the task of building a coherent, credible, Opposition. Instead, the 'Third Force' parties campaigned in November 1962 as the 'Cartel des non', reminding voters of the unregretted governments of the Fourth Republic. De Gaulle struck precisely and with timing to reinforce his position as President and to consolidate power, a task he had not been able to accomplish at the Liberation and which had defeated Mendès France (the nearest comparison in the Fourth Republic). But in doing so de Gaulle became the leader of the conservative centre-right. De Gaulle had polarised the political party system around his Presidency, but the coalition was anti-Communist as well as being pro-de Gaulle and the Communist Party had not disappeared – it remained large and well organised. After 1962, de Gaulle's coalition consolidated as a modern conservative movement with the active fault line becoming the left/right one. De Gaulle had moved from the position of crisis-leader to the crafter of a new conservative coalition based on a pragmatic domestic policy with a non-exclusive view of the nation and an active foreign policy of national self-assertion. In this process the referendum was vital and those of 1962 were indispensable.

Once again the referendum had supported the President against the Assembly and the victory was confirmed in the November general elections when the Gaullists and their allies won a parliamentary majority while voters culled many of the Fourth Republic's leaders of the centre-right as they had done those of the centre-left in 1958. However, the transition to 'normality' had an effect on the presidential coalition which then became a more conservative one backing de Gaulle and less a cross-party national one. Gaullism's claim to represent 'France' as a whole was not plausible and the fault line between Gaullism and its allies and the Opposition began to resemble the more conventional politics of Western Europe. De Gaulle continued to lay claim to a 'special' legitimacy and, although the referendums had given him that backing, it was a majority coalition around the President that was determinant (Goguel 1983, Vol. II, Ch 5).

Under the early Fifth Republic the referendums had a clear purpose: to support the increasingly dominant role which de Gaulle was playing as President as the war remained the problem for the first legislature. Framers of the new Constitution had not anticipated the eclipse of the Prime Minister and de Gaulle, not having been directly elected in 1958 and not having an explicit platform, needed this series of popular backings during the Algerian crisis. In the Assembly, most deputies were not 'Gaullist', nor loyal to the President, and would not normally have done de Gaulle's bidding. In de Gaulle's first four referendums the President asked the right questions and the public's answer was more or less predictable. Referendums appeared necessary and much was at stake. In this sense the 'dialogue' with the people, cutting out the Assembly, was an apposite analogy. De Gaulle needed popular support and it had to be demonstrated. Moreover the presidential coalition had to be pulled together and the Opposition isolated and pushed on to unpopular ground. The four referendums helped de Gaulle achieve these objectives while reinforcing his authority through the wider debate on 'de Gaulle and the government's policies' which the campaigns animated. Hence the four referendums from 1958 to 1962 dramatised the authority of the Presidency, but from de Gaulle's position of strength.

Referendums after the Algerian Crisis

Referendums had a leverage effect when used to demonstrate authority rather than to build or to bolster it. But when referendums were used to win back failing authority they had a reverse leverage and if the vote could illustrate presidential supremacy it could also reveal weakness. Moreover, after November 1962, the President had the support of the majority in the Assembly and there were no constraints from obstructive deputies nor was there a crisis comparable to the Algerian war. De Gaulle's politics had been a success; by the mid-1960s presidential supremacy had come to seem the norm in Fifth Republic politics. De Gaulle's success, which the referendum had helped establish, made the referendum superfluous. No President could afford to use referendums which appeared bogus or vindictive; Presidents who risked referendums from a position of unpopularity could be disavowed. De Gaulle's offer of a referendum on 'participation' in the 'Events' of May 1968 was met with scorn.

Five years after the referendum to amend the Constitution, the referendum of 1969 on regionalisation and reform of the Senate, which saw the defeat of the proposal and the resignation of de Gaulle is a case in point. De Gaulle had proposed a referendum on 24 May 1968 during the 'events' but this promise had been forgotten when the general elections took place (Hayward 1993). It was the May 'events' which had undermined de Gaulle and had, despite a landslide Assembly majority, made a reaffirmation of the President's authority necessary (to de Gaulle). It became necessary, in his own estimation, to restore a flagging ascendancy over the conservative coalition which he had brought together. It was less a 'suicide by referendum' than a rage against the dying of the limelight (Bon 1970). It was a referendum in two parts: a popular reform introducing regional assemblies was coupled to a less popular reform of the Senate. De Gaulle had long resented the Senate's obstruction, staffed by some of his most vigorous opponents, and the deposed Fourth Republic political class was well represented. Under its Speaker, Gaston Monnerville, relations with the Elysée had reached their nadir in 1962 and he was not on speaking terms with de Gaulle when he left his Senate office.

Had the referendum succeeded, de Gaulle would have been reconfirmed as the dominant personality on the right and continued his term until 1972 disencumbered of the troublesome Senate. If the proposal for regional reform was broadly popular it had unsettling implications for local government and the Senate reform was provocative. It was a proposal which at a stroke united the Opposition in the Senate against him. Whereas in the past de Gaulle had lined up the Opposition to demonstrate their incapacity and failings, the Senators proved surprisingly adept at defending their House and were not secondary or abrasive personalities. Moreover the (seemingly) gratuitous attack on the Upper House was deeply unsettling and the proposals called up the spectre of a Salazarist/corporatist organ. It was also very probably unconstitutional but, although that was politically managed in 1962, it was unacceptable in 1969.

Alain Poher, the newly elected Speaker of the Senate, was a Christian Democrat, a Europeanist and an unknown. Poher flung himself into a vigorous campaign in defence of the Senate which was the making of him. De Gaulle reacted to the increasing pressure on 10 April by threatening to resign if he were defeated. Opposition, however, mounted and de Gaulle even divided his own supporters. Their main ally, the Independent Republicans, who normally supported the General, were hostile: 'La France est devant le référendum comme quelqu'un à qui on a mis un oursin entre les doigts', noted Giscard d'Estaing (Chagnollaud and Quermonne 1996, p. 67). It was a campaign which never fired the imagination – as had the 1962 reform of the Presidency – and it took on an unstated dimension of a choice between de Gaulle and Pompidou, whereas previously, de Gaulle's referendums had constrained the public to face the lack of alternative to the General. Although the mobilisation of the voters was high (only 20 per cent abstained), the 'No' vote took a majority of 53.18 per cent (46.82 per cent voted 'Yes'). It was an unmistakable rebuff to the head of state and de Gaulle drew the obvious lesson: on 28 April he resigned.

Europe in 1972

De Gaulle's 1969 attempt to use the referendum thus worked a reverse leverage and, unsurprisingly, was a warning to future leaders who might be tempted. In the subsequent presidential elections Georges Pompidou, de Gaulle's one-time ally and latterly rival, was elected President. Pompidou was caution embodied, not a politician for the theatrics which had been de Gaulle's style. But President Pompidou provided another warning on how the referendum might be misused. A referendum in April 1972 was held (this time under Article 11) on the pretext of ratifying the Treaty enlarging the Common Market to include the United Kingdom, Eire, Denmark and Norway. It was inspired by a sort of naive Machiavellism which the President recognised to have been a mistake (Jobert 1974, p. 227). Pompidou's intention may have been to show that he had similar backing to the General and he was in conflict with some of the 'compagnons' for reversing one of the more distinctive Gaullist policies, but they found themselves up against the 'Gaullist' device of the referendum (Leigh 1975). There was also the growing problem of the Opposition which was uniting around the revived Parti socialiste and negotiating a platform for the 1973 elections with the PCF. A referendum would force into the open the disagreements on the left between the Europhobic Communists and the Europhile Socialists and Radicals. Thus, had it gone well, the referendum would have reinforced the President's authority in France and abroad and split the Opposition (Ibid., 1977, p. 137).

Communist Party leaders seemed to confirm this prognostic by spurning the suggestion of abstention proffered by the Socialist Party and flinging themselves and their party machine into the 'No' campaign. This provided an opposition and (from Pompidou's point of view) the right one. However, Pompidou's ploy began to go wrong from the outset although it was greeted as a coup ('bien joué'). Public opinion was not enthused about a being asked to support a negotiated treaty (if it was not good, why had it been signed?) and the momentum flagged. Other campaigners for a wider Europe (notably the Radicals) proved more enthusiastic than the 'Pompidolians' and Mitterrand avoided commitment to a damaging campaign by recommending abstention. Gaullist critics did not have any difficulty campaigning on the same side as the Communist Party and were not silenced (splits were in consequence not healed) and they, unlike the 'Yes' supporters, were well organised. Overall the public did not rally and the referendum was seen as pointless or as trickery. It was not the failure to win which undermined the value of the referendum but the low turnout. Although 68 per cent voted 'Yes' and only 32 per cent 'No', 40 per cent abstained (7 per cent spoilt ballots). Opposition differences were quickly forgotten and an alliance was sealed the following June between Communists, Socialists and Left Radicals. For the President it was a setback but Pompidou, with his habitual caution, had not put much at stake and it was shrugged off as the conservatives rallied to face the challenge of the 1973 general elections.

1988–93

With the experience of 1969 and 1972, the referendum was not attempted again until 1988 (Frears 1991, pp. 218–20). This referendum, to ratify the agreements between the settlers, the indigenous population and the government in the French overseas territory of New Caledonia, was not a presidential manoeuvre in the same way (Chagnollaud 1993, p. 382). In this case President Mitterrand had just been re-elected and Prime Minister Rocard had then engineered a settlement in the Overseas Department of New Caledonia; threatened by civil war between a settler ('Caldoches') population and an indigenous Melanesian ('Kanak') population who mostly favoured independence. It was a problem which Mitterrand's election of 1981 had encountered. His victory aroused Kanak expectations and the Socialist government had tried to conciliate by granting greater autonomy to the two populations. However, despite attempts at reform the situation deteriorated until a solution was brokered just before the Socialists lost power in 1986. When the new conservative government took power it scrapped the plan and treated the problem as one of law and order although violence restarted and worsened. It was a point of dispute during the two-year 'cohabitation' and Chirac had tried to exploit the conflict, with significant loss of life, during his presidential campaign of 1988 (*Le Monde* 22–23/5/88).

It was against this background that the Rocard government had to work and the new Prime Minister patiently negotiated a new agreement (Attali 1995, Vol. III, p. 499). Given the legacy of distrust and back-tracking, the hope was to use the referendum to give backing to the deal, to ensure that it would not be undone (or seen as ephemeral). It would be a guarantee to the New Caledonian peoples, which would bind future

French governments, and as a device it had some parallel with de Gaulle's referendum of January 1961. However, the conditions were very different and when the referendum came in November 1988 at the end of a long series of six elections, the issue was regarded as settled, the problem was intricate and went unexplained, whereas the political stakes were absent. Only the Front National campaigned for a 'No' vote (neo-Gaullists called for abstention and in New Caledonia the 'Caldoches' voted 'No') but although the 'Yes' vote was 80 per cent to the 'No' vote of 20 per cent, the abstention rate at 59 per cent was the highest ever in a French election (Frears 1991, pp. 218–20). The poor turn out and the intricacies of the negotiation made it difficult for the referendum itself to help cement a settlement. New Caledonia depended on long-term political work keeping the peace and maintaining the balance between the populations with a view to consolidating the settlement. That had to be the work of local and national leaders.

The Maastricht Trick

President Mitterrand held one final referendum and one, which fits more into the pattern of the previous Gaullist referendums, in September 1992, on the Maastricht Treaty on Europe which, accelerated integration and necessitated a small revision of the Constitution. It was not, however, necessary to hold a referendum. When the Treaty had been ratified by the Parliament at the end of June the polls showed that it was broadly accepted and a vote would probably have very substantially seconded the parliamentarians (Drain 1993).

Mitterrand may have calculated (like Pompidou in 1972) that hitching the Presidency to the popular European issue would have confirmed its centrality, reinforced its importance in foreign policy making and strengthened France's position in European Councils (Denmark had just had difficulties in ratifying the Maastricht Treaty). In addition the Socialist Party, submerging in a tide of corporate larceny, was flagging badly in the polls (on the way to defeat in the general elections of 1993) and so was the President. Europe was an issue which brought the party together and divided the right. Only something exceptional would have brought the conservative right's defeat in 1993, but the referendum might have given the President a margin to choose between possible partners in the next and inevitable 'cohabitation' of 1993–5. Whatever Mitterrand's intentions, the referendum campaign did split the French political spectrum though not just on the right, separating the Socialists from their support in their old bastions while dissident neo-Gaullists made a populist appeal.

Unexpectedly the referendum brought the Europhobes to centre stage – not the 'usual suspects' of the Front National and Communist Party (thought they were active) – but the RPR's Charles Pasqua, who also encouraged the UDF's Philippe de Villiers and, more importantly, the neo-Gaullist Philippe Séguin. Philippe Séguin emerged as the principal figure. His astute campaign, opposing the Maastricht Treaty but not Europe, was in keeping with traditional Gaullism and his common sense, if sometimes abrasive, style made conservative Euroscepticism credible. While the 'No' campaign was vigorous and active over the summer the demoralised Socialist Party was unable to provide a counter and the conservative pro-Maastricht politicians were not keen to support a Presidential referendum. On 20 September 1992 there was a high turnout of 70 per cent but a very narrow victory for the partisans of the Maastricht Treaty who took 13,162,992 'Yes' votes (51 per cent) to the 12,623,582, for 'No' (49 per cent) (Criddle 1993).

Fault lines were opened in French politics, which still remain visible. Philippe de Villiers demarked himself from the mainstream of the UDF and the RPR had a new star in Philippe Séguin, but relations between 'Europhobes', 'Eurosceptics' and 'Europhiles' in the conservative camp were appreciably worsened. These differences were not enough to halt the landslide of 1993 and the left was also divided along pro and anti-European lines (Dreyfus 1982). Communist leaders found that they had been given an unexpected opportunity to regroup after the collapse of the Soviet system and took the patriotic, workers' defence stance which they had used in the past to great effect. A schism opened wider inside the Socialist Party when Jean-Pierre Chevènement created the Citizens' Movement (MDC) dedicated to anti-European issues and led to the detachment and creation of a 'Chevènementiste' party to revive his flagging political prospects. But the Socialist Party was more damaged by a split which opened up between its leadership and its supporters. Although the 'Yes' vote corresponded to the traditional (Catholic) areas of right-wing strength, the big left-wing areas of the Nord-Pas-de-Calais, the Parisian red belt, and the Provence-Languedoc farming departments all voted 'No'.

In sum the French public came close to rejecting a Treaty which the mainstream politicians regarded as vital to France's future and the issue was not closed by the referendum. Europe was further linked, during the campaign, to unpopular effects of unemployment and insecurity and became a much less popular cause. President Mitterrand's referendum inflated suspicions of the political class in the prevailing anti-Establishment mood of scandal and hardship. Because the result was positive, France's hand was not weakened within Europe but the difficult task of persuading the public about European union remained to be undertaken (Arter 1993, pp. 215–16). It was inevitably a plebiscite on the Presidency, but if the vote was intended to solidify support for his coalition it did not do so. As Giscard acidly commented, it was only because of the strength of the European commitment that the 'Yes' prevailed and, such was the unpopularity of the government, no other issue would have been supported.

Conclusion

At a time of crisis as severe as any in French history – the Algerian war – the referendum enabled the President to demonstrate support in an irrefutable manner, effacing other questions with massive displays of popular endorsement. It was a weapon, which gave de Gaulle a crucial margin when the Republic itself was in danger, and allowed him to consolidate the Presidency of the Fifth Republic by providing it with support. It was a presidential sword when de Gaulle was struggling with the Laocoön serpent of Algeria and the threat to the Republic. After the Algerian war, voters had regular opportunities to return verdicts on the presidential exercise of power at presidential and other elections and there was less need for the further bolstering of the institution after de Gaulle's resignation. In the 1970s and the 1980s the local municipal and departmental elections were partially turned into verdicts on national (that is presidential) politics as well as on local factors.

As a presidential weapon the referendum enabled a number of tactical attacks to be made. In the first place it enabled the Presidents to divide the Opposition against itself and consolidate their own support. De Gaulle's referendums (until 1969) were positioned so as to show wide non-partisan support and to separate leaders from followers: the voters backed de Gaulle often against 'their' party. There was no other way at the time that would have permitted the manipulation out of the mass of voters of 'Gaullist' support. De Gaulle may have been confident of this backing, but it had to be shown to be available to the President. They had the further advantage for de Gaulle of splitting the other parties internally as well: some politicians initially preferred to support de Gaulle than to look into the abyss; some found themselves being driven to counsel abstention before being forced into opposition in 1962. Oppositions were split from each other, within each other and from their voters.

Referendums enabled the President to determine the question or the agenda despite the opposition of other politicians over Algeria, and enabled the President to determine the priorities of debate to their advantage. This was again related to the Algerian war. There was no more evident way of demonstrating the willingness of public opinion to follow the General's twists in Algerian policy than the referendums and no more evident way to keep the focus on the President. Using the Assembly would not have worked as de Gaulle had no stable majority then, and would have highlighted the role of the Prime Minister (who was not in complete harmony with the President on the change in policy) rather than the President. De Gaulle turned the spotlight on his own position rather than on the ballot paper question, but the effect was the same. The Assembly could not have been used as a distinctly presidential platform.

When Presidents are able to unite their own supporters, draw them together and build coalitions behind the Presidency, where the voters can be drawn onto the presidential side, the process of building support is easier and the detailed bargaining, which Assembly 'horse-trading' necessitates, is avoided. This again was crucial in the Algerian war when the General wanted a free hand. It was attempted by President Mitterrand in 1992 (Europe generally mobilises the Socialists) and by Pompidou in 1972 (also on Europe), but the mobilisation of the public is not something which can be assumed and has to be produced (usually by a party campaign).

In other circumstances the attempt to divide can work against the President. In 1969 the referendum on the reform of the Senate brought the defensive reflex from Giscard d'Estaing's Independent Republicans who urged a 'No' vote. Pompidou's referendum in 1972 briefly split the Opposition of the left but also exposed an enduring fault-line amongst Gaullists over Europe. Likewise, President Mitterrand's referendum of 1992 on the Maastricht Treaty also split the Opposition, though not enough to prevent the impending landslide which buried the presidential party in 1993's elections. It can also seriously split the presidential coalition and in 1992 the referendum provided the ailing the Communist Party with the anti-European issue around which to rally.

On the 'presidential referendums' two points emerge; neither is world shaking. Referendums must engage the public: otherwise, if they do not, they will not be taken seriously by the voters who (whatever the theory might say) do not like being asked to vote if nothing but presidential convenience is at stake. De Gaulle, during the conduct of the Algerian emergency, could convey the impression that there was much at stake, despite the abstruse questions that were asked. In the subsequent referendums only when, in 1992, the Maastricht Treaty was in danger of rejection, were the stakes considered high and that had not been foreseen. Even then, an unpopular President was unable to manipulate public opinion. For, secondly, the subject (which may not be the one on the ballot paper) must be straight. Referendums failed if voters took the view that the referendum was a 'trick'. In the use of the referendum the President needs to garner support but not through deceit. De Gaulle's threats to withdraw were real and effective – until 1969. Too obvious manipulation is as bad as guilelessness in political leadership.

If there is power in tapping into public support through the referendum, there is also danger. Presidential power was enhanced by the referendum in the immediate problem of the Algerian war and in confirming the Presidency as the seat of power. There is the danger that the referendum will stir up activity, which cannot be controlled, and there is the problem that low turn out or ambiguity may work against the President and deprive the executive of the authority needed. Of course, the danger of rejection cannot be discounted and that is direct where the public votes 'No' and debilitating if the response is insufficient.

But, returning to the starting point of this investigation, the referendum can be seen in its use by de Gaulle in the early years of the new Republic as the first phase in the determination of presidential power. Of course, the intention was not to return power to the people but to get the people to return de Gaulle. But this was a preface without a book. The referendum proved a limited weapon for the President out of the context of crisis and after de Gaulle politicians turned to other means of bolstering the institution.

–4–

The Presidential 'reserved domain'

Charismatic leaders, it is argued, tend to be venturesome in their diplomacy (Rustow 1967, p.166). This is because the international arena enables a leader to exploit opportunities to dramatic effect bolstering their personal position through appeals to patriotism. In the 1960s the deadlock between the two superpowers was particularly propitious for some middle-rank states. Yet foreign policy is not, ultimately, a matter of welfare, the normal priority in politics; de Gaulle's case, striking foreign success, could not be sustained because of limited French strength and it was not offset by a regard for the domestic situation. In addition, the international milieu was not one which could be controlled by France, as the situation in Europe turned out not to be as de Gaulle imagined or portrayed it. But in the early Fifth Republic the exploitation of diplomatic possibilities reinforced the Presidency even if there was an ambiguous legacy. As a result foreign and defence policy in the Fifth Republic were, from the Presidencies of de Gaulle to Giscard (and Mitterrand until 1986), accepted as the President's constitutional 'reserved domain'.

In fact, it is in political terms that the President has held the institutional high ground in foreign policy and defence. It has remained a political domain in which Presidents have kept the political advantage and was quickly perceived as such by 'cohabitation' Presidents. De Gaulle's foreign policy was intended to be uplifting, providing the presidential leadership which moved the society up to new levels and lifted France itself above the quotidian. In a curious reversal of diplomatic practice de Gaulle inverted the usual priorities. Thus people asked what the Presidents thought (not what France's interests were) and tried to guess or divine their intentions. By this personalisation, the President would both dramatise and compensate for the ferments of dispersion. This is where the notion of 'grandeur' has its place in the Gaullist conceptual schema (Cerny 1980). It is here that the politics of the Presidency and of its founder are determinant (Cohen 1990).

Unity and Grandeur

De Gaulle, on his return to power in 1958, stated that France's vocation was to be one of the great states (F.-G. Dreyfus 1982, p. 191). In the speeches made by the General and in the political actions of the Presidency there were, in Petitfils' exegesis, two guiding principles: unity and grandeur (Petitfils 1986). These two were intimately linked in that the unity of the French nation, through the state, would enable 'grandeur' to be attained and would in return promote further domestic unity. National harmony would emerge through the 'grandeur' of an independent, forceful France, one of the determining powers, rightfully taking its place on the United Nations Security Council. De Gaulle, in his own estimation, as set out in the *War Memoirs*, was to be the guarantor of France's destiny and of the independence of the French state (Cotteret and Moreau 1969). This vocation was passed on to successors who all maintained their sovereign responsibility for foreign affairs and defence often (as with de Gaulle) to the point of mystification.

De Gaulle set out a vision of what France ought to be, and in doing so set the foundations for future policy throughout his Presidency; lesser successors would be constrained to build on similar lines. This may not have been a calculated institution building but the foundations were so strong that the structure proved semi-permanent and subsequent Presidents found it useful to fall back on prepared Gaullist positions but also difficult to innovate within the constraints laid down by the founder (Revel 1959, pp. 46–7).

There are, however, other facets to de Gaulle's foreign policy outlook and (without necessarily assigning priority to causes) these can plausibly be seen as ways of managing de Gaulle's coalition and hence consolidating the position of the Presidency. Whatever the rationale of de Gaulle's policy (and there is no convincing one, see Gladwyn 1969) the world stage was one which de Gaulle used for the theatrical coup: to surprise, to unbalance others, to demonstrate French revival as an assertive power and to keep attention on himself. For de Gaulle the foreign stage provided an opportunity for the theatrical (something often remarked as part of the General's style) and for the creation of suspense. Who knew what the French President would do? It was a strategy of capricious unpredictability, which kept de Gaulle's opponents continually off-balance. There are few other areas of policy in which this is possible and it had the effect of leaving both the public, diplomats and even his own ministers continually speculating about what de Gaulle was trying to do. This tactic forced observers to accept the autonomy of the decision-maker in the Elysée and, of course, the independence, and autonomous policy, of France itself.

De Gaulle, here, was in his element. Diplomacy is the domain of the word: action takes place, in the main part, at a verbal level and is concentrated in the 'speech act'. 'Grandeur', which de Gaulle believed was France's due, had to be displayed within this limited context of the Cold War and the loss of Empire. At the end of the Algerian war, de Gaulle faced a decolonised world and the question of what the epochal role for France could be other than its cultural mission in its ex-Empire. De Gaulle, like many other politicians, scented possibilities in the 'Third World' of new nation-states. Revivifying French foreign policy and giving the nation a sense of its own destiny became the main difficulty. This was accomplished by de Gaulle in a way which was original and the Presidents after de Gaulle found it hard to produce the same sense of mission. De Gaulle had to change the content of the foreign policy in the Fifth Republic and in so doing used the ploys of improvisation unsettling others and keeping the initiative. De Gaulle's politics was, however, baffling – intentionally so.

A World of Nations

Part of Gaullism was the Napoleonic nation-state ideal and it had some of the same drawbacks. In this view the world was, or ought to be, a community of nations and France was the midwife of national self-determination. France would assist the birth or the emergence of the nation-states in Europe and elsewhere. To this vision of a world of nations formed through self-determination was added a maurassian 'realpolitik' which was as romantic, if not more so, than the universal nationalism evoked in the speeches made by the General. There was enough ambiguity about the proposals to keep the textual exegesist busy, but the proliferation of nation-states and independence were married to an appeal to the 'balance of power' principle. Thus 'grandeur' looks at times like a new version of *maachtpolitik*, in which States acted out of self-interest and had no friends. 'National interests' (as the theorists of today would put it) were pursued leading to switches of policy and alliances without compunction for the 'monstres froides', which had interests but no constraints. States acted without restraint and France itself might need to ally with the USA one day and Germany the next, as interest dictated (Duroselle 1966).

De Gaulle's outlook was in part a deeply traditional one and harked back to the eighteenth century, wilfully ignoring the ideological division of the Cold War world. De Gaulle conjured up the power politics of the sovereigns engaged in a stately minuet and captured it in the language he used when President (Russia, not the USSR, England, not the United Kingdom). In Europe it was the Cold War confrontation of the two blocs that prevented the natural nation-state system from reasserting itself and was in the long run untenable. 'If the Kremlin persists,' de Gaulle wrote, 'it will be against the will of the nations submitted to its government. Now, there is no regime which, in the long term, can hold out against national wills' (de Gaulle 1970, p. 47). This projection of the nationalist reaction to Soviet domination was, ultimately, correct but the gap between the 'long term' dissolution of the blocs and the short-term threat from the East was never filled. This gap became starkly evident when the Warsaw Pact invaded Czechoslovakia in August 1968 putting an end for over twenty years to that country's sovereignty. Nonetheless, as a rhetorical strategy, de Gaulle's vision was an invention of genius. It enabled a multitude of reactions and provided a flexible justification for the most eccentric action.

Nuclear Politics

There are three aspects to the presidential 'reserved domain': defence, foreign policy and Europe. For the purposes of boosting the Presidency and the politics of coalition, the most dramatic is nuclear policy, but the three are interlinked and can be seen as part of the same process of manoeuvre. Where de Gaulle's politics as theatre came to the fore, however, was in the more dynamic elements of politics where he could seize the moment or impose a definition on a situation. In these areas it is the posthumous influence of the General which is important and by commanding and dominating the high ground of national sovereignty has marked the Fifth Republic Presidency.

It was in August 1960 at Reggane (in the Sahara) that the first French nuclear device was tested and France's first 'H-bomb' was exploded in August 1968. However, the nuclear weapons programme had been set underway well before in the Fourth Republic in much the same way as the United Kingdom's but without the American aid the British government relied upon. De Gaulle inherited a process that was maturing and continued to promote it. What was not provided was a political rationale and this de Gaulle was able to give (Aron 1965, pp. 100–43). Nuclear politics became a presidential matter and a 'doctrine' was provided with the usual verve which the General imparted to matters of high politics. In this outlook the deterrent depended, it was underscored, on the determination of the user: 'dissuasion du faible au fort'. This in other words was the President in person: the greatest destructive force to be constructed lay in the hands of the Elysée.

This 'doctrine' was not without its incoherences. There were deficiencies in the size and numbers of French atomic weapons, about the delivery systems and about their diplomatic use. Throughout the 1960s, during de Gaulle's time, the Mirage IV bombers of the strike force ('force de frappe') would have needed mid-air refuelling over Eastern Europe and could easily have been destroyed on the ground. In March 1967 the first French nuclear submarine was launched (with 16 missiles) and intercontinental ballistic missiles were developed for placement in 'hardened' silos in the Plateau d'Albion. At their height the French forces were perhaps a tenth of the United States and a twentieth of the USSR's and France did not have, and never acquired, the communications infrastructure which was vital to America and the Soviet bloc. These features of the weapons programme led to flights of nuclear theology aspiring to justify the ambitions of the Gaullist programme. None of these were convincing and need not detain the observer (Aron 1990, Ch. XVI). But unlike other aspects of diplomacy in the post-war world, the atomic bomb had an effect: explosions were a visible demonstration of power. Such visible demonstrations were difficult in other realms of policy and they also provoked a flurry in foreign offices (and anger from those close to the fallout) (Chantebout 1986).

Europe

Defence has been crucial in the definition of the Fifth Republic Presidency, but then so too has 'Europe'. 'Europe' has, of course, always had French backing and it has had distinguished proponents back to Saint-Simon and before. However, Europe is an essentially Fourth Republic foundation and one supported by the centre and centre-left (Christian Democrat and Socialist). It was seen then, as it still is, as a way of promoting French interests and enabling Franco-German reconciliation. With the Fifth Republic de Gaulle's shadow fell across the policy as the President turned on the nascent institutions with unequalled determination and a rhetoric to eclipse 'Europhiles', amongst whom must be counted at least two successor Presidents (Giscard and Mitterrand). They found this rhetorical position difficult to counter and de Gaulle's Euro-doubts has had a long half-life.

De Gaulle's European stance was replete with contradictions, as the 'Gaullist' view is incoherent. From its inception as the European Coal and Steel Community (ECSC) in 1951, 'Europe' was an ambitious project which involved closer cooperation than was usual between sovereign states and a much more extended community. Yet Europe was still a set of sovereign states delegating power for common purposes, by a continual bargaining as well as an inter-state union (Milward 1984, p. 492). This process had confederal possibilities should they ever be activated but they depended on consent. France had, in this European situation, a natural advantage and could take the political lead (despite the industrial domination of Germany). Fourth Republic politicians were fully aware of the possibilities and the constraints but wagered that it was the route to a new Europe in which France (as Victor Hugo had envisaged) would be the head, always assuming that it could bring other states along with it.

De Gaulle's other rhetorical trope stood in contrast to the leadership proffered to a shiftless European flock. De Gaulle's RPF, despite claiming that de Gaulle had been the originator of the European idea, attacked the ECSC in nationalist terms from the outset (Willis 1968, p. 99). De Gaulle had been portrayed by his supporters since 1940 as the only figure who could save France and had himself opposed the European project, but in 1958 he returned to the theme from the perspective of government. Outright obstruction was not attempted. Had the General so wished the development of the European Economic Community (which had been negotiated in 1957) could have been stopped on his return to power. It had, in fact, been feared that de Gaulle would do just that but instead he promoted the new Rome Treaty and rebuilt the French position to meet the obligations hastening its application in January 1959. This period of grace was short lived and the hostility of the General to 'Europe' remained muted until the Algerian War came under control. It was not the time to start a second front and the swift acceptance had the advantage of advertising the arrival of a new – Gaullist – France.

De Gaulle took this conception one stage further by discounting 'England' as France's hereditary enemy 'from the Hundred Years War to Fachoda' (and as not being of the continent), and writing out of the record a century of conflict (Peyrefitte 1994, p. 152). He also assumed that Italy and Benelux were followers and that Germany could be made francophile and, divided, it was in no position to make policy (Peyrefitte 1994, p. 153). By the same token, the nature of the regime in the USSR was discounted as having no part in his calculations about the state system at that time. Thus de Gaulle arrogated to France the leadership of Europe (a 'European Europe'), but stripped it of its consensual nature.

There was a great deal in this view. France had a privileged situation and for Germany to re-enter the European state system it was necessary to pass the French gatekeeper. Germany was the key state in the continental European system but for historical reasons was unable to capitalise on its pre-eminent industrial and commercial power and its military potential could not be used. Germany had, since the Second World War, decided to opt for a 'Bismarckian' strategy to manage its invidious position. Its new Federal leaders wanted to play a role in the Western state system and chose to do so by reassuring its neighbours, by placating them about its intentions and by compromising to find a modus vivendi. It was not willing to lead, which would have been destabilising, it was reluctant to provoke for the same reason and the first neighbour to be conciliated was France. For Germany the forum for the reconciliation of these diverse interests was European institutions and that became under de Gaulle the support for French leadership.

Other states had to be brought along but were ultimately less crucial. Britain was outside of the EEC and had not been keen on the project in its beginnings. Italy and Benelux were important potential allies for the new Federal Republic, but France was the other principal continental power and, as France had been at the centre of the quarrels with the nascent German state, it was to France which the European powers looked. Jean Monnet's ideas of integration and the collaboration through the ECSC and EEC had made the 'European' institutions the place for the remaking of European collaboration in lieu of enmity and in those France was dominant (Duroselle 1966). On economic and monetary matters, where Germany wanted neither to take the lead nor to appear confrontational, there was room for manoeuvre, which a determined French government could exploit.

De Gaulle recognised both of these facets by making Franco-German relations pass (by Treaty obligation) through the Presidency and by centralising European affairs in the Elysée. In January 1963 de Gaulle and the FGR's Chancellor Adenauer signed a reconciliation Treaty and formalised biannual bilateral meetings. This was an important step in raising the status of the rapprochement, although it was prepared for by the unheroic work of the Fourth Republic's politicians and was largely unsurprising. In 1966, the Sécretariat Général de Coordination Interministériel was set up to oversee the work of ministries that dealt with Brussels and to prevent any sectors escaping presidential control. In this way the most important and visible of French foreign relations were conducted by the Presidency itself. These developments enabled de Gaulle to use his favoured tactic of the surprise 'coup d'éclat' on European issues.

De Gaulle's charming of Adenauer's Germany has often been described (Vainsson-Ponté 1970) but his embrace of the German Chancellor after the signing of the Treaty was high drama. This embrace, seen by millions on TV, caught the imagination, as De Gaulle must have calculated. Yet de Gaulle also decided that, contrary to universal assumption, Europe's 'great quarrel' was with the United States and not the USSR. This eccentric conception was accepted by nobody outside of the Communist bloc and by and large only by Ceausescu within it. Thus the President's attempt to give the European institutions an anti-American dimension and to develop a policy at odds with Washington's view of the Cold War was a failure from its inception. By developing the Gaullist idea of leadership on a new basis (departing from the Fourth Republic's) and by emphasising its disharmonious aspects, de Gaulle was able to mark France's position strongly but was unable to manufacture consent. In a Europe divided by the Cold War into two blocs and with the principal power being the United States de Gaulle was bound to fail. Front-line states would remain loyal to the old conceptions of the Atlantic Alliance. Germany, in particular, could not permit Franco-German understanding to impede its special relationship with the United States. This fact became very obvious when, shortly after the Franco-German Treaty was signed Konrad Adenaur left the Chancellor's office, and relations between his successors and de Gaulle's France became cool. But in France, de Gaulle had introduced the 'lyrical illusion' that Europe was there to be led in whatever direction a determined French leadership chose.

Overconfident, perhaps, of forthcoming German support, de Gaulle launched the so-called 'Fouchet Plan' in July 1961 (Soutou 1990–1). This was seen as an impetuous attempt to impose leadership on Europe. It was proposed to sidestep EEC institutions to coordinate defence, foreign and cultural affairs through a council of heads of government or foreign ministers where decisions would be taken by unanimous vote (alongside the Commission). In July 1962 de Gaulle intervened in discussions to propose downgrading the EEC Commission, depriving it of economic competence to the benefit of 'Fouchet's institutions'. Behind the detailed technicalities lay the Gaullist ambition to stop political union and protect state sovereignty. When the plan met unpersuadable opposition from those who saw dangers to the European project as embodied in the EEC (through a levelling down of institutions) and Nato, it was dropped and de Gaulle made his contempt for the 'European' project plain. The intergovernmental direction of the EEC was confirmed and the pattern of the embryonic institutions was preserved (Newhouse 1967, p. 28 ff.).

De Gaulle and the UK

A further opportunity presented itself with the first British application for membership of the EEC made by the Macmillan government in July 1961. With German support, the General had scotched the UK's floating of a European free trade area, which could have threatened the EEC, and, of course, reduced French weight within the organisation. This had consolidated the Fourth Republic's entente with Germany and it became a test for the Fifth Republic's special relationship, but it also froze out the UK. Unable to pressure the EEC from outside, the British government decided to apply to join. When it came to the application itself this had initially been welcomed by 'the EEC six' (as the UK understood it, by the French as well) and it would have opened a protected market to the continent as well as providing a counterweight to a Franco-German condominium (Young 1993, p. 76ff.)

There was, however, a basic incompatibility between Britain and Europe, which became evident as negotiations started (Beloff 1963). This lack of a meeting point came because staple foods like cereals, wheat, meat and butter were imported to the UK at world market prices which were lower than the EEC. Inside the EEC farm prices were regulated to enable the (mainly French) farming community to earn a living and restructure and this meant that prices were higher. In addition to patterns of trade being different, oriented to the Commonwealth, the UK operated a very different system of farm support. There was, it became clear, no meeting point. Either the UK would have to abandon its policy of low-cost food or the EEC would have to scrap the Common Agricultural Policy. CAP had been laboriously negotiated by January 1962 to incorporate French interests and without reference to British positions. Neither outcome could be envisaged. On the one hand the EEC was not going to abandon its hard-won and only 'European' policy (and turn on the farming lobbies) and on the other the weak British government was not ready to reorient its policy or impose higher food prices.

By the time the third round of negotiations had begun in January 1963, the six were irritated by what they saw as the delaying tactics of the British side (Lambert 1963). De Gaulle, for his part, was free of the Algerian problem and had sidelined the pro-European parties. It was France which was the pacemaker in the negotiations and the others followed. This new-found determination reflected de Gaulle's strong domestic position confirming French leadership of the negotiations and giving outsiders the impression that the key to negotiations was de Gaulle's view – whatever that might be (and it was often unclear). In making overtures to de Gaulle, who Macmillan still hoped to win over, the UK had made clear its opposition to closer union and stronger European institutions. Macmillan's outlook had failed to mollify de Gaulle and by December 1962 it was clear that the President was against the UK's entry. But Macmillan had disenchanted the United Kingdom's supporters in the EEC 'six' (Barman 1963). For de Gaulle, however, the protracted negotiations with the Macmillan government were a vital part of building the President's international reputation. Concessions from London (small or large) redounded to his credit and placed France at the centre of attention. All eyes were on de Gaulle. Various schemes had been proposed over the fourteen-month negotiations to overcome the obstacles but they only served to put off the recognition that interests were incompatible.

It was at this point that de Gaulle stepped in and issued the 'veto'. This was less of a unilateral act than it was portrayed and in effect recognised the stalemate (Beloff 1963, pp. 121–2). Shortly after the negotiations were adjourned. On the pinpoint of incompatible interests de Gaulle then erected a vast inverted pyramid of justifications. These were given at the presidential press conference of 14 January. De Gaulle's carefully choreographed 'Louis Quatorze' conferences were another stage for drama: they were the high mass, the major ceremony of Gaullist ritual, performed for an audience of invited guests, ambassadors, parliamentarians, and ministers – and before the television cameras (Vainsson-Ponté 1964, pp. 44–7). Carefully rehearsed answers to prepared questions were a serious weapon in de Gaulle's armoury and the rejection of British membership had not been left to chance. De Gaulle showed France's new status by humiliating the United Kingdom and its 'insular' nature. In de Gaulle's view the UK was the 'Trojan Horse' for American power, a view confirmed for him by the deal between Kennedy and Macmillan in Nassau the previous month, allowing the UK to buy the American Polaris nuclear system. The offer had been extended to de Gaulle. It was de Gaulle's underlining of a 'European Europe' free from American control which became the thrust although the 'Trojan Horse' was already inside the walls. None of the other six, and certainly not Germany, were prepared to risk the weakening of Atlantic solidarity. De Gaulle had, nonetheless, by humiliating a declining power, provided a brutal reminder of where power now lay in the EEC.

De Gaulle had found a way to make European politics for his own headline-grabbing matter. He had also marked out a Gaullist policy, which was European but distinctive, which did not repudiate the EEC, but reinforced French interests in it. De Gaulle may have had the support of public opinion for many of his bombastic initiatives, but the domestic politics of it were more intricate: it was both divisive and hit at the 'soft underbelly' of the Opposition. By taking this view de Gaulle had lined up against him the 'Fourth Republic' elite, the political parties of the centre: the Christian Democrats, most of the Socialist Party as well as the old Radicals and many of the conservative Independents. These were the supporters of UK membership, but also the 'Europeans' who wanted a development of the EEC and its institutions. At the same time his own Gaullist supporters were willing to go along with him in asserting France's position and backing the new diplomacy. There was an additional advantage in that the Gaullist European policy coincided with Soviet interests. De Gaulle perhaps thought that it would enable an entente with the other superpower, but in domestic politics it served to push a further wedge in between the Communists, who were the main party of the Opposition, and their potential allies in the centre. On the European issue (as on others) Moscow preferred de Gaulle to the Socialists.

Relations within the six were briefly bad as a result of the veto. The Franco-German Treaty saved de Gaulle from isolation, and the General, free from domestic constraints, was able to develop a new assertiveness which was the determining factor in the negotiation of the 'Kennedy Round' GATT tariff reductions starting in 1966. In these de Gaulle blocked the negotiations by the EEC until French demands on cereal prices (then being resisted by Germany) were accepted. Germany, for its part, needed at times a European shield for its own interests and one that would not expose it in the front line against the USA. However, the pursuit of the anti-American agenda by the French President only served to increase France's distance from the six and eliminated any possibility of 'leadership' on other issues.

De Gaulle had not, however, exhausted the possibility of the EEC for political surprise. There was a further tactical use to be made of the institutions and that was a return to a more nationalistic view, one that depicted the EEC as a threat, and, by implication, the President as the guardian. In this instance it was the delay to the EEC (more successful than had been anticipated, even by Europhiles) which was the occasion for a display of Gaullist theatrics. A third phase of the Treaty, linked to the final stages of the CAP from which France benefited substantially, would have allowed for a number of decisions to be taken by 'qualified majority vote' by governments in the Council of Ministers. If this had come into force, it would have meant that France could (in theory) be outvoted after 1 January 1966. This was something the General chose to take issue with on the grounds of sovereignty and to contrast with the Fourth Republic's spinelessness when defending the national interest. At the same time, the Commission President, Walter Hallstein, said a little too often and too loudly that the Commission was the core of a new federal Europe and over-reached itself in proposing to take control of agricultural import levies (a budget of some size) (Newhouse 1967).

This was the background to the withdrawal of France's permanent representative to the Communities and the 'empty chair' crisis starting in June 1965 and lasting seven months. French presidential elections were due in December 1965 and the farmers were anxious. De Gaulle underestimated their concern and was driven to a second ballot by their vote for Jean Lecanuet on the first. De Gaulle tried to meet the farmers' worries with the reminder that the CAP had been his achievement and by remarking in between ballots that the agricultural settlement was in the bag but that unacceptable pressures were being applied. ('Do not sell your birthright . . .' many farmers were unimpressed). But behind the detail lay the substantive problem of what sort of community was being created and who would emerge as the political directorate of a united Europe. Having failed with the Fouchet plan, de Gaulle returned to the attack and consolidated his own 'Europe des patries' (to use Debré's words). De Gaulle's unilateral reinterpretation of the Rome Treaty provoked ire from France's partners, but it resulted in the Commission's pretensions being slapped down and in the 'Luxembourg compromise'. Some of the General's demands were not met and the crisis ended with a fudge but the agricultural negotiations led to the Common Market of July 1968 (Willis 1968, p. 353). What the politicians retained from the 'empty chair' crisis was the lesson of the President's determination and the willingness of the French President to push the crisis to the brink despite the economic importance of the EEC. It was not a confirmation of the growing governmental role of the Commission and put, once again, the President in the spotlight.

France and America

De Gaulle's foreign policy was concentrated mainly on showing independence from the 'Anglo-Saxons' in various measures. This defiance of the United States (and discounting of the UK) became more pronounced as his Presidency proceeded. It started with the withdrawal of the French fleet from the Nato Mediterranean command in 1959, followed by the withdrawal of the Atlantic fleet in 1963 and in 1964 the withdrawal of French forces from Nato exercises. On 6 March 1966 came the crescendo: France withdrew from the Nato integrated command altogether. When the German government asked where this left the French troops stationed on German soil under Nato, they received the haughty reply that they would be gone within the year (a treaty enabled them to remain). This was accompanied by de Gaulle's famous Phnom Penh speech in September criticising American conduct in Vietnam, French isolation in the 'Six Day War' and the President's 'vive le Québec libre' in Montreal in July 1967.

In June 1967, the President had followed up the Nato initiative with a visit to the USSR where he was understandably lionised. Cheering crowds greeted the French President on his visits to Eastern Europe. In December the Soviet President Kosygin visited Paris and a number of treaties on technical cooperation were subsequently signed (without the German government being informed, as it should have been). Because of his internal support, the President had for about a year a free hand in foreign policy, which he used to demark France from Western alliances. De Gaulle's intentions toward the Atlantic Alliance itself were uncertain although the President announced that France would continue to participate in the structures until 1969.

Although the second British application to join the EEC had none of the resonance of the first, and not been encouraged by the French, Prime Minister Wilson provided the French President with a new platform for a lecture on geostrategy. De Gaulle vetoed the UK application in grand style in November 1967. It was followed by a French boycott of the West European Union, suspect, to the General, of being a cat's paw for Washington. France under de Gaulle would continue to be the most unpredictable of allies.

Means and Ends

Even had it been in the national interest, the policy de Gaulle had undertaken could not be sustained. It was overambitious for France did not have the means to carry through its policies. After the crisis of May 1968 the Franc came under severe pressure, and the President elected to impose import controls without consulting France's partners (in violation of the Rome Treaty). The French industrial economy could not rival those of the superpowers' (and not Germany's) and the nuclear weapons programme did not appreciably enhance France's diplomatic capacity. France's strategic position in Cold War Europe allowed it to be a free rider on Nato and American policy did not provide the 'blackmail potential' needed by the General to make the threats of withdrawal and non-cooperation actual. President Johnson's reaction to de Gaulle's ultimatum on Nato was immediately to withdraw all installations of French soil (President Johnson was, perhaps, the only Western politician not in awe of the General). Only inside the EEC did the leverage the President sought exist, and that was a power which had its limits (US positions). In sum, de Gaulle had domestic and international pay-offs for the policies but there were also charges, which would be paid by his successors.

The End of Epic Foreign Policy

With the Presidency of Georges Pompidou (1969–74) foreign policy began to change. The Soviet invasion of Czechoslovakia and then its 'normalisation' under a puppet government had exposed the unrealistic nature of de Gaulle's European pretensions. He had already indicated his willingness to see Britain enter the EEC. Moreover, the Federal Republic's refusal to revalue the DM had made difficult France's own monetary policy. Germany's Grand Coalition made Bonn less vulnerable to Paris and its 'ostpolitik' meant that the FGR turned to the Soviet bloc in the East to normalise relations, arousing French worries. De Gaulle had launched a policy of 'détente' with the East to reduce and ultimately eliminate East-West tension. Willy Brandt's 'ostpolitik' for the same purpose was a cause of tension; along with Pompidou's distrust of the German Chancellor, it led to a turning to the UK to offset German strength (if the agricultural problem could be solved) (Jobert 1974, p. 185). It was the old fear of a reunited Germany dominating Europe, a possibility de Gaulle had not taken into account (Kitzinger 1973).

Although the Gaullist old guard were on the lookout for backsliders, Pompidou needed centre support for domestic reasons and that meant low-key support for the EEC. At his first press conference, the new President suspended the General's veto on UK accession to the EEC and the enlargement process began (a refusal to enlarge constrained it to remain 'little Europe'). While France obtained the (favourable to it) final stage in the Common Market, Pompidou's other foray's into a more technical European integration of exchange rates (as a phase toward monetary union) were less successful. Pompidou's more modest style did not mean a lack of French impetus to the European process, but it was provided at another level. Regional funds were promoted and through the method of Heads of State meetings in October 1972 the EEC's competence was extended. These were all developed from an inter-governmental perspective and thus retained a flavour of the Gaullism of de Gaulle: but although the objective and method of economic integration were new, the political results were meagre. President Pompidou also tried to launch a political secretariat but this, too, failed and the lack of political solidarity remained. This was shown by France itself after the 'Yom Kippur War' when the oil producers imposed an embargo on the Netherlands and France joined the *sauve qui peut.*

Giscard's Centrism

It was, however, President Giscard in 1974 who reanimated European policy in a positively pro-Community direction, turning the Fifth Republic away from its Gaullist origins while proclaiming fidelity to the past (Grosser 1984, p. 256). Parties of the French centre had been pro-Nato, pro-Atlantic alliance and the builders of Europe. Giscard was looking for a new 'modernistic' France and found a centrist political basis in Europe – initially taking his Presidency away from the Gaullist past but finding that he lacked the support to maintain it. He was assisted in his policy by a highly personalised revival of the Franco-German relationship. Chancellor Helmut Schmidt and President Giscard contrived, after the Paris summit of December 1974, to institute tri-annual Councils. This start placated the all but the more fundamentalist of the Gaullists by obtaining what had been refused de Gaulle confirming the inter-governmental aspect of Europe. However, they subsequently became the executive for the European process which satisfied centrists, as did realising the proposal for a European Parliament elections in the Rome Treaty.

Giscard and Schmidt were determined to restore European monetary stability which had been disrupted by the Nixon administration and devised the European Monetary System in 1978. In European policy, Giscard moved the Community to consolidate economic union and in this he was powerfully supported by Chancellor Schmidt. European summits of the nine were institutionalised as European Council meetings from December 1974 onwards and in the Council of July 1975 provision was made for the European Parliament to be directly elected. It was also the decade in which the enlargement to include Greece, Portugal and Spain was begun. It was Giscard's intention, demonstrated through German support of the Franc, to create an area of European stability as a haven from the turbulence following the ending of fixed exchange rates in the post-Bretton Woods era (15 August 1971). World money markets of violently fluctuating exchange rates would not disturb a European Monetary System (EMS). This would eventually lead to a European currency – the 'ecu'. In 1971, the system known as the 'serpent' had been instituted but had been in continuous difficulties as the Franc had had to move in and out in July 1975 and in March 1976. In July 1978,

Giscard proposed the EMS to the Council and it came into force on 13 July 1979. This envisaged the tying of different participating currencies to a narrow band based on a basket of different currencies. It was a pragmatic solution to the exchange rate problem, a half-way house to monetary union and committed the Franc to an attainable (so it was thought) margin. Fixed rates would be defended by the banks but the main cost would fall on the stronger currencies, which would buy up any failing unit to maintain its value. Both Giscard and Schmidt saw the EMS as a central achievement in the building of Europe but the 'ecu' was a reflection of the exchange rates of the 'basket' of currencies, not a separate unit, and was used principally by central banks and not as a general currency.

Defence was more sensitive for the Giscard Presidency, as it bore on the Gaullist world view directly. Giscard's so-called world outreach, or 'modialisation', was a version of de Gaulle's worldwide presence of France posed in more modest terms and without theatrics: defence had to fit into that idea. In particular the Gaullists were alert to any decline in the budget for the nuclear deterrent and the delay (in 1976) in the construction of the sixth nuclear submarine was the occasion for a parliamentary revolt. Very quickly the debate moved into the realms of nuclear strategy and the question of 'sanctuarisation élargie' under which the French deterrent was conceived as protecting more than just French territory itself. Were this 'enlargement' accepted, then defence of 'la France seul' would be abandoned and France would be engaged in the defence of its allies. Following this train of reasoning collaboration with other countries might begin. This was, for Gaullists, the thin end of the wedge for it might imply rejoining Nato. There were also budgetary problems, requiring a redistribution from nuclear forces to the conventional army. The disagreement between Giscard and the Gaullists was one part in the rift between them and illustrated the problems of changing the Gaullist political stance.

Although President Giscard was increasingly hampered by a Gaullist party, which became combative and anti-European, it was under the septennate of 1974-81 that France returned to its Fourth Republic basis of cooperation and entente. Where de Gaulle had sought to form the European enterprise, Giscard and other centre politicians (Mitterrand included) looked to the consolidation of the continent on a basis which would protect French interests. In domestic politics this meant that the extremes were rejected and that the middle ground (which is where the battle was fought) was all important. It was also, as in most European countries, pro-European, but it did not mean that the Presidency was immune to attacks from the flanks, as the presidential campaign of 1981 was to show.

Mitterrand

As President, François Mitterrand also built on the politics of the centre (where he and the Socialist Party had started) but there was no dramatic revolution in French foreign policy (Ibid., p. 291). In 1981 the Communist Party had been marginalised by its poor showing in both the presidential and legislative elections; this gave the Socialists a free hand in European policy and enabled the new government to demonstrate its pro-Western credentials (because of Communist ministers, these were suspect) (Ibid., pp. 288–9). President Mitterrand had no need to conciliate a Gaullist Party, had no need to demonstrate fidelity to a leader he had always contested by promoting a special relationship with Moscow or attacking Europe (de La Serre 1996). He was free of some Fifth Republic baggage. Mitterrand did, however, use the tradition of the 'reserved domain' to conduct an active foreign policy which reassured allies. It was not surprising that the arrival of the left in power disquieted some. Vice-President Bush had arrived in Paris during the week in which the Communists were given ministerial posts. He had started by deploring American policy in Latin America but the planetary ambition of the Fifth Republic's Presidents was over and objectives were more modest (DePorte 1979).

Mitterrand did face a challenge on the European and international front (Rudney 1984). This was the deployment of Cruise and Pershing missiles ('Euromissiles') by Nato, the response to the new generation of Soviet missiles in Eastern Europe. This issue exposed the difficulties as well as the lingering importance of Gaullist doctrine. Giscard had been instrumental in promoting the Nato response (along with Chancellor Schmidt and Prime Minister Callaghan) and Mitterrand had also felt that the Soviet missiles were a threat to France itself. In January 1983, President Mitterrand gave a speech to the Bundestag supporting the deployment of 'Euromissiles': 'les fussées sont à l'Est et les pacifistes sont à l'Ouest'. Germany's repost that 'France is full of words and Germany full of missiles' illustrated the point: Mitterrand was urging others to accept the missiles but would not contemplate doing so in France. If they were a threat to France, SS20s were not going to be removed without Nato's combined effort and in this way the country avoided the clashes over 'Euromissiles' which other Europeans faced. It was the Gaullist 'opt out' again and the orientation of the French nuclear policy was still unresolved (Harrison 1984).

Gaullists argued that President Mitterrand's position supporting Nato over 'Euromissiles' ended the supposed 'special relationship' as 'interlocuteur privilégié' with Moscow (see Lellouche 1983–4). This caused some domestic problems. Georges Marchais, the French Communist leader, supported the inclusion of the French nuclear forces in disarmament talks as part of the 'Western' forces. This directly contradicted the government (and its Communist ministers) position and forty-seven Soviet spies were deported from France. Mitterrand did visited Moscow, but only after the departure of the Communists from government, and he used the occasion of the official visit to plead for the release of dissidents.

Although Europe was, in the 1980s, a popular issue which enabled an appeal to the centre ground as well as a new leadership in Europe to be developed (de La Serre 1996), it was, in fact, the failure of domestic policy (the reflation of 1981) which moved the Socialists' European policy ahead. In agreement with Helmut Kohl, the long-lasting German Chancellor, President Mitterrand promoted the Single Act which created a huge European market and in the Maastricht Treaty as a counterpart to German reunification. He thus put an end to the quarrelsome relationship the Fifth Republic had with Europe. Enlargement was continued in the 1980s.

Of course, the Single Act was not the work of France and Germany alone but of a new form of leadership that brought together the main countries and forged a consensus. By the same token the fall of the Soviet Empire in 1989 provided the opportunities for European development as had the *ostpolitik* in Pompidou's time. From this opportunity emerged the Euro and the Maastricht Treaty referendum. That referendum divided the right and the left but gave public backing to a controversial policy. Jacques Delors, whom Mitterrand had nominated to the Commission Presidency and who had remained for these ten years (1985–95) was seemingly the most popular politician in France on the eve of the 1995 presidential elections. Gaullist anti-Europeanism was far from exorcised but it had been shown where the advantage in pro-European centrist policy lay (Yost 1990–1).

Conclusion: de Gaulle's Legacy

De Gaulle's contribution to the politics of the Presidency through foreign policy became fully apparent in 1986. During the 1986-8 'cohabitation' the principal prize was the public perception of foreign and defence policy making. In this stand-off the Prime Minister started with the disadvantage of presidential practice under the Fifth Republic and the need for politics at the summit to appear harmonious. Hence in the words of one commentator: 'the "cohabitation" experience was, in this domain, particularly fascinating as a result of the inseparable mixture of politics and constitutional rules, by the more or less dextrous manipulation of symbols and of law' (Mény 1991). Because the stakes were so high – the Presidency itself – the Prime Minister paid great attention to foreign policy and had a large diplomatic unit set up in the Matignon to deal with the 'reserved domain'. There were numerous conflicts and although Jacques Chirac's request to attend meetings was acceded to, the President, because of Treaty protocol, was difficult to marginalise and maintained an effective presence. However, in some areas the Elysée was not 'in the loop' (the information provided to the President was highly selective) (S. Cohen 1986, p. 489) and the Prime Minister decided to change the policy on Iran and on South Africa and where budget questions were the key.

What de Gaulle accomplished in Europe during his tenure of the Presidency was to reduce, though not eliminate, the community-based policies by keeping the state at the crux of the decision-making process. In political terms, de Gaulle projected the Gaullist idea of a President vigilant on the state's behalf, speaking for France. This idea was extended to the notion of 'la France seul' and that became popular as well as divisive inside France itself. Splits which de Gaulle played up worked to the benefit of his position, but Pompidou was unable to finesse these divisions and a conservative/Gaullist cleavage opened in the President's coalition which remained unresolved even in the 1990s. At the same time de Gaulle stripped France of all but limited influence during the Cold War. At a time when all European societies defined their positions relative to the East-West struggle, the other Europeans worked with the USA and not with France. A door was kept open for France but Paris's position became a secondary consideration for most of the West. This, too, subsequent Presidents (starting fitfully with Georges Pompidou) tried to overcome.

In internal politics, the European issue has been used by Presidents to decisive purpose. In the 1970s President Giscard was held back by the Gaullist half of the Presidential coalition from promoting integration and he found it expedient to emphasise the inter-governmental aspect of European institutions to appease the Gaullist Party. President Mitterrand used the European issue in the crisis of 1983 to sell the U-turn on economic policy to the Socialist Party and then presented himself as the 'European' figure in his successful 1988 election. In 1992 the attempt to reinvigorate the Socialist left with the prospect of further European integration, although it divided the conservative right, did not bear fruit. French Socialists were too demoralised to respond to such treatment and a gap opened between the Socialist Party and its own supporters during the 1992 referendum on the Maastricht Treaty (there already existed disagreement with the PCF on this issue).

De Gaulle's conception of Franco-German relations was not, even in the short term, viable. De Gaulle depended on a personal commitment from Chancellor Adenauer, which did not serve to bring the Federal Republic of Germany as a whole behind the French President. De Gaulle tried to stretch the Franco-German understanding well beyond the limits of what could be sustained and it was left to subsequent Presidents to rebuild it. Under de Gaulle, the relationship was important mainly within a European Community context and broke down completely when the General moved into world affairs. Although Pompidou made some move in the direction of Bonn, it was Giscard and then Mitterrand who rebuilt the Franco-German alliance and capitalised on its positive potential for the Fifth Republic.

It is not clear that the divisions of the European national forces (not of French origin but sharpened by Gaullism) was helpful during the Cold War and the lack of progress to integration which the Gaullists fought from the EDC onwards became impediments to action in the 1990s. Although some steps had been taken to integrate operating units in the field, European states had not progressed towards strategic and political coordination by the end of the Cold War. France found it difficult to play a leadership role because the suspicion of France and its motives remained latent in European capitals and was easily provoked by unguarded actions (like President Chirac's resumption of nuclear testing). Hence, the collaborative aspects crept back into the European institutions and the Commission regained both stature and autonomy under subsequent Presidencies.

In foreign and defence policy, de Gaulle's conception of France as a superpower proved as difficult to contradict domestically as it was to implement internationally and was used by the Presidents in their assertion of authority in the domestic arena. French autonomy and independence became unattackable dogmas for subsequent generations showing de Gaulle's instruction of public opinion was effective and, on the whole popular (even though some specific policies, like the criticism of Israel, were not). Foreign policy, as no other area, was defined as presidential by the General and this was reinforced by subsequent Presidents. This public perception of the 'reserved domain' is probably the most lasting legacy of the Fifth Republic Presidents. It does not follow that, on the basis of forty years of Fifth Republic politics, a tradition has been fixed, but it will be difficult to undermine even by a determined and astute Prime Minister.

That foreign policy has its domestic sources, is well understood, but what is at issue here is the implication for domestic politics of foreign policy. In the case of the Presidency it provided a clear rationale and enabled a dramatisation of the new institution in the Fifth Republic. De Gaulle's foreign policy had its moments of Churchillain apostrophe. Thus the answer to the questions of what the President did and the justifications of the shift in executive focus were given in an effective form, which became quasi-Constitutional. Whatever de Gaulle's intentions, and it is tempting to describe them as inspired, patternless arabeques, his foreign policy became a powerful tool in establishing and maintaining presidential authority. De Gaulle was so successful in this respect, entrenching presidential power, that the subsequent tenants of the Elysée were expected to lead French foreign policy and stamp France's imprint on world affairs. Foreign policy, traditionally an executive prerogative, is also (contrary to tradition) capable of touching popular chords.

In addition to public expectations, which of course became a valuable bolster to the Presidency, foreign policy had effects on the coalitions around 'présidentiables' and Presidents. Thus de Gaulle's policy did hinder the consolidation of the Opposition and was used to break up the alliance of the left by President Giscard (though not successfully). Foreign policy could also consolidate coalitions and cement alliances and this also became a presidential political attribute. But these authorities in foreign affairs are not givens and have to be maintained. France's experience of 'cohabitation' shows that Prime Ministers also have ambitions in 'high politics' and will try to claim them. Because Prime Ministers have presidential ambitions, and because foreign policy is seen as 'presidential' they have every incentive to make a mark in an area where they wish to flourish. There is the restraint that, at the same time, they have no desire to humble the institution they aspire to occupy.

–5–

May '68

It is an old adage of political life that the two principal problems are orderly transfer of power and knowing when to go. Handing over power gracefully is amongst the most difficult tasks a leader has to accomplish. Maintaining power while the new generation waits in the wings and keeping the initiative in what the Americans refer to as the 'lame duck' Presidency (after the second election) has been beyond some of the most accomplished of leaders. Staying on too long is a danger which top leaders have been unable to resist, so strong are the attractions of office. De Gaulle, who came to power a second time unexpectedly, and at the age of 68 when most careers at the top are over, must have felt that he needed to finish the business and to see out most, if not all, of the remaining septennate. De Gaulle's physical powers were not diminished in 1968 or 1969.

The Political Position

Fifth Republic France was to all outward appearances a success. At the beginning of 1968 there was no sense of impending crisis: the end had come, but it was not then in sight. As Pierre Vainsson-Ponté famously wrote in 1968 'La France s'ennuie' and de Gaulle, anticipating the new year, looked to a rosy future and predicted that there would be no crisis. In other countries there were student problems (including in the Eastern bloc) but in France, if there were some strikes, living standards grew and the flow of consumer goods seemed endless. Moreover, the 'trente glorieuses' of post-war boom were in full swing; few recognised that the economic winds, which were still blowing strongly, bore the first hints of immobilising frost (Muron 1994, p. 197). In domestic politics de Gaulle had been elected President by a substantial margin in 1965 and the Gaullist coalition had won the Assembly elections of 1967 with a working majority. Both victories were narrower than had been expected (and that heartened the Opposition) but there was a 'margin' of support available in the centre parties which could be persuaded.

Within the 'hexagon' of France itself there was no obvious challenge to the General's position. On the left there were Mitterrand and Mendès France, and possibly Defferre, but the left's problematic coalition with the PCF looked unstable. Within de Gaulle's own conservative camp, where authority might have begun to crumble in a 'lame duck' interlude, things looked set in stone. In the Assembly majority the Gaullist Party was dominant within the coalition and the party itself had begun to take root becoming in the process a conservative party much like the British Tories. No individuals could compare with de Gaulle in stature. Not only was de Gaulle 'the most illustrious of Frenchmen', there was no rival. Georges Pompidou, who had begun to make a mark over the 1967 election campaign, had been the government's star performer putting the Opposition to the test. But Pompidou had some way to go before he could pretend to presidential stature. In the opinion polls de Gaulle remained popular, but those polled did not include the under 21s who could not vote.

Thus de Gaulle's position appeared solid and, possibly on this assumption, the President embarked in 1967 on a round of initiatives in foreign policy which were as startling as any in the previous septennate. These included a ringing call during a visit to Canada for a free Quebec ('Vive le Québec libre') and a condemnation of Israel for its aggression in the Six-Day War of June 1967. His reference to Israel as 'an elite people, self-confident and dominating' was highly controversial as was his one-sided arms embargo on the Middle Eastern states. French public opinion sided with Israel. He also developed an increasingly vigorous criticism of the United States and a pursuit of a special relationship with the Eastern Soviet bloc promoting 'détente'. It was in January 1968 that de Gaulle chose to launch the ostensibly neutralist 'tous azimuts' defence policy (which did not impress Pompidou, for one). In 1966 the President had withdrawn French forces from Nato and had vetoed the UK's application to the EEC once again in November 1967 (at a press conference, which seemed designed to stir up trouble). It was also de Gaulle's policy to undermine the dollar's position as a reserve currency. De Gaulle objected to the dollar's use as an instrument of American politics and reacted by selling the US currency and building up France's gold reserves.

The Political Problem

De Gaulle's bombast and his capricious foreign policy covered an essentially conservative regime. It was not that de Gaulle was ignorant of economic matters or that he was unaware of social problems, de

Gaulle's attention was elsewhere. He seemed to have taken the view in domestic politics that 'l'intendance suivera', that the technical problems of economic growth and modernisation would be accomplished by any half-way competent administration ('faites moi de bonnes finances'). Since de Gaulle supplied the political will and the authority, the technocrats could take care of the necessary reforms. In a period of rapid economic expansion, during which the French economy achieved rates of growth unparalleled by even the Japanese, the problems looked as if they would solve themselves. People would get better jobs and wages would rise, opportunities would become available and industry would generate the means for de Gaulle's ambitious Gaullist foreign and defence policy.

This Gaullist penchant for action and the focus on the President was part of the problem. France was stable and the Gaullists were returned at election after election, but the authority was delegated to one individual: the President. It suited de Gaulle to keep the spotlight on him, to keep people speculating about what he thought and what he would do (providing work for commentators to interpret the President's delphic pronouncements). It was a strictly one-way communication: from the President down. As a result of this 'monarchic' idea of communication the Gaullists cut themselves off from the daily problems of society. De Gaulle's politics are a big part of the reason why, in May 1968, the authority of the French state simply evaporated and for a month it was as if neither the Fifth Republic nor de Gaulle had ever been.

Creative as Gaullism was in foreign policy, in domestic politics it was under Pompidou's aegis essentially conservative. De Gaulle himself had no developed social policy. Such as it was it was vaguely Christian Democratic and there were references to 'partnership', but these ideas were not translated into concrete policy. There is a substantial exegesis of de Gaulle's thought on social matters and (where they are clear) they are humane, but they were not perceived as such at the time. People would have been hard put to it to state what was distinctive about Gaullist economic policy, but could, of course, have specified the foreign politics. Foreign policy, however, did not touch most people's lives directly although they would rally round the President when France came under attack. Prime Minister Pompidou had a free hand on the domestic side and was predisposed to a conservative, if interventionist, social and economic policy (Rials 1977).

As with the Fourth Republic, where this conservatism mattered was less in the fact of economic growth (which was unprecedented) than in the political management of it. Growth meant strains on the French social fabric and these were never fully resolved. In the Fourth Republic they had resulted in 'Poujadism'. This nihilist force was partially animated by people who were moved from old occupations in rural societies under threat from the modernisation of France which the post-war boom had set underway. Growth was disorienting, people who expected a lifetime in a secure occupation were suddenly threatened with redundancy and new challenges opened up. This was eased by the increase in better-paid jobs in new industries but, while this was a statistical fact, the people affected by change naturally did not see it that way.

In the Fifth Republic GNP grew at an unprecedented 5.8 per cent between 1959 and 1970 and society was transformed. But de Gaulle's handling of it was no more adept than had been the Fourth Republic's. In common with the rest of Western Europe, but with greater intensity, France was undergoing massive changes in social structure. Not only were the peasant farmers moving off the land, the agricultural sector was being transformed and becoming modern. In 1954 the peasantry had constituted over 20 per cent of the working population (and a further 6 per cent worked on the land) and by 1968 this figure had fallen to 12 per cent (and agricultural workers to 2.9 per cent). This movement made France less rural but at the same time new industries in petro-chemicals, electronics, 'white goods', construction and services were expanding rapidly entailing the expansion of middle management and white collar occupations. This growth in turn created a new working class and expanded the middle class of white collar and middle management. At the same time the 'rust belt' industries (and some newer ones) required unskilled or semi-skilled workers, a need which was often supplied by immigrants. Although the context was different, some of the same features of the 1950s reappeared (like Gérard Nicoud's radical shopkeepers' movement), but the main problem was that people were not persuaded of the Fifth Republic's accomplishment. In fact (as can be seen, with the immaculate perception of hindsight, from polls and surveys) there was considerable disquiet about the future and about employment prospects (Muron 1994, pp. 198–9).

Even at the height of the economic growth, the public did not think their living standards or their quality of life was getting better (IFOP 1970). Polls were, with a rating or over 50 per cent, showing high support for the President although if opinion is probed deeper it appears that the public remained unimpressed by the Fifth Republic's record on social matters. In part this was a presentational problem which had never been addressed by the governments of the Fifth Republic (and in which the President was not greatly interested) but there was also a difficulty with the hierarchical and old-fashioned nature of unmodernised French society. This touched people in many occupations (even those normally conservative) and the burden of complaint there was the stifling hierarchy and the quality of relations in the workplace. In some areas, like television, the state's inhibiting presence was only too evident. Then there was the youth problem.

Fifth Republic France was youthful, as was the rest of Western Europe, but the post-war 'baby boom' had rejuvenated the country even more than its neighbours. In 1968 over 33 per cent of the population was under 20 years of age. There thus was a disproportionately large population under 21 and this population was disenfranchised (suffrage started at 21). In addition France had also participated in the expansion of higher education and the universities had expanded faster than elsewhere in the West. In 1959 there were about 200,000 students in France and in 1968 there were over 600,000 (Braudel 1982, p. 997). Not only had this led to a 'devaluation' of the degree itself, the facilities were often poor and university education was not what it was. This problem in Higher Education was recognised in the Education Ministry, but was not tackled and became a serious difficulty for France. It was not tackled because de Gaulle's presidentialism had created a circle of subordinates keen to please the General and to pass on his ideas to the public but not to be expected to relay dissatisfaction or raise problems. This centralising trend around the Presidency was increased by the downgrading of the Parliament and the sidelining of interest groups and parties. One of the interest groups which was split and then ignored (because of its radical position on the Algerian war) was the student union, with the result that no student grievances were being listened to in the mid-1960s.

De Gaulle by 1968 seemed to be a figure from another age. He was 78, his ideas had been formed in the Edwardian era and his preconceptions were not those of the new France over which he presided. De Gaulle had been in power for ten years (a long time in a Western system) and domestic issues had not been put on his agenda. Other figures had a more acute ear for the problems of the society being created, but they had little influence. Prime Minister Pompidou had a background in the education system but his conservative instincts were not the same as the new generation.

There were also issues which, while not inimical to conservatism as broadly conceived, were not Pompidou's concern. These so-called 'libertarian' issues were a revolution in social attitudes and included issues such as divorce law reform, abortion law reform, gender, feminism, freer relationships and so on. Through May 1968 there is an unmistakable thread of individualism challenging and demanding a change in social outlook. Frontiers of behaviour were changed, the Church was pushed out, and relationships took on a new meaning. De Gaulle excluded a close associate from power because of his philandering and the Catholic outlook was deep in Gaullism despite its secular origins. It is significant that the first stirrings of student 'troubles' were over mixed residences and not workers' power (Posner 1970, p. 59).

When de Gaulle did express the outlook of French people there was a 'grandeur' in his pronouncements but by 1968 there was an unrecognised 'décalage' between society and President. This came about because the perspectives of President and people were different and an overconfidence crept into de Gaulle's world view. This was the background to the 'events'. Disaffection amongst students and sixth formers had built up and had not been tackled. At the same time the nature of Gaullist power had led to a dissatisfaction which was unrecognised because it was not a presidential preoccupation. Although the public later supported the return to law and order, there was a failure of public opinion to rally to the government in the initial stages of the crisis which points up a failure of Gaullist politics. In that May-time failure de Gaulle, as the principal architect of the presidential system, must bear the ultimate responsibility. De Gaulle's government should have had public support in the circumstances, but instead there was a tendency to turn on the regime itself. A movement against de Gaulle was a distinct feature of the 'events' and the centralised presidential system was a root cause. To this generalised but unarticulated dissatisfaction and potential of dissent was added a series of difficulties caused by the misunderstanding of the nature of the problem from the beginning.

May '68

De Gaulle, no more than anybody else, recognised what was happening. It must have looked, to the former leader of the Free French and the saviour of the Republic, like a minor problem of law and order (Grimaud 1977, p. 150). It was treated as such at its origins and that proved to be the initial problem when, instead of siding with the police taking action against occupying students, the public sided with the youthful 'revolutionaries'. Students were, after all, middle class and the police action was characteristically brutal. It was the same 'technocratic' insensitivity to political realities which was the next step in the burgeoning crisis. Officials at the end of March, trying to cut the drop-out rate, decided that the way to prevent these failures was to stop the underqualified from entering the Universities (by reinforcing 'selection'). Selection looked like a good idea and it periodically resurfaced as a 'solution' to the high drop-out rates of 50 per cent or so (repeated in 1986). In one view the only lack was determination on the government's part to impose it. However, selection mobilised the sixth formers who recognised in 'selection' a threat to their own futures. Sixth-form students in France are well organised and they formed a large bulk of 'student' crowds in May '68. These 'crowds' were consequently much younger and less able to be coerced than might be expected (the effect of the police firing on schoolchildren would have been devastating).

But, inadvertently the government had mobilised the main part of the younger generation against it. Its next step was to cause more problems. On 2 May, following disturbances which made the campus ungovernable, the University of Nanterre in the suburbs of Paris was closed. As a result students flooded into the centre of Paris and the disruption spread from the outskirts to the Paris campus. These problems were intensified by the absence of the Prime Minister and the presence of relatively junior ministers in charge of the state machine. They had neither the inclination nor the authority to change the government's response from one of law and order to enable the situation to be recovered by police on the streets (Tournoux 1969, p. 31). This intransigence led to the 'night of the barricades' of 10–11 May. A more considered response had to wait on Pompidou's return while de Gaulle pushed for a quick solution to the masquerade ('chienlit'). When Pompidou, absent for the first ten days of May, arrived back from Afghanistan on Saturday 11 May the situation had deteriorated and the university system as a whole had been brought to a stand-still; building occupations also increased. However, the Prime Minister, flying into a great calm, changed the strategy to the one which would eventually bring the 'events' to a conclusion (Balladur 1979, pp. 74–5). He declared that the Sorbonne would reopen on the following Monday and extended an olive branch to the students (Tournoux 1969, p. 77).

This, from Pompidou more conservative in outlook than others in government, was no mark of sympathy, but a tactic. Pompidou had calculated that the situation had to burn itself out, that public opinion would have to be turned back to support the government and that the way to do this was to 'pay out the rope' to the students. A disorganised and anarchic student movement would sooner or later lose public sympathy by its excess and in the meantime the government had to appear reasonable and to be seeking solutions. De Gaulle's preferred and unrealistic response of 'sending in the police' to clear out the troublemakers was not a possibility (Grimaud 1977, p. 209). Apart from alienating the public, the police were exhausted and battles resulted only in ephemeral victories for the police (the students reappeared in another place). Pompidou was, in most accounts, the perceptive spirit on the government side in May 1968. This opinion was shared by the public which saw in Pompidou the architect of the peaceful outcome and the return to normality. But the coalhammer blows continued to fall: on 13 May there was a massive demonstration and a public service strike. On 14 May, as the strikes were spreading to other industries starting in Sud-Aviation and Renault-Billancourt, de Gaulle departed for a state visit to Romania. But over the next week about ten million went on strike. These strikes were not animated by a desire to join the students, but by more mundane matters like rates of pay, working times, and working conditions. Pompidou's response was to seek out union leaders to negotiate a return to work. In this the Prime Minister was aided by the Communist Party's decision not to take part in the 'events' and its worry that 'its' workers would be won over to the student cause. (As early as 2 May the PCF's daily *L'Humanité* had condemned the disturbances.)

Meanwhile, de Gaulle in Romania (and not without misgivings) delivered his message condemning the blocs to cheering crowds. This visit was cut short on 18 May by anxiety about the deteriorating situation and de Gaulle returned to France. De Gaulle did not immediately react in public, creating an expectation, but prepared a parry. On 24 May there was a television broadcast by the President. This announcement was badly misjudged and set the 'events' on another downward spiral. De Gaulle was expected to take some initiative reflecting the gravity of the situation. Instead, the President announced a referendum on reform 'de haut en bas' and, as he had done in the past, linked it to his continuation in office. A Cabinet meeting had been informed but Pompidou was unconvinced (Tournoux 1969, p. 136). This 'méprisant' broadcast brought thousands onto the streets chanting 'adieu de Gaulle' and the Presidency was at stake. De Gaulle's broadcast inspired a night of rioting in the Latin Quarter and students crossed to the right bank where they tried to set fire to the stock exchange. These new incursions had the effect of turning public opinion further against the students and played into the government's hands.

The Situation Turns

Pompidou, who had urged that the only appropriate response was a dissolution, was justified in his view that a referendum was neither adequate nor organisable in the generalised chaos of May '68 (Pompidou 1982, p. 197). As the May crisis entered its last week the strategy Pompidou had set came into its own: people tired of disruption and violence and opinion hardened against the students. In addition the negotiations between the Communists, the unions and the employers (at the Ministry of Labour, rue Grenelle) went ahead under Pompidou who led his chosen team (but excluding the mercurial Minister of Finance Debré) (See Balladur 1979, p. 225). These negotiations were concluded on 27 May to the benefit of the workers who were to receive an immediate 7 per cent pay rise to be followed by 3 per cent in October (and other benefits), and the government, which expected a return to work. CGT leader Séguy was, however, heckled by Billancourt workers accusing the unions of a 'sell-out' but, although other factories threatened to reject the agreement negotiated by a union which – after all – did not represent them, Pompidou was not sidetracked from pursuing negotiations (Pompidou 1982, p. 191 and Balladur 1979, p. 266). There was, later on 27 May, a mass student meeting at the Charléty stadium.

Students were contemptuous of the 'Stalinists' and the Communists were the object of ridicule and heckling during May '68. But it was not just the Communist Party which had been sidelined by the 'events'. Gaullists, centrists and the mainstream opposition parties were all forced to the periphery during the 'events'. As long as that was the case the government had no purchase on the politics of the situation. Opposition politicians, for the most part, wanted an electoral resolution to the crisis which was in a sense what the government also wanted (though on terms it could win). On 28 May Mitterrand was to make the first mistake, more gauche than sinister, by offering to form an interim government while the situation in the factories also began to change. It was becoming a more recognisable political crisis and the government was beginning to find a success along the lines Pompidou had worked out.

It was at this point in the 'events' on 29 May that the situation was dramatically resolved in the President's favour. It is still unclear what the motivation of the 'coup de théâtre' by the General was, but the effect was clear (Charlot in Hanley and Kerr 1989). On the 29 May de Gaulle disappeared leaving even Pompidou in the dark (the Prime Minister was annoyed. See Pompidou 1982, p. 193), going to the army Headquarters in Baden Baden where he met General Massu (Massu 1983, pp.142–3). Whatever de Gaulle's spirit at the meeting, the disappearance of the dominant figure dramatised the vacuum of authority and people waited for the next move by the President. De Gaulle, in his absence, became the focus. De Gaulle returned and announced, in a magisterial radio broadcast on 30 May, that there would be general elections. This was a backdown of sorts by the General who had seen a referendum as a solution and had wanted to send in the police to end licence. However, it at one swoop displaced the issue from the confused revolutionary demands to the institutions of government. That evening massive crowds, assiduously prepared, flooded onto the Champs Elysées to support de Gaulle. De Gaulle, reportedly, had no illusions and did not interpret the crowd's cheers as an endorsement of him (Tournoux 1969, p. 286).

General Elections

It was very much a law and order election with the Communists taking the place as the main target of the Gaullist Party. A steady drift back to work was underway from the beginning of June and students abandoned their occupations of buildings and went on the long vacation. In the mainstream left there was disarray and the leadership was largely discredited by their over-reaction at the end of May and by their inability to capitalise on the régime's crisis. As a result the Gaullist Party ran a 'law and order' campaign and won an absolute majority (without their Giscardian allies). With 296 seats, it was the first time that a single party had won an absolute majority in the Assembly (Giscard's RI, in coalition with the Gaullists as the Union pour la Défense de la République, also won 64 seats). On the left Mitterrand's Federation was crushed and was reduced to 57 seats while the Communist Party was reduced to a rump of 34 seats (Goldey in Williams, P.M. 1970). It was a vote for stability in the first place and – possibly – for Georges Pompidou in the second (Pompidou 1982, p. 203).

De Gaulle dismissed Pompidou. This act of vindictiveness did not suit the figure de Gaulle aspired to cut, and it has been suggested that it was a misunderstanding (Pompidou had asked to go). But de Gaulle's appointment of the loyal but uninspiring Couve de Murville as Prime Minister in place of the 'victor' looked mean minded and the inference could be drawn that the President had no intention of changing his style – or of listening – despite the 'events'. (Pompidou may have considered that it released him from some obligations to the President who had promoted him from backstage to front stage.) But de Gaulle also promoted the masterful Fourth Republic 'fixer' Edgar Faure to reform the universities. Faure's reform was pushed through the very conservative 'chambre introuvable' of 1968 with the government's backing and made some changes to the universities although the measures did not end what proved a continuing crisis.

De Gaulle was the principal victim of May 68. Others recovered but the President never did. De Gaulle said of his actions that he was 'not proud of himself' (Pompidou 1982, p. 201). His personal position was weakened by his bewilderment at the 'events' and his inability to master them. Moreover, the stability the President seemed to incarnate had been eliminated by students and government authority had collapsed. In addition the 'special relationship' which the President claimed to have with France was, in 1968, clearly an illusion.

De Gaulle's Last Months

The inevitable aftermath was that the domestic economy was subject to crisis measures. Imports were taxed and the Franc was under threat (and in no position to attack the Dollar) although the President refused to entertain a devaluation. In the early autumn the flight of capital increased and the government compounded this problem by removing exchange controls. Pressure on the Franc was relentless, but the government did not generate the confidence that could stay the speculative process. A test of resolve in November 1968 was passed when the government refused to bow to pressure to devalue and that staved off the crisis in the short term. De Gaulle's régime was synonymous with the 'new Franc' and sound money and to devalue shortly after the débâcle of the United Kingdom's devaluation would not have been the President's way. In this case political resolve and an adept reversing of expectations of devaluation enabled de Gaulle to avoid domestic cutbacks and overseas humiliation. But then de Gaulle's monetary crusade against the Dollar (and the move to gold) was also abandoned.

De Gaulle's attempt to respond to the domestic malaise by turning to the old idea of 'participation' was also revealed to be hollow. The 'participation', such as it was, made little impact and did not justify the emphasis on it as the Gaullist 'middle way' in social relations. 'Participation' had been mentioned in May and again at the press conference of 9 September 1968 and it was an old notion intended to overcome industrial strife. Although it aroused the employers' suspicions it was too late in the second septennate to try to give the slogan of 'participation' any real substance. For the President to present himself, after ten years in supreme power, as a thwarted radical was implausible. Some of the agreement made with the unions was honoured, parts were slowly put into place and other bits were postponed. Unemployment began to rise and increased the price of the deal negotiated with the government. Neither the unorganised workers nor the unions were in any position to do anything about the disillusion but industrial production recovered.

Abroad de Gaulle's stature was substantially reduced by the crisis of May 68, but a more serious crisis was to follow. On 21 August the Soviet Union invaded Czechoslovakia; this invasion disposed of the pretensions of the Gaullist foreign policy to engineer détente with the Eastern bloc. De Gaulle's response, and that of the ministers, was an attack on the bloc system and an attempt to disguise the failure of policy (by blaming the wartime 'Yalta Agreements') (Aron in *Le Figaro* 28/8/68). All the same it was a fatal blow to the policy de Gaulle had pursued and his main claim to originality in the political field was eliminated. His press conference on 9 September was as assured as ever but lacked impact and, overshadowed by the Soviet Union's imposition of power over its bloc in August, was not an event in itself; words could not, this time, substitute for action.

Pompidou as 'Présidentiable'

After May 68 de Gaulle faced another threat and one which he had not had since the War: a rival. This rival, from within his own camp, was Georges Pompidou who had been replaced as Prime Minister and put by de Gaulle 'in the reserve of the Republic'. Pompidou did keep off stage but was present in the wings as a critic of the President. There was a serious problem of relations between de Gaulle, who thought Pompidou had a responsibility for the deterioration which led to the 'events', and his old Prime Minister who resented what he saw as rank ingratitude (Pompidou 1982, pp. 200–8). This became bitter over the 'Marcovitch Affair' (Alexandre 1970, pp. 305–9). This obscure 'affair' of a murdered bodyguard was the object of rumours, most of them disobliging to Pompidou, and was allowed to rumble on by the government and some of de Gaulle's 'compagnons'. Pompidou took the view that by not stifling the 'affair' the President was actively hostile and undermining his former compagnon (Pompidou 1980, p. 256 and p. 260). On 9 January de Gaulle invited Pompidou to the Elysée where relations were somewhat mended – but not enough. Pompidou was treading a difficult line between loyalty and disloyalty but by 1969 (after the 'affair') he did not feel a strong obligation to the President (Jobert 1974, p. 82). This became more fraught during the referendum campaign when the Gaullists needed all the support that could be mustered. Pompidou managed to keep on the right side of all but the most passionate Gaullists.

In the meantime Pompidou had started a campaign for the Presidency and part of that was, as was realistic for a 'présidentiable', a series of meetings with foreign leaders. On a visit to Rome on 17 January 1969 Pompidou reiterated that he would, when the General retired, be a candidate for the Presidency. This, hardly a secret, was taken as a declaration of war and provoked from de Gaulle the reponse that he had been elected for seven years and intended to see the septennate out. But Pompidou was now posing as an alternative to the General and in February even repeated his intentions to stand at the next presidential election.

The 1969 Referendum

In the end de Gaulle's defeat in April 1969 was a 'tragedy'. In the short term two incompatible expectations had been set up. On the one hand in May 1968 he held out the prospect of a referendum and had felt impelled to repeat it in February 1969. It was possible that, confronted by a massive Assembly majority which was not his own, he felt it necessary to reinforce his authority and Pompidou's shadow might have been removed by a big victory in a referendum. In May the subject had been 'participation' but this was dropped for the subject of reform of the Senate and regions. This topic had the benefit of yoking together the unadventurous (but popular) reform of regional government with cutting down the Senate's pretensions. De Gaulle distrusted the Senate which was a stronghold of his centrist opponents and had been a persistent nuisance (as the President saw it). It was, however, the General himself who was being judged.

On the other hand there was no constitutional need to hold a referendum and by 1969 there was no urgent political need to hold one. It could have been quietly buried after May 1968. Although almost forgotten, this promise was repeated and could not be sidestepped a second time and de Gaulle could not escape being bound by it when a 'no' became probable. It was a promise which could not be watered down or neglected, but as the hour approached, defeat seemed increasingly likely. At the beginning of 1969 de Gaulle could not survive a defeat (and would not want to) but neither could he afford a narrow victory. Either way, reneging on the referendum or being defeated, it was a bad way to end an illustrious career. De Gaulle chose to go ahead and to risk a double or quits which would rid him of the Senate's obstruction and rebuild his authority or end in his departure. Pompidou loyally, but without sentiment, supported the General's last campaign (Pompidou 1982, p. 273).

As it transpired de Gaulle encountered a strong opposition led by Alain Poher, the Speaker of the Senate, and could not mobilise his own supporters in a referendum in which his future was at stake. On 27 April the referendum was rejected by a vote of 53 per cent to 47 per cent. De Gaulle left the Elysée as he promised. De Gaulle's immediate resignation when the 1969 referendum was defeated opened up the presidential race. As stipulated by the constitution, Poher as the Speaker of the Senate became interim President and once installed in the Elysée saw his popularity rise to astonishing heights. However the left divided by personal and party disputes failed to field a credible candidate and the real choice was between Pompidou and the interim President (Charlot and Charlot 1986).

The Presidential Election

At the same time as being a choice of political orientation (Poher represented the anti-Gaullist centre), the 1969 presidentials were a choice of regime: between the continuation of the active executive Presidency and the more passive Fourth Republic-style Presidency. With the Poher/Pompidou duel the left/right head-on clash was minimised (the PCF called for abstention) and the differences in policy and 'choice of society' were much less (some would say virtually negligible) and their stance on the institutions of the Republic was correspondingly heightened.

Poher had become the 'reconciliation' president, the defender of the 'arbitrator' role of the Presidency and 'le champion du retour aux chrysanthèmes' – not a role Poher was happy with (*Le Monde* 9/5/69). But Poher was supported by many on the left who hoped to see the Presidency reduced in its pretensions as well as by right wingers of the same persuasion (*Le* Monde 20/5/69). In a book written before the opening of the race for the succession to the General, Pompidou put it this way: '. . . nous n'avons pas d'autre alternative que le retour camouflé mais rapide au régime d'assemblée ou l'accentuation du charactère présidential de nos institutions' (Pompidou 1974, p. 65). Pompidou was able to play on the ambiguities in Poher's position (which he implied meant a regime crisis) and on the lack of majority for the Speaker of the Senate in the National Assembly with telling criticisms. Pompidou's intention was to consolidate a wider majority and enlarge the coalition (*Le Monde* 30/4/69). He obtained the backing of all but a few intransigent Gaullists and of Giscard's (hesitant) Independent Republicans as well as centrists in Jacques Duhamel's Progrès et démocratie moderne who had declined to follow Poher (Jobert 1974, p. 90).

On the first round Pompidou polled 43.9 per cent to Poher's 23.4 per cent and the Communist candidate's 21.5 per cent. On the second ballot Pompidou polled 57.5 per cent to Poher's 42.4 per cent but a massive 31 per cent abstained (Goldey in Williams, P. M. 1970). Pompidou's hand-some majority was misleading, it was a low turnout, the left had been fragmented and the result was not a foregone conclusion. Hence the General's successor was obliged, after the Presidential elections, to continue his strategy of 1967 of widening the coalition to include both the centrists and Giscard. Pompidou thus stood at the crucial cusp, that far, in the history of the Fifth Republic: at the point where the institutions moved out from the legitimacy provided by de Gaulle ('Gaullisme épique') and the personal coalition put together to support the General, into the mainstream of modern conservative politics.

Part II
Ordinary Presidentialism

-6-

Georges Pompidou

With Georges Pompidou's victory in the presidential elections of 1969, the Fifth Republic left behind its heroic origins to enter its phase of 'ordinary Gaullism'. Unlike de Gaulle who had had the stature of a 'historic leader' even before re entering the political arena in 1958 to found the Fifth Republic, Pompidou's public political career began only in 1962, thanks to presidential patronage. It is a measure of Pompidou's success that the transition was perceived as natural. However, although the Presidency had been provided with political resources by the General, it was not yet taken for granted that the Fifth Republic was the Republic of the Executive Presidency. Georges Pompidou had, as will be seen, to work on all fronts to reassert presidential authority, something which was not a foregone conclusion even in 1969.

Georges Pompidou

Born in 1911 in Montboudif (Cantal) of peasant stock from the Auvergne, Georges Pompidou liked to remind people of the virtues of obstinacy and prudence (Roussel 1984, p. 83). His father was a left-leaning but politically uninvolved schoolteacher. A bright schoolboy, he went to the Lycée Louis-le-Grand in Paris and on to the prestigious Ecole Normale Supérieure and became a politically unengaged teacher of literature in the prestigious Lycée Saint-Charles of Marseilles and then in Albi. In 1938 he was moved to the Paris Lycée Henri IV, where he was able to indulge his interest in modern art and to frequent the fringes of the artistic world (he edited books on French literature). Although he completed military service from 1939 to 1940, he returned to teaching and during the war kept out of any active engagement. In this he was like most ordinary French people but unlike the historic Gaullist 'compagnons' of the Resistance or London. It was in 1944, when the General (according to legend) sought 'un normalien sachant écrire', that his old boy network ('normaliens') brought him onto de Gaulle's political staff (Decaumont 1979, p. 3).

Although Pompidou did not get to know de Gaulle well during this brief Liberation governmental interlude he had attracted his attention. When de Gaulle resigned from government in January 1946, Pompidou was made head of the de Gaulle family foundation and a confidence then sprang up between the General and the young teacher. Subsequently, Pompidou was a member of the Executive of the *Rassemblement du peuple français* and played an important but discreet backstage role in the first Gaullist Party along with Jacques Foccart, François Mauriac and others in the RPF's policy group. When the RPF was wound up in 1953 (possibly Pompidou played the key role in this decision) he remained at de Gaulle's command, for example negotiating the publication of his memoirs, and then joined the Rothschild frères bank as a Director in 1955 (Roussel 1984, p. 87). Nevertheless, in 1958 Pompidou was again at de Gaulle's side, negotiating with the politicians of the Fourth Republic and smoothing the General's return to the helm. Pompidou played an important role as head of de Gaulle's political staff in the foundation of the Fifth Republic, but he declined to join Debré's government and instead moved into the Constitutional Council intending, so it seems, to return permanently to banking. However, he still frequented the corridors of power and was negotiating with the FLN in 1961 (Droz and Lever 1982, p. 296–8).

In April 1962 Pompidou was asked by de Gaulle to form a government. In many ways this was a surprise nomination: Pompidou was not well known, a literature teacher, an administrator, but not an experienced public politician, and had never even stood for Parliament. Pompidou had to cope with the end of the Algerian war, OAS terrorism and then the vote of censure in October 1962. In one respect, however, Pompidou's task was straightforward: the elections of November 1962 returned a solid Gaullist majority to the Assembly giving his government the reliable support to pursue the President's policies that Debré had lacked. Pompidou, initially ill at ease in the front line, grew into the role and quickly developed the political skills he was so lacking on appointment. Pompidou was the first to discover the potential of the Prime Minister's role in the Fifth Republic for the creation of a national political stature and thus the furtherance of presidential ambitions. De Gaulle's interest in foreign affairs and his consequent lack of interest in the domestic arena (other than as a means for his foreign policy) gave Pompidou a much freer hand than subsequent Presidents gave to their Prime Ministers. Pompidou had, after all, run the 1965 and 1967 election campaigns (he may have hoped de Gaulle would not stand in 1965).

To Pompidou also fell the duty, which the President somewhat neglected, of ensuring the organisation of the Gaullist Party for local and national elections and of promoting the new generation and by the Lille conference of the UDR in 1967 the rebuilding was well in hand. At the Gaullist Party's 1967 conference the Prime Minister emerged, after the General himself, as a principal force in the UDR (Charlot 1971, p.125ff.). Pompidou stood for his native Cantal constituency in the general elections of 1967 and was easily elected then and again in 1968. Thus by mid 1967 Pompidou had reorganised the Gaullist Party and widened the majority to include some non-Gaullist supporters of the President. Most of the younger promotions in the Gaullist governments were Pompidou's. However, the ' events' of 1968 and their aftermath proved a breaking point in his relations with de Gaulle. Although – or because – Pompidou had played an essential part his relations with the President deteriorated and after he had won the 1968 general elections he was replaced with the loyal Couve de Murville. When he won the Presidency in May 1969, de Gaulle kept a disdainful silence (Debré 1996, p. 194).

Pompidou's Truncated Septennate

When Pompidou won the elections, he moved the Presidency out from the shadow of one man onto the less personal ground of coalition politics – 'Gaullisme politique' (Roussel 1984, p. 318). All the same, coming in the shadow of the General, 'twice saviour of France', and lacking the Resistance background of many of the 'compagnons' (the so-called 'barons'), Pompidou's problem was to conquer authority within the movement and the centre right and to impose presidential authority on the country. Pompidou had made his reputation during the six years he had been de Gaulle's Prime Minister but to no small extent this authority had also been made attainable by Pompidou's role during the crisis of May 1968. Moreover, Pompidou also had the inestimable advantage of having managed the party and run the General's election campaigns. Of Fifth Republic politicians, Pompidou had had more 'hands-on' experience of party organisation and electioneering than any contemporary or rival (except, perhaps, François Mitterrand). He was also, like Mitterrand, troubled by ill health and incapacitated at some points. In Pompidou's case it was a rare blood disorder which was first evident in 1967 and became debilitating in 1973 (Ibid. 1984, p. 505).

Notwithstanding, the President was to be dogged by an unclear mandate and a shaky political position in the first years of the septennate: in the Assembly elected with a massive UDR contingent in 1968 many looked to him as well as the General. The 1969 election victory had (despite the clear second ballot majority) been an uncomfortable one, based on a backlash against disorder. This 'law and order' majority was more conservative than de Gaulle's electorate had been and Pompidou accentuated the conservative drift of the majority. In keeping with his instincts he abandoned the ambiguous social legacy of Gaullism and bid for the floating vote of middle-class opposition centrists. The Assembly was an insecure one as many deputies, elected in normally opposition constituencies in the aftermath of May '68, were unsure of their re-election at the next legislatives – due in 1973; certainly many of them were likely to lose their seats. In the Gaullist Party itself the necessary widening of the coalition (to include centrists who had campaigned against de Gaulle in the referendum but supported Pompidou in his presidential campaign), necessitated a dilution of the Gaullist component.

Pompidou's conservative almost reactive reflexes (suspect to left Gaullists and to partisans of an adventurous Presidency) caused difficulties which continually resurfaced in factional disputes (Nay 1980, p. 55). It is often forgotten just how uncertain the political climate was at the end of the 1960s: the ' events' of May '68 had badly shaken society and it was not taken for granted that the exponential French economic growth could be continued. And, if Pompidou's knowledge of the Gaullist movement was intimate and it was his success, which provided the UDR with election victories, he was never able to wholly dominate it. Caught between an uncertain economic and social situation and the conservative demands of his majority, he had no real leeway in nominating his first Prime Minister (Jobert 1974, p. 89).

The New Government

With the need to bring the Party and movement into line with the new President there was a renovation of the ministerial team. Pompidou appointed his supporter in 1969 the long-standing Gaullist 'baron' Jacques Chaban-Delmas as Prime Minister. Negotiation of the composition of the government was a delicate affair, in which the combination of the various factions in the Gaullist Party (and 'barons') had to be managed with the newcomers, the centrists who had previously fought Gaullism. These centrists included René Pleven (Justice), Jacques Duhamel (Agriculture) and Joseph Fontanet (Labour), Giscard, accused of having brought down the General, was rewarded personally with the Finance Ministry (to the dismay of some Gaullists). Raymond Marcellin, a Républicain indépendant but not a 'Giscardian', was made Minister of the Interior. He had supported Pompidou through the 'Markovich affair' and Pompidou's aide Xavier Ortoli became Minister for Research and

Development, while Albin Chalandon became Minister of Equipement. Olivier Guichard, de Gaulle's political staff officer but a supporter of Pompidou, replaced Edgar Faure in the key position as Education Minister. It was a government marked both with the presidential stamp and with the new policy of extending the coalition.

At first sight the appointment of Chaban as Prime Minister looked like a coup: to Pompidou's caution and introspection would be added the romantic side of Gaullism expressed in Chaban's mercurial style. But Chaban was a reformist who was faced by a conservative President and an even more conservative Assembly and he was regarded with suspicion by some of the orthodox Gaullists who remembered his willingness to enter governments in the Fourth Republic. But Chaban knew the Assembly Gaullists and was expected to smooth over difficulties (Muron 1994, p. 274). However, Chaban, also keen to widen the coalition (with an eye on the 1973 general elections and his own presidential prospects), mistakenly took the UDR for granted (rarely meeting its leaders) and determinedly wooed contacts with the centre and left.

Chaban's independence, even against de Gaulle (who had not made him a minister), had been demonstrated on several occasions and, although he had a close relationship with the Gaullist movement, he was not a lightweight and nor was he biddable. In this politics was uppermost: the new President needed Chaban, but Chaban needed Pompidou too. Chaban was a living symbol both of continuity and the enlargement of the Presidential coalition. In political terms the Prime Minister was one of the 'barons' who owed nothing to the new President – before his nomination as Prime Minister – and in policy terms Chaban-Delmas was left-leaning and intent on widening the presidential majority to the Radicals and perhaps beyond. In the Matignon the Prime Minister installed two key advisers: the former CFDT union reformist Jacques Delors and the ex-Mendésist Simon Nora. These two aides were to put their own leftist stamp on government policy taking it in a direction away from the Elysée's chosen path.

Pompidou had other ideas: reform was not Pompidou's preoccupation (*Le Monde* 19/6/69). At the press conference on 10 July, sitting at a desk, with only his Prime Minister and the 'porte parole' of the government, the President answered unscripted questions from a small number of journalists. Pompidou had the knowledge and confidence to undertake this (Americanised) transformation of the 'Gaullist' occasion. What Pompidou said was intended to set the tone for the septennate: build a powerful modern economy (Martinet 1973, p. 7). Pompidou did not intend to pursue Gaullist 'grandeur'. France was to continue, and accelerate, its mutation from a rural economy into an industrial one, but not forgetting the difficulties of change in, for example, the smallholding farm sector (which continued to decline rapidly: *Le Monde* 24/9/69). Pompidou's coalition included sectors pressed by modernisation as well as modern France and looked to increased prosperity to smooth the difficulties and anxieties of change. With no hesitations and few reserves, an expansionary objective was made the central presidential concern with the result that inflation was relatively high but interest rates were low and investment vigorous ('saint-simonisme retrovera ses lettres de noblesse' as the President's economist Bernard Esambert put it) (Esambert 1994, p. 74). This philosophy of 'corporate' state-industry partnership and promotion of growth was an active one (see L. Stoleru 1969 for its exposition of this view).

It was Pompidou's Prime Minister Chaban-Delmas who had been responsible for the persuasive encapsulation of the relations between President and Prime Minister with his definition of the Presidential 'reserved domain'. That Pompidou had no intention of being confined to the 'reserved sector' was to become evident through the first four years of the septennate. For example, Pompidou, who had a special interest in modern art, promoted the Paris modern art centre (Centre Pompidou) with determination. In a further extension of presidentialism, the new President had shown, by his actions in arranging the successful devaluation of August 1969 (and the subsequent economic measures), that there was no limit to the potential interventionism of the Elysée. There was, however, a Prime Minister who was unpersuaded.

'New Society'

When, in September 1969, the Prime Minister unveiled his 'nouvelle société' programme for a series of social reforms to deal with the stalemate society ('société bloquée') he came up against the President's own particular interests (Peyrefitte 1976, pp. 95–6). Despite Pompidou's outlook, the éclat with which it was presented, and with virtually no prior notice to the Elysée, Chaban's declaration was a slight to the President. Pompidou was displaced from centre stage: the Premier having made a presidential declaration, the Head of State was reduced to making a prime ministerial response (Roussel 1984, p. 353). There were three scourges which the 'nouvelle société' was intended to remedy: the overbearing state, social rigidity and industrial weakness. For the small opposition centrist party PDM the 'nouvelle société' was welcome, but for many in the UDR, and the President, this was an implicit criticism of the years of Gaullist rule and it aggravated difficulties with the party.

But the septennate had started with the concept of 'modernisation'. This presidential theme, which meant efficiency and increased competitiveness, did not exclude Chaban's project of the 'nouvelle société', but there was a tension between them and they could not be run at the same time. In setting out the government's programme in this manner, as a social and philosophical project underpinning the concerted action of the team, the Prime Minister had usurped (consciously or not) the privilege which de Gaulle had claimed and which Pompidou had erected into a constitutional principle and intended to exercise (Jobert 1974, p. 160). Where Pompidou's campaign had appeared to promise a retention of the Executive Presidency, the initial practice was more like prime ministerial rule than had been anticipated.

Worse still for Pompidou, the social aspects of the programme, put together in the Matignon political office by Simon Nora's team, were inspired more by the left's Mendès France than by de Gaulle, and after initial acclaim, encountered outspoken opposition in the Gaullist movement (Chaban 1975, p. 368). Chaban started another series of debates, by starting the freeing of the ORTF, the state broadcasting system, from government intervention. This had been one of Pompidou's campaign promises, but Chaban also nominated the independent journalist Pierre Desgraupes to head the First TV Channel (Jobert 1976, p. 113). It was at this point that Chaban's own agenda began to displace the President's while the Matignon's links with the Assembly became dangerously weak through neglect. Lack of sympathy between Prime Minister and President enabled the Gaullist 'loyal opposition' to exploit the space between the Matignon and the Elysée with quasi-authorised attacks on the 'nouvelle société'. Chaban, who had been Speaker, was expected to keep the Gaullist parliamentary party in line but, curiously, chose not to do so. However, even if he could sense a profound conflict with Chaban, Pompidou could not dismiss the Prime Minister so quickly after appointment: the uneasy tandem had to continue. But by the beginning of 1970 the split between President and Prime Minister was an open secret.

If the 1969 devaluation of the 'Gaullist' Franc (managed by the Elysée) was a success and was followed quickly by a resurgence of growth in the French economy, the social side of the President's programme, under the aegis of the Matignon, also began to bear fruits. Led this time by Jacques Delors, the negotiations with the unions in the public sector moved ahead. The sought-after consensus in society, easing social divisions and the threat of 'class war', began to materialise with a series of 'contrats de progrès' intended to take confrontation out of industrial relations. At the same time the minimum wage was reformed to redistribute the fruits of success to the lower paid in industry and give them a bigger stake in the growth of the economy. Coming, as these measures did, at the same time as the tightening of the budget and the austerity which were intended to reorient French businesses to the export market, the Pompidou Presidency had begun to make a distinctive mark in the domestic arena.

Pompidou's 'Reserved Domain'

Foreign affairs, clearly in what Chaban called the 'reserved domain', were not neglected, and the first months saw a flurry of overseas visits, but the activism of the Elysée was confirmed across the whole policy front. Pompidou's activity in foreign affairs was more low key than that of the General and without the spectacular and theatrical which so distinguished the first President's style. Foreign affairs was the dossier which Pompidou knew least well: in the General's time, Matignon had not been fully conversant with the President's foreign initiatives, in contrast to its close 'tutelle' of domestic business. Pompidou was under close scrutiny from the Gaullist 'barons' for signs of backsliding, particularly the guardian of Gaullist orthodoxy, Michel Debré, not at the Quai d'Orsay but Minister of Defence, was a critical presence.

Pompidou, in the words of one commentator, had an inclination to 'les attitudes prudentes et les démarches réservées' (de Gaulle 1970, p. 112). Placed in a modest, pragmatic and calculating context, amongst the first measures was the appointment of the centrist but European Gaullist Maurice Schumann. Schumann had been a fanatical supporter of de Gaulle but was also the first president of the MRP. His nomination as Foreign Minister was a sure sign of a receptiveness to any move to enlarge Europe to bring in the United Kingdom, Denmark, Norway and Eire in a new entente (Rials 1977, p. 136). Pompidou was worried by the growth of West German confidence under Brandt (to whom he had a personal antipathy) and expected the UK to balance the FRG and enable French leadership of Europe to continue (Fontaine 1982, p. 248). In Britain, Prime Minister Harold Wilson still led a Labour government looking for entry. After the elections of June 1970 the new Conservative government of Edward Heath made overtures to the French and found a receptive ear. Pompidou's position favoured enlargement and a second entente cordiale inside the institutions if Britain accepted the Common Market as it had developed (CAP included). In one of these personal understandings which are important in a Presidency, Pompidou found himself able to come to an understanding with Edward Heath (Jobert 1976, p. 176).

In 1969, at his election, Pompidou was, to use a later idiom, in favour of 'deepening' as well as of consolidation and enlargement: the Elysée was determined to see that the agricultural policy was consolidated before any detailed negotiations began and then the institutions would be unscathed by a new addition. These negotiations between EEC partners to complete the market were quite rapidly accomplished and the discussions with the UK were able to begin ahead of schedule. In the institutional debate, Pompidou (in a speech in Strasbourg in June 1970) set out his long-held position and was able to pose as a Gaullist defender of inter-governmental relations and to repudiate any element of federalism – also the UK position. However the enlargement might please the centre (and the Socialists), it did not please the keepers of the flame, inside the Gaullist movement – the very people Pompidou had trouble with on other matters.

Other matters included defence policy. With Michel Debré, guardian of the Gaullist continuity, as Defence Minister the Gaullist orientation of defence was initially carefully maintained in a stance of wary acceptance of the authority of the Elysée (Debré 1996, p.112). Pompidou had less interest in – and use for – nuclear diplomacy than had de Gaulle, but France's stance vis-à-vis Nato was maintained as was the nuclear priority within the defence budget. All the same, within the restrictive framework, the French defence outlook began to change. In particular defence policy began to acknowledge the importance of the European dimension (without, however, following through the evolution into cooperation) and the climbdown from exclusive reliance on the deterrent was begun. French suspicion of America was also evident in Pompidou's Presidency, although the first few steps seemed to indicate a desire to 'normalise' relations with the superpower. At the same time Pompidou did not neglect to cultivate the Soviet connection and visited Moscow in October 1970 to reaffirm the 'special relationship'.

Conceived as a way to rebuild Franco-American understanding, Pompidou's visit to the United States of February 1970 became tangled in the problems of French policy in the Middle East. France under Pompidou continued the Gaullist policy in the region and maintained the arms embargo but decided to supply weapons to Colonel Gaddafi who had just ousted the King and taken power in Libya. Israel was furious at this policy (and cocked a snook at France by making off with five embargoed boats from Cherbourg) as was public opinion in America (and elsewhere). With this in the background, Pompidou thought of cancelling the visit but it went ahead and in Chicago the presidential entourage was jostled as it left an official function. Pompidou's accusation that the

American authorities were responsible for the insulting treatment was not without consequences (Pompidou refused to return to the USA) but his first experience with foreign policy had been the infusion of a measure of realism into the old Gaullist line, though without any corresponding public relations success.

The Split Between President and Prime Minister

In private dismissive of Chaban's 'nouvelle société', but reserved in public, the President's distrust of the Matignon team and his dislike of the Prime Minister's direction began to grow. By the autumn of 1970 the Gaullist Party was factionalised and the Prime Minister was not in full command of a majority which (by Pompidou's own precedent) he ought to have led and mobilised on the President's behalf. Within the 'majority of the majority', the UDR, the reservations about the Prime Minister grew and there were some warnings to the Matignon of the size of this problem. Despite the 'nouvelle société' left-wing Gaullists quit the movement and despite Chaban's status as a 'baron' of the party, the ultra Gaullist *fronde* was not pacified. Meanwhile civil disorder continued in the universities and in the streets through 1970. University reform had not calmed the situation on the campuses and there were several incidents including further unrest on the Nanterre campus in the spring of 1970. There were problems with truckers (who blocked roads at Easter in 1970) and with the farmers and shopkeepers, necessary to the President's majority.

Given the reticence of the Prime Minister in matters of law and order, the President was obliged to come to the fore in April to appease anxious deputies. Strikes (despite the *contrats de progrès*) remained a feature of industrial relations and the rise of a more violent 'gauchisme' was accompanied by bombings and attacks on police. May 1970 saw the replay of incidents between police and students in the Latin Quarter and Alain Geismar's Trotskyite Gauche prolétarienne was dissolved in June. To appease the more hard-line of the Gaullist Party (and the President and Interior Ministry), a crackdown was instituted after several months of trying to avoid a confrontation; law and order measures (the so-called 'loi anti-casseurs') were adopted, after some difficulty, to deal with the surge of violence and a tough stance was ordered from the Minister of the Interior (Raymond Marcellin).

In early 1970 the President and Prime Minister still remained relatively buoyant in the polls with no indication of a collapse of government popularity. Opposition in the streets was matched by the attempt to regroup the centre in the shape of the revitalised Radical Party of Jean-Jacques

Servan-Schreiber ('JJSS" the 'kennedillon'). They took the opportunity of a by-election in Nancy, caused by the resignation of the deputy contesting a government decision, to capitalise on the unease in French society (de Tarr 1993). Chaban, who had been patronising about the Radicals' new manifesto Ciel et terre, had supported the widening of the presidential majority to the left by bringing the Radicals into it and had provoked the ire of the Gaullist faithful for doing so. A Radical revival under 'JJSS' was thus a blow to him. 'JJSS' won the Nancy by-election at the end of June in a Gaullist 'safe seat', in what appeared to be the beginning of a 'JJSS' tidal wave which risked undermining the Gaullist majority. But as the Prime Minister was eclipsed, Pompidou became more assured and the Elysée took up the reins. In the polls, where Chaban had regularly outshone the President, Pompidou's ratings began to pick up. The Prime Minister's days were numbered.

By chance the Prime Minister was given an extended tenure on Matignon when a by-election became necessary in his own constituency in Bordeaux. Faced by the 'JJSS' mania then sweeping the country, the Gaullist Party had to rally round against the Radical enemy and support the Prime Minister in his own city. Unlike the situation at the beginning of the year (or the June UDR national council meeting in Versailles), when the critics were given free range, the Gaullists closed ranks at their September parliamentary group meeting. Bordeaux returned Chaban-Delmas to the Assembly on the first ballot with a massive 64 per cent, the 'JJSS' bubble was pricked and the Prime Minister was temporarily safe. Pompidou, however, dropped the regional reforms to which the Prime Minister had committed himself.

In November General de Gaulle died and, at an emotional time, Pompidou fell under the scrutiny of the 'historic' Gaullists vigilant on behalf of Gaullist principle. Pompidou had not been extravagantly praised in de Gaulle's posthumous volume of memoirs, in which Chaban had been rehabilitated. In the Assembly and in the country, historic Gaullists were on the lookout for backsliding by 'Pompidolians' and the tension between the President's men and the supporters of Chaban in the UDR worsened. Left Gaullists, more disenchanted by Pompidou than the 'barons', tended to quit the Gaullist movement and set up their own associations which in turn enabled a presidential reconciliation with the more orthodox UDR. But the Prime Minister had not found grace with the UDR majority and nor had his 'nouvelle société'.

In January 1971 a government reshuffle took place in which the Gaullists in Cabinet were reinforced. Not only were Pompidou's associates promoted so were several 'compagnons' of the Gaullist movement. Key here was Hubert Germains' orthodox 'Présence et action du Gaullism', supported by about forty deputies. Chaban's enlarged government had forty-one Ministers. René Tomasini, no shrinking violet and an opponent of the 'nouvelle société', became secretary general of the Gaullist UDR Party in succession to Robert Poujade (who became Environment Minister). Tomasini, a defender of the 'Pompidolian' orthodoxy began to retrench on the widening of the Gaullist coalition for the municipal elections due in 1971 and laid into the 'nouvelle société' criticising the spinelessness of judges and the 'lack of patriotism' of the ORTF (and the general secretary was pulled back into line). Another of the Elysée's faithful was promoted: Jacques Chirac became Minister for Relations with Parliament to fill the gap left by Chaban in liaison with deputies, replacing the 'Chabanist' Roger Frey. Promotion for the 'bulldozer' Chirac was a slap to the 'barons' and the reward to a loyal 'Pompidolian'.

But the possibilities of opening out the presidial majority were not forgotten by a President who had had to struggle to capture the centrist vote in the elections of 1969. Centre Démocrate et progrès, a small party of 'Pompidolian' centrists (who had supported Pompidou's candidature in 1969), were promoted as were the Giscardians of the Républicains indépendants despite a tendency to criticise the Elysée and even more virulently, the UDR (through the voice of Michel Poniatowski). This secured the President's position for his own Parliamentary majority, which was ensured at the expense of the Prime Minister. Meanwhile a series of financial scandals ('la République une et immobilère') sapped the government and even touched the Prime Minister (both his private staff and personally). This was the point, in 1971 after the unexpectedly successful local elections, which marked the apogee of Pompidou's political power.

Yet even as the 'coup' of the United Kingdom's entry into the EEC was being concluded, the government began to lose its way. In mid-January 1972, the *Canard enchaîné* revealed (using unexplained leaks) that Chaban-Delmas, had (quite legally) paid no income tax over the last four years (Chaban-Delmas 1975, p. 393). Coming on the heels of revelations about financial and property dealings a bit close to the wind in other sections of the Gaullist Party, the authority of the Prime Minister could not but be weakened. Within the Presidential majority the Républicains indépendants (and Michel Poniatowski, in particular) began to make capital out of the Gaullist Party's problems and to promote their own leader. Meanwhile, a threat from the left appeared: the Socialist Party had been taken over by François Mitterrand at its Epinay Congress of June 1971, and was being reorganised; a consolidation of a credible opposition was underway. This new-found Socialist unity around the 'présidentiable' of the left, François Mitterrand caused the Gaullists to temporarily close ranks.

Their harmony was not to last: in July 1971 the Gaullist 'compagnons' (five chairs of the Assembly's committees and Hubert Germain) denounced the government's lack of consultation with the legislators and excessive courting of the union movement. A feeling was also evident in the UDR that a party president should be appointed: such a head would undermine the authority of the Elysée (to which the party looked for leadership). But the movement, promoted by Chalandon, Sanguinetti and others, did not develop sufficient momentum to succeed. In addition the UDR also risked being reduced to one (though by far the largest) of the components of the majority coalition. Giscard's Républicains indépendants, on the margins of the majority squabbles, organised their first party congress in Toulouse in October 1971. This was the beginning of the transformation of the Républicains indépendants Assembly group into Giscard's presidential party.

Pompidou's Referendum

President Pompidou decided to go onto the offensive and on 16 March 1972 announced the organisation of a referendum to endorse the enlargement of the EEC. It proved a disappointing damp squib: there was a majority of 'yes' votes for the President but an exceptionally high abstention rate of 40 per cent. President Pompidou had taken a knock and the Prime Minister was designated the scapegoat. Jacques Chaban-Delmas, a month after the referendum, and protesting loyalty to the President went to the Assembly to demand a vote of confidence on the government to protect himself from the President. Chaban received the support of the Assembly by 368 votes to 96 but it was an empty victory (after this direct challenge to the President) (Decaumont 1979, pp. 109–16). Presidential politics did not allow for a Prime Minister to usurp the limelight from 'their' President ('cohabitation' was still distant) and Chaban had tried to place himself in the front rank, rivalling the President, rather too often (recalling, rather uncomfortably, Pompidou himself in May 1968) (Jobert 1976 p. 102).

Pompidou could not summarily dismiss Chaban immediately after the referendum and relations between the Elysée and the Matignon worsened (Muron 1994, p. 293): an investigation into the state televison service (on the pretext of the corruption criticised in André Diligent's Senate report) was transferred from the Prime Minister to Philippe Malaud, a

'Pompidolian' minister, and 'Chabanists' were moved out by the President. Other Gaullists spoke up to denounce the liberalisation of the ORTF. It was becoming impossible to avoid the 'Chaban problem' of declining public popularity, scandals and distrust by the UDR. There were many in the majority who wanted a change of Prime Minister to give the government a new vigour for the forthcoming general elections. On the left the Socialists and Communists agreed their joint manifesto (the 'Common Programme') at the end of June 1972.

Messmer's Government

On 5 July 1972 Chaban was sacked. Pompidou had not found 'his' Prime Minister to work on the details of dossiers under the shadow of the President. In keeping with the spirit of the Gaullist movement, the Prime Minister went quietly, making no difficulties for the President and the government was reshuffled to some limited extent: Chirac was made Agriculture Minister, Edgar Faure was brought in (to head Social Affairs) along with Jean Foyer at the Health Ministry, Guichard (a potential Prime Minister) was put in charge of a 'super ministry' of Planning and Public Works and Jean Charbonnel and Roger Frey quit. But this was no ordinary reshuffle: the surprise was the new Prime Minister, Pierre Messmer. In taking on Messmer and not one of the more widely talked about possibilities, nor the most popular choice in the UDR (unlike Guichard, for example) (Chaban-Delmas 1975, p. 426), Pompidou created a surprise and a contrast. Pierre Messmer, a dour but combative figure, although not a 'baron', was with Louis Joxe and Michel Debré active in the orthodox Gaullist 'Présence du Gaullisme' Assembly group.

Pierre Messmer was a man of impeccable rectitude (free from any hint of impropriety), and was a historic Gaullist but a 'legitimist' who would recognise presidential supremacy. In 1958 he had been made Defence Minister by de Gaulle to put into practice de Gaulle's edicts (in the sector closest to the General's heart) and was trusted to oversee the difficult transition of the Army during and after the Algerian war. He had remained at that post until de Gaulle's departure in 1969. In 1971 Pompidou had brought Messmer into the government as Minister for Overseas Departments; even at that stage the President may have envisaged not just 'bringing a critic into the tent' but also making him Prime Minister. He became a critic of Chaban-Delmas and the 'nouvelle société' project as well as of the watering down – as the orthodox saw it – of Gaullism. He was also more sceptical than Chaban about the need to widen the presidential coalition. When, later in September, a property scandal broke (the 'Aranda' affair), the wisdom of appointing the upright figure of Messmer became evident. At the same time René Tomasini (not thought to be 'above suspicion') was, at the Elysée's behest, replaced after some difficulty by Alain Peyrefitte as UDR General Secretary in September and the Party set about organising for the 1973 general elections in concert with the President's office.

Messmer's remit was to lead the outgoing 'majority' into the battle against the 'Common Programme' of the left. His pugnacity against Chaban-Delmas might have been thought to be useful if it could be turned against the opposition in the run-up to the keenly fought 1973 elections. ('Messmer: mission impossible', ran a *L'Express* headline). In sum, Pompidou was taking no risks with his own position by appointing Messmer who was an exécutant and saw himself as such and the potential for a clash between Elysée and Matignon was eliminated (Jobert 1974, p. 206). To use Michel Jobert's expression: a Premier *'ne doit pas trop bien réussir* (Jobert 1976, p. 110).

As Prime Minister Georges Pompidou had managed the presidential majority from 1962–8 and had pursued the strategy of steadily widening the coalition to bring in the centrists. It was a reactivation of the major left/right fault line to the President's benefit. After his election to the Elysée in 1969, Pompidou remained head of the coalition (Union des Républicains de Progrès pour le soutien au Président de la République – URP) although the Prime Minister took charge of the intra-coalition negotiations. Both the power of the Presidency as well as the nature of French society were at stake in the 1973 elections which would see the end of the absolute majority for the UDR alone. With the consolidation of the alliance of the left between the Socialists and the Communists this process of polarisation was intensified as the centrists reacted to the negative pole of the PCF by moving towards the Gaullists. Within the majority, however, the presidential pressures were becoming evident as the Gaullist Party struggled to maintain its dominant position in the coalition: on the one side were the 'fundamentalists' of the Gaullist movement and on the other were the Giscardians.

On the Gaullist side were those, hostile to other formations, who wanted to close ranks to keep out new coalition members. On the other side were Giscard's Républicains indépendants who were mounting a campaign for 'primaries' on behalf of their 'présidentiable', intended in the fullness of time to reinforce their position in the coalition, and they did not neglect to criticise the Gaullists (for example, M. Poniatowski's *Cartes sur table*, 1972). This forthright position by the Républicains indépendants threatened the principle, outlined by Pompidou in 1966, of single candidates in each constituency representing the 'presidential majority' (avoiding destructive 'primaries' – run-offs). Giscard broke a year's silence by declaring in a speech in Charenton in October 1972 that France 'should be governed from the centre'. Ostensibly above the political battle, Pompidou was careful to cover the campaign in its various aspects from strategy to choice of candidates and had to intervene at times personally to maintain the coalition. For example, Pompidou discreetly imposed one coalition candidate in each constituency: this limited the destructive 'primaries' to only fifty.

The Conservative Campaign

In January 1973, the Prime Minister set out the URP programme (the 'Provins' manifesto). But the elections, in addition to the choice of social programme (disputed by antagonistic and very different ideologies), also turned on the working of presidentialism. As in 1967, the elections of 1973 would make, or prevent, the continuation of presidential domination. Opinion polls were favourable enough to the left-wing opposition (now united and credible) to make it a real test. But, in the last resort, the centrists around Servan Schreiber and Lecanuet, would have been driven to the Gaullists (on the second ballot) because of the Socialist-Communist alliance. In the circumstances, therefore, Pompidou was more directly involved in the general elections than was de Gaulle, but not to the extent of putting his own position on the line (*Le Monde* 11–12/3/73).

President Pompidou appeared on televison on the eve of the second ballot to indicate to the public that: 'Le choix est simple. . .ici le communisme marxiste et les alliés qu'il s'est assurés; là, tous les autres' (F.L. Wilson 1973; J. Hayward and V. Wright 1973). For some time the President's strategy had been to play upon the fear of the leap into the unknown: both the untested 'marxist' Common Programme of the left and the institutional uncertainty, which would be created by a victory of the Opposition. This was emphasised in the eve of poll TV broadcast from the President. Now currently used to describe the co-existence at the top of the Republic of a President of one party complexion and a Prime Minister of another, 'cohabitation' was not a term used at the time. In 1972-3 the tendency was more to allude to the possibility of an ensuing crisis, and increase the pressure to swing behind the URP, rather than to debate the possible outcomes (*Le Monde* 4/1/73). Pompidou, in any case and true to his prudence, wanted as free a hand as possible in the case of the unexpected.

A repetition of the landslide of 1968 was never in question, but the results were a reinforcement of the President's position at the expense of his detractors in the party. The majority was reduced to 276 out of 490 seats but it was a working majority. His strategy, of opening out the coalition and negotiation with the centrists, had been followed and given the full weight of the Elysée (Roussel 1984, pp. 487–90). All the same, there had been progress on the left and the centrists had had to be mobilised in between ballots to bolster the presidential majority: the Assembly of 1973 resembled that of 1967. In 1973 there were 73 Communists (73 in 1967), 89 Socialists (91 in 1967), and 12 Left Radicals (as against 25). For the President there were 185 Gaullist deputies in 1973 (as against 200 in 1967), 54 Républicains indépendants (as against 42) and 19 non-party (as against 11 in 1967). Whereas in 1967 there had been 41 centrists 'in between' the blocs, in 1973 there were 32. However, although in 1967 the bulk of the centre had been aligned with the Opposition in the presidential elections, in 1973 the centre was split and even those (Réformateurs) who had not made a deal with the Gaullists could be called on to support the government – though they were not brought into the new government. If the President had a comfortable majority in the Assembly and his supporters were still the dominant party in the coalition, the Gaullists had suffered a drop in support and their allies in the centre had withstood the receding tide. (Only two of their ministers, Schumann and Pleven, were ousted by voters.)

Within the Gaullist Party the discord and the problems of succession (after the General departed) had not been entirely dissipated by the 1973 elections. Following the elections Prime Minister Messmer handed in his resignation and was renominated in what was, however, a lackluster continuation. But all of the Gaullist 'barons' (Guichard excepted) were replaced and, for reasons of expediency, the President brought new personalities into the government to broaden the coalition even though these same politicians had previously opposed (or not helped) de Gaulle. For example, Michel Debré left government, and was replaced by Robert Galley while Michel Poniatowski entered the Cabinet. In the UDR there were further calls for a 'president' of the movement to be elected to distance the Gaullists from government.

Pompidou's close supporters – Alain Peyrefitte, Maurice Druon, René Pleven, Jean Taittinger, the eccentric conservative Jean Royer and Michel Jobert (as Foreign Minister) – all entered the government. The close allies of the Gaullists in the coalition, the Républicains Indépendants, were in contact with the Réformateurs and a possible enlargement of the majority by an alliance between them was kept as a possibility, reinforcing the non-Gaullist component of the majority and thus the presidential ambitions of the Finance Minister Giscard d'Estaing. At the same time the 'Pompidolian' centrists of the CDP kept out of the Giscardian orbit apart from the Gaullist Party, even though they had a large role in governement. Inside the Gaullist Party itself, the parliamentary group was not appeased and the 'Chabanists' regrouped even though the Elysée's choice, Edgar Faure, was elected to the Speaker's Chair. In fact the race for the presidential nomination was on and inside the UDR it became partially a movement to stop Giscard.

Pompidou's Last Year

In May 1973 the French President went to meet President Nixon in Reykjavik. Photographs of the meeting, showing a Pompidou bloated by cortisone, encouraged speculation about the President's deteriorating state of health. This uncertainty was not ended by the proposal (made in the spring session) to reduce the presidential term to five years. It was moving through the parliamentary process when it was dropped. Pompidou, meanwhile, let it be known that he would be standing again for a second term in 1976 (the end of the septennate).

Events in 1973–4 did not give any respite to a, by now, seriously ill President (Jobert 1976, p. 231). Pompidou had ensured that Pierre Messmer would not take unsanctioned initiatives. Thus there was a period of drift in the government which lacked direction as turbulence hit the exchange markets, inflation mounted and the economic difficulties and social problems. There were the occupation of the Lip watch factory and its evacuation and the sacking of the ORTF director Marceau Long, for example, during which the drift of the country became apparent. And in October 1973, following the Middle East crisis, the oil producers increased prices by 17 per cent. France was 80 per cent dependent on imports for its energy requirements (Roussel 1984, p. 500).

While the President was away (recovering) during July-August, internal party opposition mobilised. In the October 1973 UDR congress in Nantes the President's rivals won positions on the executive (Chirac and Lecat were not elected) while Chaban-Delmas (cheered to the rafters) more or less declared his presidential candidacy and was virtually declared the successor by the party. A UDR, worked by Chaban's supporters, had became even more 'Chabanist' responding to the 'barons' increasing suspicion of Pompidou. Hence a sign of the President's failing grip was that the UDR – the President's party – had moved into revolt and at Nantes his emissaries (Bernard Pons and Jacques Chirac) were even heckled by some Gaullists.

Alain Peyrefitte's successor as Secretary General of the UDR in October was Alexandre Sanguinetti (an old opponent of Pompidou's) and the party elected its orthodox 'barons' to leadership positions in November 1973. Pompidou had constantly been one of the inner group and had – even as President – taken a close interest in the party machine. Yet, with his health failing and the succession question unavoidable, Pompidou lost control of the party as the politicians quarrelled and his grip on policy weakened (*Le Monde* 16/5/73). As Jean Charbonnel, who was Minister of Industrial Development 1973–4, noted the country seemed to drift (Charbonnel 1976, p. 224).

Michel Jobert, as Foreign Minister supported by the President, stepped into the policy gap and promoted a distinctive and forceful foreign policy line in response to the crisis. However, Pierre Messmer would not step into the President's shoes and that left the way open to the presidential staff to take up the reins. Pompidou's private office was devoted to the President and was accused of playing an unwontedly active role in policy making. Pompidou had been at the summit in French politics since the beginning of the Fifth Republic and, at least initially, had no need of council and was well able to ignore unwanted advice. When his health failed, however, the Elysée staff began to play a more dynamic role speaking 'on behalf of the President'. Not all of these staff members were particularly close to the Gaullist movement itself and some were outsiders who had been promoted through an association with Pompidou (not de Gaulle). They were mostly young and unelected, but they were Pompidou's staff and not the General's – or the Gaullist movement's. This presidential staff has been accused of all manner of political interference and misjudgement. But even in Pompidou's last year the actions of the Foreign Secretary Michel Jobert, combative but isolated (in February 1974) appeared to been in the main approved by the President (*Le Point* 21/1/74). Even as late as March 1973 Pompidou visited the Soviet leader Brezhnev at the Black Sea, in May he had met Nixon and he undertook a voyage to China and to Tehran in September (as well as meeting with the UK's Edward Heath and with Germany's Willy Brandt).

The Expanded Presidency

Presidentialism as a system had taken another turn during the Pompidou years. Such was the strength of the presidentialism Pompidou built up that when he was ill the Elysée staff (not Matignon) acting in his name held the authority. De Gaulle had an office of forty-five or so staff which rarely took initiatives and went through the Prime Minister who give direct instructions. Pompidou worked with the relevant minister and with those experts and advisors whom he chose and delegated presidential authority to the Elysée staff. Chaban-Delmas and his ministers chose their own political staffs but Pierre Messmer saw this choice overseen by the Elysée. There were two sections to the office in the years 1969-74 (leaving aside the shadowy role of Jacques Foccart who dealt with African policy: Foccart 1999): one for policy questions and the other for political questions (they had their difficulties of collaboration). On the policy side there were Edouard Balladur (who looked after Social Affairs) and Michel Jobert. Jobert was at Pompidou's service until the President's death through such upheavals as May 1968, the setting up of the Vietnam Peace talks and UK entry into the EEC. It was Jobert who rallied the European states to respond to the American decisions on alliance policy in the 1974 energy crisis (Jobert 1974, p. 288).

If, in Jobert's phrase, the Secretary General 'était le conseiller du jour' then the political tandem of Marie-France Garaud and Pierre Juillet were 'les conseillers de la nuit '. Much has been written about these two political advisers and most things have been said. They were hostile to the 'nouvelle société' and to Chaban personally as well as to the 'barons' and they were conservatives in domestic and foreign policy with a brutal but effective manner of dealing with problems. Pierre Juillet's work in the Elysée as *chargé de mission* was in the Gaullist Party where he worked to try to keep it out of Chaban's control. Mme. Garaud, like Juillet was on a short fuse, and was liable to start as the ordinary lady who cannot tell Stork from butter and end up in barrack room style (Nay 1980). She had moved with Pompidou to the Elysée in 1969, also as a *conseiller technique*.

The year 1974 ended badly for most Western countries and France was no exception. Inflation mounted and the Franc floated downward on the exchanges as social problems worsened in response to the turbulence. Taking their cue from the general malaise, the centrist Réformateurs voted for the censure motion tabled by the left in the Assembly. Government drift in the face of the beginning of a period of crisis and a further scandal (telephone tapping of the *Canard enchaîné*) was condemned as was the Prime Minister's lack of grip (*Le Monde* 15/11/73 and 19/12/73). Pompidou's response was to reinforce his own authority by undertaking a government reshuffle on 28 February on the pretext of reducing the size and increasing the cohesion of the team. Pierre Messmer was reconfirmed as head of the government but, although there was not a major change in composition, the Cabinet team was reduced in size to sixteen (from twenty-two). Roger Frey (a Chaban supporter) was 'promoted' to the Constitutional Council where he would be effectively silenced. Other contenders for the succession were kept waiting for their chance to enter the Matignon; in this way Pompidou tried to stop the race for the Elysée encouraged by his continuing illness. But Giscard d'Estaing emerged as a Minister of State and as the principal figure after a series of initiatives placing him at the centre of politics; and Jacques Chirac was made Minister of the Interior in charge of the Prefects, police and elections. Pompidou died unexpectedly on 2 April 1974.

Pompidou's Term

The President's incapacitating illness blunted his initial sense of direction and outlook, which was quite different from de Gaulle's overarching ambition. Chaban-Delmas summed up the position as follows: 'The undeniable restarting of growth through the systematic development of industrial power, a forward looking development of contemporary art, a leap in the architectural domain with the Pompidou Centre, Parisian urbanism and the reinforcement of national security and of alliances with the entry of Great Britain into the Common Market' (Muron 1994, p. 290). Of course, the Pompidou Presidency was at first favoured by international circumstances, but the priority given to industrial growth was still distinctive. Other societies, worried by the beginings of inflation and wage demands began to slow down expansion, but Pompidou, anxious to buy off popular protest, took a different decision with the result that France had record growth (of 7 per cent per annum) in the early 1970s. But Pompidou's ambition to overtake Federal Germany by size of industrial GNP at the end of his term (which would have been 1976) was undone by the end of the 'trente glorieuses'. In addition to a slower growth rate the next President faced rising inflation and a backlog of social problems, 'libertarian' as well as industrial, with a majority increasingly divided against itself.

In politics, as in other arts, the 'ordinary' is underestimated. This is because, in politics as in craft, the art lies in concealing the artistry. Georges Pompidou's Presidency did not aspire to the heights reached by de Gaulle but it was in its way as artful and effective as the politics of the General (of which Pompidou had, in reality, been part architect). Pompidou's poll ratings had fluctuated but in 1974, just before his death, he was popular (Roussel 1984, p. 542). Pompidou was not given the time to develop this aspect of the Presidency and it may have eventually established the Executive Presidency as a permanent but undramatic feature of the Fifth Republic. This was not to be and Pompidou left his own party in turmoil and his own coalition directionless.

But Pompidou had at the same time moved against the less dramatic aspect of the Executive Presidency by polarising the party system and it would become more difficult to subsequently depart from the narrow conservative path he had cut. In striving to save the situation for his side, Pompidou had intensified the division of the country into left and right (and had raised the stakes in the recession after the oil crisis). This was too tempting a route and too obvious a tactic to be passed up by competitors and the presidential struggle of the 1970s was easily dramatised and came to be depicted as a 'choice of society'. Given that background the Presidency was depicted as the saving institution, the focus of authority and the President as the fount of wisdom. It was the next President, Giscard d'Estaing, who inherited these contradictions: between dramatising and dedramatising, dividing and reconciling, and Presidency above politics but active in its intervention to deal with a turbulent coalition.

Giscard d'Estaing

Valéry Giscard d'Estaing Giscard, although a quintessentially Fifth Republic figure almost, an 'identikit' of its ruling elite, was not a Gaullist. He was born on 2 February 1926 in Koblenz (then under French occupation) into a family of provincial financiers on his father's side and (the 'd'Estaing' was added in 1923) politicians on his mother's. Married to Anne-Aymone de Brantes, granddaughter of a steel magnate, flanked by Prince Poniatowski and Count d'Ornano, the pseudo-aristocratic d'Estaing in fact had followed the *cursus honorum* of the ambitious Fifth Republic technocrat. Giscard was one of the first political products of the tiny ENA, graduating as one of the top 100 graduates in his year into the prestigious Inspection des Finances, and with an intellectual capacity and technical confidence (sometimes affecting an attitude not so much laid back as horizontal (Nay 1980, p.41).

Giscard was Finance Minister in the Fifth Republic just as France opened its borders and began to compete in European markets without the safety net of protection. For this he was well adapted: Giscard was a free market liberal in economics, he carried none of the baggage of Gaullist Republicanism – 'participation' and 'planning' – and he was keen to reduce the French state's role in the economy where possible, although not by reducing the state's responsibilities (Giscard 1976, p. 40). Thus, as Pompidou's Finance Minister, Giscard created the Direction de la Prévision in his Ministry, to remove economic forecasting from the Planning Ministry. Giscard during the 1960s cultivated the famous 'oui, mais' to Gaullism and it was the Républicans indépendants Party which enabled Giscard to build a presidential platform as a 'loyal opposition' within the conservative camp: supporting Gaullist policy, but not uncritically, and intervening at decisive junctures himself or through lieutenants like Michel Poniatowski and Roger Chinaud.

Giscard's Campaign

Giscard thus emerged as one of the principal 'présidentiables' in the government and then as the main centrist on the government side. In a series of deft speeches he arrogated to himself the years of growth but dissociated himself from the negative aspects of the 'trente glorieuses', adroitly associating himself with the centrist criticisms of the Gaullist governments and their reform programme while continuing to woo Pompidou's party. Giscard had criticised excessive presidentialism and the division of France into two blocs as well as conducting an increasingly indiscreet presidential campaign after the 1973 elections. He launched himself on the trail to the Elysée with a memorable sound bite: 'Je voudrais regarder la France au fond des yeux'.

In the 1974 presidential election caused by Pompidou's sudden death, Giscard, in contrast with the unfortunate Chaban-Delmas, had a slick, well-organised campaign supported by the small Républicains indépendants Party as well as by centrist figures like Lecanuet. Mitterrand was the candidate of the united Socialist and Communist left from the first round and Giscard was aided by the fear of a lurking Communist threat: something which provoked an unprecedented mobilisation of 84 per cent on the first round and 87 per cent on the second. Interior Minister Jacques Chirac organised a desertion of forty-three Gaullist deputies to Giscard's camp (Nay 1980, p. 114–5). That, and the rallying of the remaining opposition centrists led by Lecanuet and Servan-Screiber to him on the first ballot, sank the candidacy of the Gaullist Chaban-Delmas. Conservatives seeking the candidate best placed to defeat Mitterrand, increasingly moved to Giscard and he was the right's front runner on the first ballot with 32.6 per cent to Chaban-Delmas's 15.1 per cent and Royer's 3.17 per cent. Although Mitterrand had polled 43.24 per cent, the combined votes of the right provided a tiny theoretical margin over the left. It was a feature of the second round that Giscard's television debate against Mitterrand served him well (with another sound bite: 'vous n'avez pas le monopole du coeur'). On a high (87 per cent) turnout, Giscard won the run-off by the narrowest of victories: 50.8 per cent, a mere 425,000 votes. It was, however, a more conservative electorate than Pompidou's had been in 1969 and Giscard wanted to move policy leftwards.

Centrism Inherits Fifth Republic

These were the circumstances in which Giscard became President in 1974. Gaullism under Pompidou had been under challenge from the rising left-wing coalition and Giscard was, therefore, the residuary legatee of a centrist thrust which would have had to be continued were the right to maintain power. However, whereas Giscard was from the small pro-

Gaullist centre-right party (the Républicains indépendants), Pompidou was an orthodox Gaullist: Pompidou could take chances with the Gaullist Party. Giscard's strategy set up a tension in the internal coalition politics of the Fifth Republic right that was overlooked in the short term but which in the medium and long term was debilitating. With a centrist politician in the Elysée, the problems of the centre dominating a split coalition governing the Fifth Republic were to be explored *in extenso*.

After the nomination of the 42-year-old Prime Minister Jacques Chirac (who could not overshadow him) Giscard's authority over the government was not in doubt. Chirac had little say in the composition of the first government which was smaller consisting of fifteen ministers including one woman, Simone Veil, and with an accent on youth and technocracy. In composing the new government (and it was Giscard not the Prime Minister) the President also produced some ministerial changes. Servan-Schreiber, Minister for Reforms, who was cordially detested by the Gaullists, was sacked on 9 June after an intemperate criticism of the nuclear test programme, but the appointment of *L'Express'* Françoise Giroud as head of a new Ministry for Women and the creation of ministers with responsibility for immigrants (who resigned after two months) and the handicapped were well received in reformist circles.

But this was a government which was overwhelmingly centrist: quite at odds with the balance of the Assembly where the Gaullists dominated the majority. Michel Jobert, for example, the Foreign Minister who talked up a storm in the last months of Pompidou's life, was replaced by the emollient, highly diplomatic Jean Sauvagnargues. He was replaced in 1978 by Jean François-Poncet (who was Elysée secretary general) but in both cases foreign policy was decided at bilateral meetings with the President on Friday mornings (A. Duhamel 1980, p. 29). Giscard travelled on official visits more than his predecessors (Grosser 1984, p. 295). Gaullists noted that, although they held the Matignon and defence their role in the Presidency had been sharply downgraded and the key posts were held by Giscardian loyalists: Michel Poniatowski at Interior, Lecanuet at Justice; Fourcade at Economics; d'Ornano at Industry and Christian Bonnet at Agriculture (Giesbert 1987, p. 222). Other posts such as Defence (Senator Soufflet), Foreign Affairs (Sauvagnargues) and Culture (Jarrot) were held by second-rank 'technocrats' able to put into effect presidential policy. Although Chirac delivered the Gaullist vote in the Assembly 100 per cent, Gaullist sensibilities were being trodden under in the drive for the centre ground. But so too, were Chirac's: Giscard announced his intention to deal directly with ministers and not through the Prime Minister who was cut out of the decision making. Chirac discovered that he had only a partial view and control over very little and the Chirac-Giscard tandem, which promised a new era and which started as a honeymoon, quickly became conflictual. Giscard had taken Chirac to be a devoted 'dircab' and treated him as such. That mistake, the underestimation of the Prime Minister and his sensibilities, cost the French conservative right dear in the next two decades. Giscard had the merito-crat's failing of underestimating other people.

100 Days

On his election Giscard announced: 'de ce jour date une ère nouvelle' (Giscard 1988, p. 68); and, true to the 'Kennedyesque' style then in vogue, started a furious first 100 days ('Vous serez surpris par l'ampleur et la rapidité du changement'). There followed measures designed to mark out a new politics and a style that was both reformist and modernistic (Fabre-Luce 1974, p. 54). Some of these reforms were ill-prepared and others not properly implemented, but fifty bills had been passed by the end of 1975. Giscard's reforming zeal lasted over a year, and then ran out of impetus and the government returned to a more cautious con-servatism. Immediately after his election the Paris Expressway construc-tion was stopped, the voting age was lowered to 18, Foccart (the Elysée 'Africanist' inherited from de Gaulle) was sacked and without precedent the President met Opposition leaders and visited two prisons (after summer riots) (Giscard 1976, p. 170).

On 14 July the Marseillaise was made less martial and the monolithic government-controlled ORTF was broken up into seven divisions, though the President would like to have gone further (Bothorel 1983, p. 85). October of the same year saw the amendment of the Constitution to en-able 60 deputies or Senators to put a proposed law to the Constitutional Council, opening the process of judicial review to the Opposition. In the same way the Presidential press conferences ceased to be magi-sterial and haughty affairs and became American-style informal ques-tionings of the Head of State – not choreographed in advance. Giscard had the confidence and the experience to deal with the press and the informality was to his advantage, enabling the direct explication of policy at which he initially excelled and the citation of statistics which usually both threw the audience and gave an imposing impression of mastery. Informality continued to be the keynote of public appear-ances. On 24 December 1974 Giscard had breakfast with the dustbin men of rue Faubourg St Honoré. He also started a carefully planned programme of 'dropping in' on ordinary people for dinner, 'taking pot luck'. These were stopped when they attracted increasingly sarcastic comment.

Where Gaullist social policy had been relatively conservative, Giscard began to make the 'advanced liberal society'. Simone Veil's November 1974 reform of the abortion laws were central to this new society. It was a project which then put the centrist 'Giscardians' at loggerheads with the President (47 of 65 voted against). But the Gaullist majority also caused Simone Veil great difficulties through which she was helped by the Prime Minister and Michel Durafour. At issue here were the Catholic sensibilities of a majority relatively conservative in religious matters and disinclined to vote against their consciences or their constituents on this of all issues. Gaullists were torn between the 'ultras' (like Maurice Schumann) who rejected change and those who (like Jean Foyer) wanted to decriminalise medical abortion. Schumann and Debré emerged as the principal opponents of the Veil law and almost the whole of the Gaullist group were prepared to vote it down. It was passed with the help of Opposition votes, but without the clause allowing for reimbursement of the operation by the social security funds.

Education Minister René Haby, an educationalist, who had been plucked from the administration (he had been running the schools in Giscard's region) was less fortunate. Although in the highest rank as a teacher ('agrégé'), he underestimated both the opposition to his attempt to introduce a comprehensive equal opportunity principle and its cost. This was despite his positions in Fifth Republic political offices dealing with education and a long-nourished plan for comprehensive schools. Haby managed to push through the comprehensive policy for the public system and to establish the principle of supplementary teaching but the combined opposition of the teaching unions and the Treasury meant that the main provisions were never fully applied and the new government of 1978 did not include him (*Le Nouvel Observateur* 28/2/77).

Republican Formality

There was a contradiction between style and substance which worked to undo the Giscard Presidency: the public informality belied a formality in official affairs which was hierarchical and obsessed with protocol and linked with an hauteur in political dealings which was Gaullist in standing if not in inspiration. In fact, anybody less man-of-the-people than the conservative and upper-class Giscard would be difficult to imagine and as the septennate wore on the Castillian count in the President signalled more wildly to be let out: although Giscard started with high hopes and much goodwill this mismatch was soon to show in a Presidency bathed in a 'climat de revérénce frondeuse.' Whereas the 'informal' and approachable had been made the initial thrust of the septennate, this slowly turned to a quasi-monarchical style obsessed with prestige and pre-eminence. Giscard's decision, for example, contrary to normal usage to have himself served first (as Head of State) at table hardly touched people although this (and other protocol matters) were lampooned. No President of the Fifth Republic was to stretch the ambit of the Presidency as Giscard did in the first two years, but dispersing energies on everything meant that it was increasingly difficult to follow through on anything. Giscard's 'monarchical' comportment started undermining the sedulously promoted idea of a people's Presidency, modest but modernist, decisive but not divisive and authoritative but not authoritarian. Self-confidence easily became over-confidence as the presidential practice set up by de Gaulle of setting out the main lines of domestic policy and leaving to the Prime Minister the daily administration became a generalised intervention. Giscard's pretension became fatal when he overreached himself.

For example, Giscard re-established good relations with the USA and to cement these visited President Ford for a bi-lateral summit in December 1974 at which the situation in Vietnam was to be discussed. Giscard took no Cambodian expert at a time when this little country was, as a result of the Vietnam war raging next door, at the centre of diplomatic attention. Secretary of State Kissinger, using his habitual dexterity, wrote a communiqué (in English) which Giscard then signed without realising that it completely contradicted France's policy in the area (Shawcross 1979, p. 335–43). When the communiqué was welcomed with across-the-board outrage (especially by China) Giscard had to backtrack (but to no avail). All the same, de Gaulle's 'domaine réservé' was replaced by an intervention 'tous azimuts'.

The Deepening World Crisis

But President Giscard's problems were not confined to the management of the coalition of the right on the one hand and the mounting threat from the left on the other: the world had been hit in 1973 by the first oil crisis and by rapid inflation which threatened the prosperity of post-war economic growth. Giscard had no better solution than other politicians but used a two-pronged attack: on the one had dealing with social reform ('advanced liberalism') and making a more humane and equal society (see L. Stoleru, then Giscard's right hand, in *Le Monde* 20/5/79), On the other hand trying to reanimate the economy through freeing it up and stimulating market competition (but retaining social justice). These promises appealed to different constituencies and partially cancelled each other out politically.

In political terms this 'shock' to the economy was symbolised by the abandonment of the optimistic VIe Plan (1971–75). Yet rather than diminishing, the 1970s saw the extension of the economic crisis and witnessed the failure to recapture the early post-war growth rates. At the same time, with rising inflation (which rose from an average of 5.5 per cent in 1969–72 to 8.7 per cent in 1973 and to 15.2 per cent in 1974), balance of payments problems (a deficit of 6.4 billion francs in 1973) and the steady ascent of unemployment (to half a million at the end of 1974), were damaging to optimism, presidential ratings and to Giscard's proclaimed intention to provide social justice (Frears 1981, p. 136).

Yet Giscard changed the thrust of economic policy from the emphasis on the industrialisation of France to a restructuring to meet the needs of globalisation and regulation and the energy price rises. France was particularly sensitive to this last problem as the quadrupling of the price of petrol in Pompidou's last year had made evident France's external energy dependence for which the much-vaunted Gaullist Middle East policy had not provided any special protection. Giscard's promotion of a policy which opened France to competition and abandoned French 'lame ducks' to European competition and to the products of the Third World (then growing in traditional areas such as textiles) ran against the strong current in favour of protectionism (see, for example, Barre's article in *le Figaro Magazine* 7/10/78). French deputies felt the pressures from their constituencies hit by oil price rises and unemployment and sought to defend their local industries. Thus protectionist demands came from all parts of the political spectrum, not just the left (see, for example, J.-M. Jeanneney 1978). From 2.6 per cent in 1973 unemployment grew to 7.5 per cent in 1980 and its average duration extended from 9.4 months to 12.3 months during the same period. In 1974 the number of bankruptcies was 11,964 and by 1980 this total had risen to 20,840 (Bartoli 1981, p. 174). Giscard's policy of edging the value of the Franc upward, to help keep inflation down, further hindered the efforts of French businesses to sell abroad and contributed to the mounting unemployment.

Crisis Measures

As the crisis deepened the reassurances from the Elysée that the light was at the end of the tunnel became increasingly implausible and 1975 was a year of social upheaval. A second Fourcade Plan, launched in

September 1975 to promote internal expansion, was a response to this political imperative (from business and the jobless) but it ran into balance of payments difficulties and in March 1976 the Franc was forced out of the 'snake' the European monetary coordination. Attempts to deal with the crisis resulting from the 'oil shock' were hampered by the rivalry within the majority as the responsibility for taking necessary but unpopular decisions was evaded. A return to 1960s growth rates and full employment was still anticipated for the 'crisis' was regarded mainly as being a result of the petrol price rises which would be overcome in time. The abandonment of the second 'Fourcade Plan' was thus criticised by Gaullists who still saw a role for national strategy in economic policy and a reflation was supported – after his resignation – by Jacques Chirac and then attempted again by the incoming Socialist government of 1981.

Thus Giscard's policies after the 1973 crisis was threefold: to defend the Franc, to tackle inflation and to liberalise. An anti-inflation plan led to the strengthening of the Franc on the exchange markets and to the rejoining of the European monetary 'snake' in May 1975. This was a septennate which started with the rigorous 'Fourcade Plan' and was characterised by a series of measures designed to free up the economy and remove state controls, including the free circulation of capital internationally and the progressive elimination of price controls on industrial products, so that by 1981 they were an exception. At the same time, the public sector was not reduced but was subject to market discipline and to competition where possible and a Competition Committee (a sort of Monopolies Commission) was set up.

It was also decided to promote strategic alliances with overseas companies to enable specialisation and market penetration by the more active French concerns. In the process the state took an active part in facilitating the alliance of Peugeot-Citroën and the rebuilding of Elf-Aquitaine. French investment in foreign countries grew substantially over the septennate to become an integral part of the business of the big French companies (foreign investment in France also doubled between 1973 and 1978) and the turn-over of the same companies became increasingly oriented to selling in foreign markets which were then growing faster than the French economy (Ibid., p.146).

Cutting out the Matignon

In the government, the 'strong man', approaching in function to the Prime Minister, was Giscard's old associate Michel Poniatowski – a man of bracing coarseness. He had recognised the rising star of the young Giscard and devoted himself to the promotion of Giscard's career from the late 1950s. 'Ponia' had an old grudge against the Gaullists and he set about reducing their status in the coalition with apparent relish. Poniatowski was Remirro de Orco to Giscard's Prince: a 'cruel efficient man' who in short order removed the main opposition and in doing so made himself highly disliked (Machiavelli 1961, Ch. 7). His work accomplished, Remirro was summarily removed, this pleased the public who were reassured that the excesses of power were not the Prince's: the role was played out by 'Ponia' from the text book; he became Giscard's principal lieutenant, usually in the role of saying things which Giscard found it diplomatic to leave unsaid (especially his attacks on the Gaullists: 'copins et coquins') (Bothorel 1983, p. 24).

Previously in the Fifth Republic, the Prime Minister had coordinated government policy and had run the ministerial team implementing the presidential programme except in the 'reserved domain' where the tradition of presidential decision making on foreign policy prevailed. In general, Presidents set the main routes and left the governments to decide on the details and on the distribution of tasks (even if Pompidou's private staff at the Elysée surveyed the work of each ministry). From de Gaulle Presidents had made the key choices even in domestic affairs, such as devaluation or other contentious issues, but Giscard was at home with detail when it took his interest and presidential intervention was pushed to new extremes with direct phone calls and letters setting out the priorities and details to the Prime Minister as the President felt it necessary. These public 'lettres de cadrage' to the Prime Minister indicated a serious weakness in a relationship which should have been a strength not a liability.

During 1974–5 some eighty 'conseils restreints' of ministers' advisers and presidential staff were held in the Elysée (Pompidou had twenty or so each year) and were another indication that the President feared to leave the Prime Minister to his own devices. These 'conseils restreints' of ministers, civil servants and the Premier were held weekly in the Elysée under the President. Important problems were decided by the relevant minister directly with the Elysée and cabinet meetings were emptied of all but formal significance (Giesbert 1987). Despite Giscard's desire to seem to decentralise and to free up hierarchies, the appearance of Presidential domination was accentuated by the frequent television appearances which before the year was out began to grate. After Giscard's ill-judged dismissal of the rout of the right on the night of the cantonal elections of 1976, as a little local difficulty, they became less frequent and the presidential TV address 'En direct de l'Elysée' was abandoned.

Giscard's extreme extension of presidential domination was possible because the Prime Minister, at first, had no independent support. But Chirac as Prime Minister thought more of his position than of the President's and at the same time Giscard discounted his Premier as a negligible force (Giscard 1991, p. 124). Almost Chirac's first move was to control nominations and, helped by Garaud and Juillet and by the nomination power and funds of the Matignon, he moved to control the UDR (*Le Monde* 29/9/74). Chirac became secretary general of the UDR in December 1974. Gaullist demoralisation and Matignon's backstage manipulation goes far to explain the UDR's acceptance of the Prime Minister who had been instrumental in depriving them of power. Giscard also neglected to keep his minister up to the mark by giving him 'honour to the point of surfeit' so that he 'could not but fear change'. Giscard did the opposite: Chirac was kept out of the inner circle, patronised and prevented from leading the 'presidential majority'.

'Giscard the African'

African policy was run from the Elysée as it had been under de Gaulle and Pompidou. Giscard's first visit as Head of State was to the capital of the Central African Republic, Bangui. For a long time Giscard had been interested in Africa (which, as he declared to the Elysée dustmen, 'j'aime bien') and had enjoyed hunting parties. When he was elected President the interest (and the hunting) redoubled. Jacques Foccart may have departed the Elysée, but he was replaced by a close associate and Giscard's African policy was a continuation of the special relationship run through the Presidency more than a break with the Gaullist past (Grosser 1984, p. 258). African policy was run by Foccart's friend, René Journiac, who was 'Conseiller à la Présidence pour les affaires africains'. Active neo-colonial intervention in 'French Africa' from the Elysée continued through the support of tyrannical régimes and an imprudent closeness to dictators like Bokassa 1er. Giscard continued Pompidou's Franco-African summits but made them a yearly affair involving about twenty countries, most of them francophone African but including some former Portuguese colonies and a few Commonwealth ones. Ultimately this led, in 1979, to the creation of a multilateral Association concertée pour le développement de l'Afrique to support development in agriculture, mining and infrastructure. Despite reducing aid to the Third World, Giscard tried to continue a policy of reinforcing France's position and of independence (Wauthier 1995).

In July 1974 the 'Abelin report' confirmed this mission and over the septennate the securing of supplies of primary materials and of industrial markets in Africa was reinforced while over the same period the conditions in the poorer countries worsened and debts grew as a result of the onset of world crisis. In the first government of the septennate the Ministry for Cooperation was recreated and two of the new sections of the Quai d'Orsay (which had been reorganised into five geographical divisions) were for Africa: North and sub-Saharan Africa along with Europe, America, Asia and the Pacific. This was an active policy in which the Minister was personally involved and which deployed the resources of the French Army and state mainly in the former French Africa and Zaïre. French troops were in action in Zaïre (April 1977), Mauritania (December 1977) and in Chad (April 1978). It was a policy which suited the United States, then in post-Vietnam self-doubt, and operations such as the capture of Kolwezi in May 1978 were only possible with American logistic support. In addition to the 11th Parachute Division (specialising in African campaigns) there were troops stationed in Gabon, Central Africa, Ivory Coast, Senegal and Chad (where the crisis was burgeoning) and military councillors elsewhere.

Foreign Policy

In foreign policy Giscard continued the centrist orientation, the key feature of which was the furtherance of European integration – helped by a close friendship with the German Chancellor Schmidt (*Le Monde* 4/6/74). Friendly relations, which had gone through a bad patch in Pompidou's time were re-established . Their European interests reflected the former Finance Minister's worry about the turmoil in the world economy, and especially inflation, but political integration also moved ahead. Giscard's centrist revival of Europe came under increasing constraints from the conservative coalition's Gaullist component. In world affairs Giscard hastened the move back towards the Atlantic alliance and patched up relations with the United States under Kissinger, Ford and Reagan. It was Giscard who institutionalised the summits of the major Western powers and he continued the practice of Pompidou's bi-lateral meetings – although at an accelerated rate. In July 1975 Giscard achieved agreement for the first economic summit meeting of the main Western powers (USA, France, Germany, United Kingdom, Japan and, later, Italy and then Canada), held in Rambouillet in November of the same year.

At the same time Giscard believed that he could maintain privileged relationship with the USSR. Brezhnev's visit to Paris in June 1977 was fêted and détente was reaffirmed – although there were few tangible results. After the invasion of Afghanistan by the USSR in 1979, and the suppression of Polish Solidarity, the continuation of contacts was not accepted by the French public (or by conservative opinion in France). France was one of the few Western countries not to boycott the Olympics in Moscow in the summer of 1980. In particular the meeting between Giscard and Brezhnev in Warsaw in May 1980 was derided by both 'Cold Warriors' and the Opposition (who referred to 'Brezhnev's telegraph boy'). Giscard's seeming indulgence to the Soviets by persisting in détente was an element in his defeat (Grosser 1984, p. 281).

M. Chirac and M. Barre

Meanwhile Jacques Chirac had been neither 'pampered nor crushed'. Giscard should have been circumspect because, having to hand the RPR as a means of action, Chirac would exact a price for his previous real or imagined injuries. There is a good deal on record about the personal relations between Chirac and Giscard and about the slights Chirac felt while Prime Minister. Resentment piled up (as several witnesses testified) but the fundamental problem was that the situation made them political competitors. Chirac was invited to the presidential retreat at Brégançon in July 1976 and shortly after that the break became definitive and the war then became open. A malicious description in a weekly (*Le Point* 9/8/76) described Chirac arriving to discuss matters of state, but subject to a long weekend of petty humiliations culminating in a dinner with Giscard's ski instructor. Giscard repudiated this account, but by mid-1976 both Giscard and Chirac felt betrayed: Giscard by the Gaullists and Chirac by the President (Giscard 1991, pp. 90–2 and Giesbert 1987, p. 276). At the end of July 1976 Chirac became the only Fifth Republic Prime Minister to resign rather than be dismissed. His position had become impossible. But the (Gaullist) family of the old Prince was not extinct; it had been revived by the Prime Minister as his personal vehicle the RPR.

Giscard's nomination of Raymond Barre as Prime Minister to replace Chirac was, at first sight, in keeping with the Fifth Republic tradition in which a political Prime Minister of some weight is replaced by a 'technician' who is the President's creation. He was, however, no mere placeman and was given the powers (which Chirac had been refused) to put into effect the deflationary strategy the President wanted. Barre was born in Réunion in 1924 and came to France in 1946 to study in the IEP Paris after which he was a university economics teacher in France and the United States and wrote one of the principal economics text books in French. Barre was a 'safe pair of hands', had an internationally formidable reputation as an economist, was a reliable administrator who crucially shared the President's outlook on economic policy and who had no political base of his own: he would be unable to cause problems for the majority in the way that Chirac, the party politician, had done. Barre was a distinguished politician for not being like a politician. This was not widely appreciated at the time, since imposing budget discipline made him unpopular, but it made Barre a politician to be reckoned with as Mitterrand discovered when bested in a 1977 TV debate. Barre grew to politics and mastered the milieu with assurance and his authority grew. As with others in the Fifth Republic, residence in Matignon led to dreams of the Elysée (Servent 1988).

Barre's principal task was to force through the austerity programme designed to consolidate the Franc and to deal with inflation. He returned to what could be called 'Giscardian orthodoxy' (the first Fourcade Plan) and proposed a new anti-inflation strategy. In September 1976, the first 'Barre Plan' froze prices and utility tariffs as well as capping higher salaries, increasing some taxes and providing incentives to investment. Barre's plan was to continue to hold down wage growth and to penalise companies which permitted excessive rises: 'les salaires devront progresser *au mieux* comme les prix' (Bartoli 1981, p. 87). Monetary policies, then coming into vogue, were also introduced restricting monetary growth to 12.5 per cent for 1977; it was a reduction.

There were also measures taken to reduce inflationary expectations, but the precise figure anticipated was carefully fudged. Implicitly the Barre plan abandoned the priority of the fight against unemployment and was based on the postulate that the control of inflation was the priority instead. Inflation, it was argued, undermined the value of the Franc and was at the root of contemporary problems. Once inflation was controlled, the balance of payments would return to equilibrium, investment would take off and growth would restart: that would mean a reduction in unemployment. With the exception of the two years in 1981–3, the policy has been followed grosso modo since then, rechristened 'competitive deflation' in the 1990s. A strong Franc was defended against the other currencies in industrial Europe which were experiencing worse inflation (Britain and Italy) but the 'Giscardo-Barrist' policy kept the Franc slightly undervalued relative to the Mark of France's main trading partner (In *Année économique et sociale* 1978).

The Conservative Division Consolidated

Just when the government needed full support (the unions and the Opposition were in arms) the Gaullists went onto the offensive. In this

Barre made no concessions to the Gaullist deputies whom he treated with disdain and at times open contempt. In the autumn Barre called the Gaullist bluff and forced them to support the government against the combined Socialist-Communist censure motion. In the new government only two ministers came from the Gaullist Party. A riposte was in preparation. Two months after his resignation, Jacques Chirac made his 'Egletons' speech calling for a 'refoundation' of the Gaullist Party as a mass movement capable of bringing together all the conservatives, and defenders of essential values, who rejected the Giscard/Barre austerity programme. In December 1976 a massive rally at the Porte de Versailles launched the Rassemblement pour la République and Chirac was voted its president by 96 per cent. Chirac had created his own party, sidelined the Gaullist 'barons' (from de Gaulle's era) and put himself at the centre of the conservative political stage. Chirac's resignation, to create a position for himself on the right could only be done at Giscard's expense. Dividing the 'presidential majority' between them was a zero sum game and if the president was not in full control of his own majority it meant the beginning of a new phase in the Fifth Republic. Chirac's appeal to a new 'travaillisme' made at Egletons, should be seen in this light as a declaration of war against the 'liberalism' which Giscard represented and a disputing of the centre ground.

The Battle over Paris

But the revival of the Gaullist movement enabled it to fight the 'battle of Paris' (*Le Monde* 9/3/77). Giscard had promised to restore Paris as an autonomous municipality, a status it had lost in 1871. Christian Taittinger, a secondary but popular politician, led a Gaullist fiefdom but Giscard had other ideas for what was (given the presidential election results) a 'Giscardian' city. Michel d'Ornano (Minister of Industry and then mayor of Deauville) was announced as the Giscardian candidate on the steps of the Elysée in November 1976 (Giesbert 1987, p. 295). It was a mistake. Michel d'Ornano, personable enough, had neither the authority nor the capacity to face down a determined Gaullist challenge and the search for a Gaullist candidate started backstage.

On 19 January Chirac audaciously announced that he would be candidate for the mayorality of Paris and the battle swung into full action with the Gaullists leading the battle against the 'socialo-communiste' united left. Paris was by no means an easy conquest and it was a very bitter campaign in which the 'aristocratic' d'Ornano was derided and in which several reputations were severely battered. Chirac's astonishing energy was deployed on the RPR's behalf and d'Ornano did his best but on the first round on 13 March Chirac took 26 per cent to the Giscardian 22 per cent and on the second round the RPR led with 52 councillors, the Giscardians won a meagre 15 and the left took 40 (d'Ornano himself was defeated). Chirac had taken a prize which would enable him to set up a 'government in exile' and to act as a world leader meeting all the politicians who passed through Paris. The left had polled over 52 per cent and had swept to power in other cities and towns and that, along with the list of beaten ministers, only cast Chirac's victory in a better light. Chirac was elected mayor by the Paris Council by 67 votes to 40.

Giscard reacted to the municipal elections with sang-froid, but reshuffled Barre's government moving out Jean Lecanuet, Olivier Guichard and the combative anti-Gaullist Poniatowski but promoting the Gaullist Alain Peyrefitte and (later) the Paris local boss Jacques Dominati. This government introduced a second austerity 'Barre plan' but it did nothing to enthuse and was roundly criticised by an RPR which had rediscovered its confidence. Meanwhile Giscard had given Jean-Pierre Soisson the task of rebuilding the Républicans indépendants (renamed Parti républicain) into a presidential force capable of rivalling the RPR in a cold war which was capable of becoming 'hot' with a dissolution at any moment. This was confirmed when, in order to pass the legislation electing the European Parliament by direct suffrage, Barre had the first occasion to use the 'package vote' (Article 49–3) against a Gaullist obstruction animated by Chirac's newfound Euroscepticism.

The General Elections of 1978

But Giscard, although unpopular by the standards set by predecessors, was fortunate. In particular, the French Communist Party decided to end its alliance with the Socialist Party around a joint manifesto (the 'Common Programme') in 1977 and to reinforce its own position on the left even at the expense of the victory of the right. After the municipal elections of March 1977, when the Communists had profited from the popularity of their Socialist allies to win council seats and town halls, the PCF recommenced its polemic with the Parti Socialiste but this time with such vigour that it drowned out the discord on the right.

Jean-Pierre Soisson's work on the Parti Républicain had been successful but not to the extent that it needed to balance the RPR which, with a candidate in almost every constituency, appeared likely to dominate the conservative right after the 1978 elections. Over the summer of 1977 a centrist electoral cartel was put together to combine forces and prevent the self-destructive first ballot run-offs from which the Gaullists would profit. Prepared in secret by the President's closest advisors, the UDF took shape, federating the Parti Républicain, CDS, Radicals, Social Democrats and Giscardian Perspectives et réalités Clubs, as the left bickered (Petitfils 1981, p 28). It was a very weak Giscardian confederation but, although not a political party, it would help rebalance the right in the President's favour by limiting the number of first ballot contests among the president's own supporters almost guaranteed to allow the RPR to come ahead on the right on the first ballot. Yet even after the collapse of the left's coalition on 23 September they still seemed likely to win (according to polls). Giscard played his own version of de Gaulle's 'me or chaos' under 'cohabitation' indicating that he would not be able to prevent the application of the left's programme if they had a majority in the Assembly. In other words the President would not be an overseer vetoing the more unrealistic parts of the manifesto but would be an onlooker. This 'warning' (which is what it was) against an unrealistic and dangerous programme was made with a forceful intervention at Verdun-sur-le-Doubs on 27 January (Maus 1985, pp. 18–19). Raymond Barre produced his own carefully judged programme of 110 measures at Blois. Giscard intervened again on the Saturday before polling to point out the 'choice' which confronted the voters.

As was usual, Prime Minister Barre tried to lead the election campaign, but when it came to electioneering Chirac was in his element and Gaullism became the effective force of resistance to the left mobilising the conservative electorate. Giscard and the UDF were not inactive but they had nothing to compare with Chirac's sixty-nine meetings and 413 speeches over five months which gave the impression to the RPR at least that the right's victory was mainly a result of the revived Gaullist movement (Giesbert 1987, p. 309). In a high turn out of 83 per cent the conservative parties kept their majority – by a tiny margin. On the first round the left took 49.87 per cent and the UDF and RPR combined won 45.26 per cent (RPR 22.19 per cent and the UDF 21.39 per cent). Although it came ahead of the PCF, the Socialist Party's 23.03 per cent (21.25 per cent for the PCF) was disappointing and Communist tactics had succeeded in driving the centre-left voters from the PS back towards the centre. If the Socialist Party had come first of the main parties it had not a high enough poll and it was not ahead of the PCF in enough constituencies to overcome the suspicion of the Communists. It was not in sight of the 30 per cent promised in opinion polls; the UDF had kept the margin of floating voters within the presidential camp.

On 19 March the 'divine surprise' of the second round confirmed the presidential majority with 153 seats for the RPR, 137 for the UDF and a combined left of 201 in which the Socialists had 103 (Frears 1981, pp. 69–74). In 1973 Pompidou's supporters had won 268 seats and the left had won 176 and there was a 'cushion' of 34 centrists most of whom could be mobilised for the President's side. Giscard's majority was thus lower than in 1973 and the Gaullist weight in the coalition had diminished, but it was a working majority. Giscard's hopes of replacing the RPR as the main party of the right were not realised but not only were the 'Chiraquians' not rewarded for their part in the victory, Giscard then made a more determined effort to replace the Gaullists in the state and public sector with 'Giscardians'. Giscard's conclusion was that the voters had endorsed his government and his approach and that if there was a need for a change of direction it was to open the 'majority' out to the left and he made no overtures to the Gaullists. This complacency after two narrow victories against the trend (in 1974 and in 1978) was, in the long term, costly. It was rendered fatal by the divisive war, amongst conservatives this time unrestrained by approaching general elections, for the RPR began to believe its only hope for salvation lay in Giscard's defeat in 1981 (in the same way the PCF preferred a victory of the right to that of their 'enemy brothers' the PS).

A third Barre government was then nominated, but the government reshuffle did not promote the Rassemblement's politicians and Chirac concluded that nothing could be hoped for from the Elysée. After a bruising battle, the Elysée's candidate Chaban-Delmas (who had a score to settle with Chirac from the 1974 presidential elections) became Speaker of the Assembly defeating Chirac's nominee (Edgar Faure). Chirac's attack came in May 1978, RPR leaders suspect of 'Giscardisme' were summarily removed from posts in the movement. But the RPR could afford to be no more than was semi-detached: it criticised the government and made things difficult for it waging a procedural guerrilla war in the Assembly, at times supporting Opposition amendments, but the RPR could not risk voting a motion of censure: the conservative electorate would not have forgiven an open sabotage. A long campaign of anathema had begun.

Europe Divides the Right

It was the European issue which proved the next and serious bone of contention dividing the parties of the right. In November 1978, Jacques Chirac, hospitalised after a car accident, made a declaration from the

Cochin Hospital in Paris which was in effect a call to arms against the European project accusing pro-Europeans (in effect the UDF) of being the 'parti de l'étranger'. These pressures forced Giscard to temporise (for example over the 'Southern enlargement'). France, which had been in a virtually permanent state of election fever since 1973, experienced a further rise in temperature (Pickles 1982, p. 14). With the first direct European elections due in 1979, the nationalist and populist tone which had animated the RPR's general election campaign was revived for the purpose and salted with anti-Giscardian sentiments. These were judged excessive by many on his own side.

Thus Chirac, declaring himself a supporter of 'Europe' warned against he 'inféodation' of France, the 'abaissement' of the country, and that 'le parti de l'étranger est à l'oeuvre avec sa voix paisible et rassurante'. This appeal to the more Europhobic and anti-Giscardian Gaullists in the RPR made life difficult for its remaining Giscardian Europeanists. But it was a far from ideal posture for the first direct elections to the European Parliament, leaving the Giscardian UDF in prime position to pick up the (majority) pro-European vote amongst the conservatives. Moreover the declaration was taken (despite a denial) for what indeed it was: a virulent condemnation of the President and the Prime Minister and their European policy (with the EMS taking the brunt of attacks). Giscard did not immediately respond to Chirac's immoderate attack, though he later deplored 'xenophobia' and 'hatred'.

In the European elections of 10 June 1979 which were, in reality, a sort of national popularity poll of the parties and their principal 'présidentiables', the quarrels within the majority and Opposition were the scene stealers but predictably failed to mobilise the voters (abstention at 39 per cent was high). For the Giscardian UDF list led by Simone Veil the result was a triumph: they took 25 seats and 27.55 per cent of the vote but the RPR with 16.25 per cent and a mere 15 seats came behind the Parti socialiste (23.7 per cent, 22 seats) and the Communists (20.57 per cent, 19 seats). Chirac sacked his two overbearing and anti-Giscardian councillors (Garaud and Juillet) after this RPR setback. Simone Veil, one of the most popular politicians in France, was elected to preside over the first directly elected European Parliament and Giscard, his eyes fixed on distant horizons, took a further step to ensure monetary union. But the European elections, with little at stake and a low turnout, were misleading: there would be no easy victory for Giscard in 1981.

Scandals

In September 1979 the Emperor of Central Africa Jean-Bedel Bokassa was overthrown by French forces. Bokassa, initially supported by Giscard, had become a repressive tyrant and an international scandal, isolated from neighbours and from the OAU. When Giscard stopped French loans to Central African, Bokassa turned to Colonel Gaddafi who, eager to make inroads into Francophone Africa, offered to help. Bokassa's flirtation with Libya was what caused the Elysée to react and depose the Emperor and reimpose (with virtually no opposition) the former President David Dacko as President. Bokassa's regime was ready to fall; by ensuring that his replacement would be favourable to France, the Elysée was acting in a way that was, while not routine, not unique.

Things might have remained there had Bokassa regarded the moves as just another turn of the wheel. It was the beginning of the 'Bokassa diamonds affair': the satirical weekly *Le Canard enchaîné* revealed that the Emperor had given Giscard a present of diamonds, which Giscard had not declared as a gift to the Presidency as required. Giscard's response was to admit that he had received diamonds but to dismiss them as of little value and to refuse to reply to accusations based, he affirmed, on forged documents. This response of outraged dignity, as allegations continued to tumble out, proved inadequate and the President's standing was damaged. The suicide of Robert Boulin, a Gaullist minister under Giscard, and the murder of Jean de Broglie were undermining. The atmosphere was soured and people were less forgiving in bad times than in good: 'colomniez, colomniez, il en resteira toujours quelque chose'.

All the same, the Communists and Socialists remained on bad terms. The Parti Socialiste was at daggers drawn over its future presidential candidate with Rocard challenging Mitterrand until the autumn of 1979. Preoccupied with the RPR's war of attrition in the Assembly (holding up the budget for 1980, for example), Giscard did not take Mitterrand's campaign seriously enough (he appeared to be a 'two time loser'). The polls did not seem to exclude a second term for Giscard although by-elections in autumn 1980 were not good for the UDF. As the election approached, Giscard's supporters introduced a new series of 'law and order' measures ('Sécurité et liberté') to crack down on crime, in response to growing fears. Problems were growing in the steel-making districts as the restructuring of that industry, decided in 1979, led to increased unemployment and social despair (there were continuing strikes and demonstrations). In October 1980 a bomb exploded killing four people outside the Synagogue in the rue Copérnic in Paris. Giscard's reaction to this terrorism was, unlike every other major figure, slow and perceived at best as indifference and at worst as an insult to France's Jewish population – while Barre insensitively sympathised with the 'innocent victim' of the blast, as if to imply that the synagogue was a legitimate target (*Le Monde* 7/10/80). Giscard's distant monarchical comportment began to work against him and to undermine his standing with a public which, in 1974, thought it had elected a young, modern and approachable candidate to the Elysée. At the end of 1980 both Giscard and his Premier were very unpopular but a Socialist victory seemed distant and the President was thought the likely winner (*Pouvoirs* 1981, No. 19).

The 1981 Elections

Giscard had a problem similar to de Gaulle's in 1965, how to run for election while still President. How could the outgoing President preserve the Presidential function and prestige while descending into the arena with the political mob to exchange blows? Giscard, like de Gaulle, tried to enter at the last possible minute (on 2 March) and like de Gaulle lost votes in consequence (but de Gaulle could recoup on the second ballot and Giscard did not). Giscard's campaign (like de Gaulle's in 1965) was a poor one. Declaring himself to be a 'citoyen-candidat' Giscard did not use all the attributes open to him; his campaign was badly organised, without the backing of an effective political party (which the UDF was not) which formed the backbone of the campaign for the other main candidates (Chirac, Mitterrand and Marchais).

By 1981, Giscard's economic credibility, and particularly his ability to deal with unemployment, had been eroded to the benefit of the Socialists (Bartoli 1981). But the war with the Gaullists was critical. Farmers, when they were Gaullist supporters, felt that the economy under Giscard had not benefited them and farming income fell – the first time since the War – in 1980. Not only had Chirac entered the fray in February 1980 determined to revenge himself and to remedy the RPR's marginalisation, but his campaign immediately took on an anti-Giscardian tone. Chirac went onto the offensive against the deflationary policies of the Barre government. In addition Marie-France Garaud also set out as an anti-Giscardien candidate as did Michel Debré who, being a 'historic figure of Gaullism', gave no gifts to the President. Chirac had some interest in ridding the conservative right of the President to save his own party and to replace him as the conservative right's titular leader.

On the first ballot, on 26 April 1981, Giscard polled 28.31 per cent, Mitterrand 25.84 per cent, Marchais 15.35 per cent and Chirac 17.99 per cent (Garaud took 1.33 per cent and Debré 1.65 per cent). Giscard had a theoretical possibility of victory but needed the full complement of votes from the right's combined 49.28 per cent to transfer to his name on the second ballot on 10 May. Giscard might have turned the tide in his favour in between ballots and placed his hopes in the TV debate with Mitterrand: a genre in which he was (as in 1974) normally superior. Giscard did not perform well and the tone of his presidency (its de *haut en bas*) was turned against him by Mitterrand's: 'Vous n'êtes pas mon professeur, je ne suis pas votre élève.' For his part Chirac chose not to give any instruction to his supporters on how to vote adding, instead: 'A titre personnel, je ne puis que voter pour M. Giscard d'Estaing' (hardly an endorsement). Remembering the lack of recognition for the RPR's efforts in 1978, Chirac also refrained from throwing his party or himself into the support of the President on the second ballot and did not attend the President's last meeting.

With 51.75 per cent of the votes, Mitterrand, on the second ballot, had almost a million more votes than Giscard. Some 16 per cent of Chirac's voters had switched to Mitterrand while a further 11 per cent of them had abstained. But it was Giscard's defeat rather than Mitterrand's victory (*Le Monde* 11/11/81). The reasons were numerous. The presidential coalition had split and the division had worsened as the parties warred with each other into the presidential campaign itself. Giscard's image had been progressively eroded and had not withstood the inexorable rise of unemployment. Overall there was an exceptionally high level of discontent with the state of the economy and economic management and this tipped the balance against the incumbent (Lewis-Beck 1983). One indicator of the shifting mood was that more women had voted for the left than the right for the first time in the Republic's history. On 19 May Giscard made a farewell presidential broadcast (ending with an empty chair) and on 21 May transferred authority to the new President.

Political Mismanagement and Disjunction

Giscard promised a lot on his accession to the Elysée and delivered comparatively little. This was partially a result of the splits in his coalition, splits which he should have tackled vigorously and immediately and which he was not able to overcome and which he made worse. It was also attributable to the disintegration of the coalition, the 'disjunction', in which the young President found himself (Skowronek 1993, p. 39). It was a septennate which, at the time, seemed unable to tackle the increasing crisis. But then there was no follow-up to the repeated promise to reduce the ideological tension and, like others, Giscard found a heightened conflict between left and right (Goguel 1983). To some extent the problem was not of the President's making but the inability of the 'centrist' President to reshape the coalition for his own purposes was ultimately fatal to his ambitions for a second term. Some reforms which might have been promoted were rendered impossible by the fragmented and faction-alised presidential coalition and on many issues (such as Europe) Giscard was forced to temporise. Other measures, which were expected (like the reform of radio and television), were disappointing or abandoned (a change in relations with Africa). Some of the measures Giscard promoted were well intentioned but failed because the political backing was inadequately prepared or absent (the 'Haby reforms' are a case in point). Thus in addition to the widening political splits, Giscard did not carry through the modernisation of France which the election of 1974 seemed to promise and the 'ordinary presidency' reverted to the 'regal presidency' and became authoritarian and overbearing (Duhamel 1980, p. 23).

Giscard after 1981 found himself in the unprecedented situation of being a relatively young ex-President and kept alive hopes of a return to power, but having his plans for a comeback thwarted by his first Prime Minister (Chirac) and his then second (Barre). On leaving, Giscard failed to find an appealing register and to mark out his own distinctiveness on the conservative right. Barre, the 1976-81 implacable 'Mr Austerity', took the role of economic expert and Chirac became the 'coming man'. Giscard's U-turns to keep himself in the presidential running did not help his reputation. In 1991 Giscard complained of an invasion of 'immigrants' and called on a family policy to help redress the population balance (French: *sous entendu*) (*Figaro magazine* 21/10/91). Giscard is not the forgotten President, his continuing presence at the front stage since 1981 has kept him a familiar figure, but his septennate has not been remembered as positive.

—8—

François Mitterrand

Counterfactual history is a precarious business. But if François Mitterrand were removed from the politics of the Fifth Republic, the resulting system would not look 'presidential'. Put another way, if Mitterrand's career had failed at any one of a number of dangerous turning points the Presidency would not have developed as it has. It is with Mitterrand, therefore, that presidential leadership on the left in the Fifth Republic becomes determinant and that politics is what will be examined here. For the left it was Mitterrand who for the first time organised support for a directly elected President, by the nature of his 1965 campaign; putting together the support for a personal bid for the Presidency and making the capture of the institution the left's focus was his doing. In this section the argument is, simply, that the Presidency was sustained in important respects by Mitterrand's style and was also weakened in crucial ways by the same approach. This is an examination of what Mitterrand attempted and achieved within the Presidential framework. Hence once again this is an examination of the mechanism of authority. The nature and value of the achievement itself is another topic (see, for example, Cole 1994).

François Mitterrand's political path has been traced by many bio-graphers and from many different aspects, and with attention to both the incidents and the outlook that have characterised a long involvement in French politics. In fact, Mitterrand's political life was a long and involved one which was more than ordinarily replete with paradox and masked by obscurity (There are excellent summaries in Jean Lacouture 1998 and W. Northcutt 1992.) More than with Presidents de Gaulle, Pompidou, Giscard or Chirac, there are with Mitterrand remaining dark areas which future biographers will have to investigate. It is not the intention here to revisit that ground, but a preliminary résumé of the main outlines of Mitterrand's career will be useful background. With that limited purpose in mind, and in order to provide context, a brief review will be attempted.

Mitterrand the Politician

François Mitterrand was born in October 1916 into a modest but comfortable provincial and Catholic 'barrésien' family in Jarnac, Charente, near Angoulême. His father was a stationmaster, but the family had enough property to ease their circumstances. Nothing particularly distingushed the family or the young Mitterrand, but his move to Paris to study began to suggest a modern Rastignac with ambitions greater than Julien Sorel's (Nay 1984). As a university law student, the young Mitterrand attended the Ecole libre des Sciences Politiques and lodged in the Marist residence where he made influential friends. Mitterrand was a maker of networks to which he had access which was a feature of his politics subsequently, whether through the Church (as in Nièvre), veterans' associations or his own 'clubs' of committed activists. His pre-war right-wing politics was the starting point for a later drift leftward which, however, did not start until the War was underway.

He was mobilised into the 237e R.I.C. and in 1940 he was taken prisoner, though not before having won a Croix de Guerre. After (he claimed) three attempts, he escaped and regained Vichy France where, helped by political friends, he entered the service of Pétain's régime. He was no minor official and was awarded the *Francisque* medal for this work for French prisoners of war and organised them into an effective network which he could deploy for his own purposes. These purposes changed progressively to become support of the Allied cause and the rejection of Vichy, although he never accepted the leadership of General de Gaulle. Mitterrand's antipathy for de Gaulle and differences with the Gaullists are well known but the upshot was that he was made general secretary for prisoners of war in the Provisional Government, entered the War Veterans' Ministry pistol in hand at the Liberation of Paris and then after the Liberation presided over the National Movement of Prisoners of War. As Howard Machin points out, at only 27 years of age Mitterrand emerged from the War with 'a Croix de Guerre, a *Francisque*, the prestigious *Rosette de la résistance* and brief ministerial experience'. He also edited *Votre Beauté*.

With the backing of the important Veterans' Association and a Resistance record the young Mitterrand was well placed for a position in the Fourth Republic political class. On conservative Senator Edmond Barrachin's suggestion he started by alighting in Nièvre, where he had no attachments, and acquired a political base in this right-centre region, getting elected to the Assembly in 1946 as Rassemblement des Gauches Républicaines against the Communists. His ascension was as rapid as his consolidation of his local fief: he was elected to the city council of Château Chinon in Nièvre in 1947 and the department council in 1949 and in between these he had entered the Cabinet (of the Socialist Ramadier) as Veterans' Minister in January 1947. With the exception of the 1958 elections (when he opposed de Gaulle's return to power and was defeated), he was deputy for the Nièvre until he was elected President.

As a rising star of the Fourth Republic, the still very young Mitterrand was one of the perpetual 'ministrables', minister in eleven governments from 1947 to 1957 (though he resigned from Laniel's conservative Cabinet). In his ascension he was aided by the small Union Démocratique et Socialiste de la Résistance (UDSR) which was initially a small centre-right/centre-left parliamentary group, which exploited its hinge position to advance ministerial careers. Mitterrand, already an adept at the Assembly tactical game, took it over in a coup in 1953 and although it moved leftward it remained a small band of notables. In 1954 Mitterrand was made Interior Minister in the formidable, if short lived, Mendès France government. This left-centre government was the one truly radical, determined and effective governments of the Fourth Republic. Mitterrand's leftish drift fitted in with the mood of the Radical leader in its attempting decolonisation, loosening Imperial ties and being both pro-European and pro-Atlantic Alliance.

It was as Minister of the Interior in 1954-5 that Mitterrand faced one of his first real tests. His action, as Interior Minister, to repress the uprising in Algeria was not a disadvantage at the time. However, the leak of defence secrets was. In this so-called 'Affaire des fuites', somebody had passed secret Defence minutes to the Communist Party and Mitterrand was whispered to be the source. It was investigated and the Minister was absolved, but the rumours had circulated. At the back of it was, it is assumed, the right's unforgiving attitude to his stance on decolonisation. Prime Minister Mendès France investigated his own Minister of the Interior and that opened a rift that was never really closed. It also testifies to a suspicion of Mitterrand by the most upright of men, Pierre Mendès France, even if it was unjustified. This feeling was widespread at the time of the '*affaire de l'Observatoire* ' in 1959 which was almost fatal to the career of the 'ministrable' and it has never been fully explained and it never came to trial (P.M. Williams 1970, pp. 74–9). Mitterrand claimed to have been the victim of an assassination plot (from which he had escaped by climbing the gate of the Observatoire) but evidence was produced that he knew of it in advance. He was able after a 'mauvaise quarte d'heur' to re-enter the political mainstream, though not without a reputation for deviousness and some bitterness (see Montaldo 1993).

Mitterrand, however, after a brief stumble continued to progress. He was Justice Minister in the Guy Mollet government of 1956 and had the Fourth Republic continued he would certainly have been Prime Minister at some stage. However, the collapse of the Republic and the return to power of General de Gaulle effectively halted a brilliant parliamentary career on the rise. Mitterrand would have no place in a Gaullist government or Gaullist-dominated France. The consequences of what that perception meant for him personally were worked through in his subsequent political career from 1958. He chose to go onto the offensive from the first, making clear his hostility to the return of the General, thanks to which he was beaten in the general elections of November 1958. He did, however, get elected as Mayor of Château Chinon in March 1959 and was elected a Senator for Nièvre in the autumn of the same year. He was completely on the outside of the Fifth Republic Gaullist ruling circle although not completely out of the opposition networks. In that he was like many other Fourth Republic politicians, notably the admired Mendès France, but they had parties to back them and Mitterrand had only friends and contacts.

Fifth Republic Politics

As a politician, Mitterrand was not ideological or policy oriented. This lack of political definition was a help in remaking himself for the second part of his career under the Fifth Republic. While being vaguely left of centre and a reforming minister, he was free from the ideological baggage that encumbered most of the mainstream party politicians. A persuasive and sometimes stirring orator, tactics and negotiation were Mitterrand's forte but he was a loner. These facets of Mitterrand's character, while they have sometimes been portrayed as devious or as unrestrained pragmatism, did constitute strengths in the highly charged political atmosphere of post-war France. Mitterrand is the one tactician of genius produced by the French left, in itself an accolade. Most Socialist politicians were mindful of a whole history of relations between them and the Communists (as well as of a whole theology of internal disputes); Mitterrand was not burdened by that complicated history. They were conscious of their anti-clerical tradition (and supporters) when dealing with the MRP; a Catholic himself, Mitterrand had little time for the moral scruples of his Catholic colleagues, but nor was he a visceral anti-clerical. He would deal with and manipulate whoever was useful to him. Mitterrand could also rise above the quotidian and seek out concordances and mutual interests where others could not see them. This is what he did in the Fifth

Republic, first in creating the CIR, then the Federation of the left and then refashioning the Parti socialiste for his presidential ambitions.

Mitterrand's perception was a strategic one. From the early 1960s onwards the strategy was constant although the tactics varied according to circumstance. If de Gaulle and the Gaullists were to be defeated at the polls then a coalition had to be put together. Whatever the General might pretend, the Gaullists dominated the conservative right and were essentially a conservative coalition (if a startlingly successful one). Most of the politicians of the centre-left could see that, but hesitated about where to move or made untenable strategic choices. It was the Communist Party which was the problem. It dominated the left amputating a third (or even a half) of what would normally be the social democratic left elsewhere in Western Europe. Its rapprochement with the Socialists was difficult enough but too close an association with the Communist Party frightened away the centre, the floating voter and even some Socialists. Opponents of de Gaulle had to contend with the dilemma that there was no alternative majority without both the centre and the Communists. In 1956 the PCF had supported the Soviet suppression of the Hungarian uprising and had been duly punished at the polls in 1958, when it also opposed de Gaulle. It remained unpopular but was still the best organised and best funded political party in France. At the beginning of the Fifth Republic (despite its drubbing) the distrust of this massive party was pervasive.

There were three possibilities and all were tried. Guy Mollet, the Socialist leader, wanted to keep the local government alliances with the centrists but accept Communist votes to win parliamentary seats. Mollet hoped that a non-Communist and centrist Third Force would form in the Assembly and would at some point evict the Gaullists from power. This assumed a conventional and powerless Presidency without de Gaulle. The second was the notion that the Fourth Republic centre could be rebuilt around the SFIO, adding to it the MRP and the Radicals; then the Communists would be compelled to deal with a strong non-Communist left. It became clear, as the Mayor of Marseilles, Gaston Defferre, discovered that it was not possible to perform this feat against the leaders of the PCF, MRP and the Radicals and against the leader of his own party, Guy Mollet. Both the centre (MRP) and the Communists rejected it and the leadership of Defferre's own SFIO was very reluctant to back the enterprise although it appeared the most threatening to continued Gaullist hegemony. Defferre's failure seemed to give comfort to the Gaullist expectation that the construction of a counter coalition to theirs was difficult, if not impossible, and that the participation of the Communists would force the hesitant into supporting the General.

Mitterrand, however, had formed the view that an alliance with the Communist Party was necessary and possible, and that notwithstanding its marxist aspect a winning coalition could be built with it in time. Most political leaders surmised that such an alliance, between the weakened centre-left and the Communists, would lead to domination by the PCF; radicalisation of the programme would mean that winning with the PCF would be impossible. Mitterrand saw the possibilities to rebuild the non-Communist left for the presidential elections. As Mitterrand anticipated, the Communists were willing to compromise and Mitterrand was able to use that weakness to limit the radicalisation and where he was innovative it was on his own terms (not the Communists'). Squaring of the circle in this way was disguised by a radical *marxisant* language but was not completely achieved (see below). Mitterrand used the materials which were to hand, and that meant mainly the SFIO and its traditions, and allowed the assumptions and outlook of the socialist left to continue unchallenged as the coalition was put together.

In other words, there was a misperception at the outset: a coalition was structured on a shifting foundation, part radical and part centrist. Mitterrand's strategy, alliance with the Communists but then to limit or tone down the programme, hardly varied but his reputation as a visionless machiavel was confirmed by the tactics to reach this outcome. Mitterrand himself spoke in a sphinx-like style, using his impenetrability in private; giving little away in public he maintained his ambiguity to the last. Like the Sun King, Mitterrand's personal authority was heightened by his inscrutability. Like de Gaulle, Mitterrand had a supporting cast of lieutenants who spread the message. They were able to adapt the appeal to the audience and they referred back to the source of their authority (they were listened to because they 'knew' what the master wanted). Different (or incompatible) messages were transmitted and coalitions were put together with the leader speaking with several voices.

Mitterrand had other advantages, however. One of these was the Communist Party itself. In 1956 the Communist line in Western Europe had changed at Khrushchev's instigation. Western Communists, from that time (including the French), were urged to make their way to power through alliances and elections: this was the 'parliamentary road to power'. Once that had been decided the Communist Party sought allies and in the French context that had to mean in the first place the non-Communist left. At the same time the relaxation of the international scene led to 'détente' and a less threatening atmosphere prevailed. In the Fifth Republic, unlike the Fourth, the lines in Europe were consolidated and the challenge from the Communist Parties was reduced (though not eliminated). But it was a basic problem that between the Communist outlook (totalitarian and Soviet) and the Socialist (Western and reformist) there was very little in common other than their position on 'the left'.

Mitterrand and 1965

Mitterrand was also assisted by the introduction of presidentialism and direct elections. Other leaders had rejected the Presidency (as had the most eminent leader on the left, Mendès France), but Mitterrand was prepared to use it and to work with it. In 1965, when Defferre withdrew his candidacy, Mitterrand was able to propose himself as an alternative acceptable by the Communist Party and then by the SFIO, because he had no party organisation of his own, and they thought he would pose no challenge to their own. It required time, however, and Mitterrand was prepared to wait for his chance ('laisser le temps au temps' as it was portentously put), supporting Defferre until he failed when lesser politicians might have been impetuous, and given the impression of power-hunger, or given up.

It was, therefore, Mitterrand who stepped forward as the left's candidate for the first presidential elections by direct suffrage. It was a gamble: de Gaulle was unbeatable, and Mitterrand was an isolated figure. On the other hand the Communists, desperate for an alliance of the left and keen to avoid a humiliating result for a PCF candidate, were willing to back Mitterrand while the Socialist Party had no candidate of stature. On this meagre basis, he was given a free hand as the left's candidate, and used it to produce a number of planks (Atlanticist and European) which would not have been accepted by the PCF in other circumstances.

It was the 1965 presidential election which gave Mitterrand his status on the left and as the 'présidentiable': the vote against de Gaulle that forced a second ballot was seen as a victory. Although de Gaulle won on the second ballot by a wide margin, Mitterrand profited from Lecanuet's candidacy which forced the General onto a run-off with Mitterrand thus becoming the principal figure on the non-Communist left. It was also an apparent vindication of his strategy and a promise that the next time (with de Gaulle out of the way) a victory of the united left would be possible. Thus he emerged from that trial as the incarnation of left-wing reconciliation ('left union'), an object so ardently desired by the Communist and Socialist left that he was able to call on substantial capital. Unity appeared to place Mitterrand as the point of reconciliation, the healing of the division which had split the parties in 1920, and gave him a moral authority on the left comparable to de Gaulle's on the right. Divisions between the 'people of the book' were felt to be, in some sense, unnatural. In this matter the symbol was very important and went beyond persuasion and rhetoric giving Mitterrand a potential position of dominance on the left for the rest of his life. Only Mendès France had a comparable stature amongst de Gaulle's opponents, but he had refused to deal with the Presidency which he maintained, with unbending rectitude, was an institution contrary to the Republican spirit.

Mitterrand used this success to consolidate the alliance with the Communist Party and to bring together a confederation of the non-Communist left which roughly equalled it in representation in order to 'rebalance' the left away from the PCF. Communist leaders were not overly worried by the new confederation of the FGDS. They had regained some of their support lost in 1958 and, along with many others, felt the strategy of a united left would continue to benefit them. Their party had been the main beneficiary of the influx of new members after 1965 and still controlled the main levers of working-class power: the unions, their newspapers and, despite the invasion of Hungary, Communism still retained some intellectual prestige. However, Rome was not destroyed in a day and Mitterrand looked to the longer term.

Consolidating the alliance with the PCF was the first step to a general renewal. Communist leaders, helped by the continuing climate of détente in Western Europe were willing to continue the alliance. In electoral terms the cooperative strategy paid off. Both the Communists and the non-Communist left gained in the 1967 elections. Although centre politicians began to slip to the Gaullist camp, and the left's vote did not increase substantially, centrist votes for non-Communist left candidates contributed to an impressive gain in seats. The government looked in danger of losing its majority but it had a 'reserve' vote of centrist deputies, when it came to it. Again this near victory provided Mitterrand with further authority and a 'Shadow Cabinet' was formed followed by the signing in 1968 of a joint platform of the Communist and non-Communist left.

1968

This fragile construction fell to pieces in 1968. Mitterrand overplayed his hand during the May 'events' and the Warsaw Pact invasion and 'normalisation' of Czechoslovakia pushed the centre even closer to the conservative coalition and the SFIO away from the PCF than had the student riots. When de Gaulle resigned in 1969, Mitterrand was in no position to profit from the lack of a candidate on the left and the weakness of the conservative right and there was no prospect of a united left presidential platform. Mitterrand thus stayed out of the limelight. Without the backing of a party even as well placed a 'présidentiable' as Mitterrand in 1969 was vulnerable. Although the Communists ran Jacques Duclos and a good campaign, they could never win. But by winning away Socialist votes, they polled an impressive 21.5 per cent to the Socialist candidate Defferre's 5.1 per cent and the PSU's Michel Rocard who took 3.7 per cent. Georges Pompidou led the first ballot with 44 per cent and the centrist Alain Poher came second with 23.4 per cent. Defferre had repudiated Mitterrand's strategy for dealing with the Communist Party and his humiliating poll made him a belated backer of the alliance with the PCF, for which there now appeared to be no alternative. Yet at the same time, Mitterrand's absence in 1969, the Socialists' humiliation, and the absence of the left from the run-off, made him appear to be the left's unique and indispensable unifier and coalition builder.

It took two years for the consequences of the defeat to become institutionalised. In 1969 the SFIO was reformed as the Parti socialiste with the intention of bringing together the scattered parts of the non-Communist left, and renewing the leadership. Although some small groups joined, Mitterrand, who had never been a Socialist, was frozen out and the new party, led by Alain Savary, included neither him nor his supporters. Despite a renovated leadership and a partially reshaped party, the new Parti socialiste was only a partial success. In a presidential system a party, as the PS then was, lacking a presidential candidate or unable to bring in new blood, could not prosper.

The Parti Socialiste

This lack of progress, despite a bruising rebirth, led to the formation of a coalition of the right and the left within the party looking to Mitterrand's leadership. There was only one 'présidentiable' on the left and that was François Mitterrand who was able to negotiate his entry into the new party as its leader. Following a very unfraternal coup, he entered the party in June 1971 at the Congress of Epinay and took it over evicting those of the old guard who did not rally to him (Nay 1988, p.19). With Defferre and Mauroy, Mitterrand imposed a new Party personnel and a determined strategy aimed at propelling him into the Elysée. It was the strategy of left-wing alliance and that was the basis of Mitterrand's appeal to the new party although (again) there hung over it the uncertainty of what the implications were. For Mitterrand they were strategic, not doctrinal or ideological. It was the beginning of the myth of the 'party of Epinay', of the hope for a new socialism – but also continued the distrust of its 'florentine' leader. Mitterrand had to work on parallel lines to bring together the non-Communist left and to deal with the Communist Party. Almost immediately the effect was of a gathering snowball as the Parti socialiste dominated the scene and attracted the ambitious and ideological. This rallying could not be accomplished in a short time for the left had been dispersed over the previous twenty years. It tested Mitterrand's skill in reconciling quarrelling groups and in jockeying between left, right and centre in the Party itself. Disputing factions might have been a debilitating weak point for the new Party, but Mitterrand built up his own base and played them against each other and used their squabbles to become the ultimate decision maker. Already in the takeover of the Party, the question of influence in the Socialist movement became one of the person's or group's relation to Mitterrand rather than the formal distribution of power through mandates and votes. Manoeuvring groups was integral to Mitterrand's style of party leadership, so much so that it was not until the 1990s, when his authority was flagging, that significant groups or individuals quit the movement.

After the Epinay Congress there were two years to the general elections of 1973 for which the Parti socialiste was not prepared. Mitterrand had to prove himself within a Party shaken by the takeover and to the outsiders like the PCF who were not sure what to expect. There began a flurry of activity which saw not only the promotion of a new generation within the party, but the writing of a party programme, a new left-wing platform and a recasting of alliances. In the first instance came the new manifesto in March 1972, *Changer la vie* written by the Party's left around Jean-Pierre Chevènement and truffled out with 'soixante-huitard' notions. It was the basis for negotiation with the PCF for a joint manifesto and one of its organising concepts (self-government or 'autogestion') became a rallying standard for the PS. Self-government, although impossibly vague, differentiated the Socialists from the Communists and put the PCF on the ideological back foot in the 1970s. What issued from the negotiations was a barely credible programme of anti-nuclear measures, nationalisations and 'progressive' promises which might have become 'the longest suicide note in history' but did not. This 'Common Programme' (signed later by the Left Radicals) seemed to vindicate those who said that no deal could be cut with the Communist Party which would lead to victory: the assumptions were so inimical to Western life that it would be rejected at the polls.

Mitterrand was not, however, the 'useful idiot' or the 'fellow traveller', that Leninists sought. It was a step in the process of plucking the Communist chicken or, as Mitterrand put it to the Socialist International at Vienna, to bring three of the five million Communist voters to the Parti socialiste. Seen as a short-term initiative the Common Programme was a failure but in the long term the seeds of success had been sown. By September 1974 it was over, but it benefited the PS at the expense of the PCF (as Mitterrand had calculated) though not without giving hostages to the Communists. In the general elections of 1973 the left did not win the victory it had expected but the Parti socialiste and its allies surged to 20.8 per cent (101 seats) while the PCF only just kept their first place with 21.4 per cent (73 seats). Mitterrand had already begun to appear as the leader of the left as a whole. Mitterrand also began to use the Socialist International and the Party's connections to bring him into contact with key leaders and to develop a presence on the world stage. Communist leaders viewed these unexpected developments with apprehension.

It was the continuation of what was in effect a presidential strategy. Direct elections to the Presidency had given Mitterrand the opening to develop a personal ascendancy over the parties and groups of the left. While shaky, and unsupported by a major party, the presidential campaign established Mitterrand as the leader and pacemaker. Another politician with the backing of the Socialist Party or the PCF would have been able to undercut this position but Mendès France was unwilling and there was no Socialist contender while the Communists preferred to back Mitterrand than go it alone. Mitterrand was able to bring the parties of the left to the support of the Presidency as an institution (with a promise of victory) and they may have felt that even a left-winger in the Elysée would have been subject to the demands of the party line up in the Assembly. By the time Mitterrand had taken over the Socialist Party the spotlight had moved to the left's presidential contender and onto what he might do.

1974 Presidential Elections

In fact the scheduled 1976 presidential election was in the process of purposeful preparation: Mitterrand's campaign was being carefully planned, efficiently modernised and properly financed (Colliard 1975). But Mitterrand's use of the long term to build up to the next presidential elections of 1976 was interrupted by President Pompidou's unexpected death in April 1974. Mitterrand was the calm centre of preoccupations while others were disoriented. The early vacancy had not been foreseen, but it had its benefits for the candidate. To start, the Communist Party was still confident of its superiority to the PS. It was still prepared to play the role of the supplicant and back a Mitterrand candidacy on his terms, if that was necessary for the advance of the alliance as a whole.

Communist self-effacement was a paying prospect for the left as a whole but less so for the PCF itself. The PCF leadership were not introduced into the inner councils of the campaign and felt slighted, which later developed into extreme distrust. But its leadership was a new one (Georges Marchais had only recently replaced the ailing Waldeck Rochet) and remained confident in its alliance strategy. Gaullists and the centre squabbled and disputed the succession; Chaban's first ballot defeat meant that the Gaullist left were homeless. From this confusion, Mitterrand was able to gather the backing of the important groups on the left to his own person, not as a sectoral candidate. Presidential campaigning enabled him to write his own programme sidelining the Common Programme and to pick his own team which was an impressive gathering of all the talents of the non-Communist left.

Although the Communist Party was not a presence (other than to mobilise its voters), the campaign soon polarised into a dramatic confrontation between two concepts of society (Hincker 1981, p. 124). On the one side there was the conservatives' principal challenger, Giscard d'Estaing offering a liberal and reformed society based on the free market; on the other was Mitterrand's socialism. What exactly Mitterrand's 'socialism' might be was not clear except that it was not Soviet-style centralism and not the Gaullist top-down and unequal society (then entering the first phase of the oil crisis) but it included many of the traditional Socialist elements of European unity and Atlanticism. This radicalisation of the campaign, polarised between the two candidates Giscard and Mitterrand, mobilised the conservative right behind Giscard, who was not a Gaullist, but it also mobilised the left. It gave Mitterrand's credentials as the left's leading figure a further boost and brought the Communist Party's voters and activists behind him, particularly on the second round. Again there was a short-term price, but the long-term gain was that Mitterrand had assured his position on the left and as the left's pre-eminent figure.

On the first round Mitterrand polled 43.26 per cent. He was the front runner, ahead of Giscard who polled 32.6 per cent, but it was not a convincing lead and it was an open election. On the second round Giscard was elected President by 50.8 per cent, a margin of 400,000 votes. Although a narrow defeat, the dynamic imparted by the campaign gave the Parti socialiste an impetus which outpaced its rivals. This time recruits flooded into the Parti socialiste and the remaining pieces of the non-Communist left were brought back into the fold (at the Assises in October 1974, Rocard and his supporters joined). During the 1970s the Party's support at the polls soared and it was France's most popular party in opinion polls and in local elections by 1976 (*Le Monde* 16/3/76). Mitterrand himself was reinforced as the left's leader but a second defeat meant that he was in danger of appearing to be a loser (Nay 1988, p. 387).

Alliance Problems

But, even as Mitterrand had reached unexpected heights, the strategy of left-wing unity on which his campaign since 1958 relied was coming undone. Mitterrand's success in winning 13 million votes meant that the PCF was now the junior partner in the alliance. That failure, their treatment as subordinates by a leader they distrusted, the Kremlin's pressures or a change of Party balance, all inclined the Communist Party to criticise its partner. Communist restraint had been a factor in Mitterrand's two election campaigns. The Party decided in September 1974 to open a campaign of criticism of the Socialists based on the old accusation that they were 'reformists' and in thrall to the 'bougeois' forces in France and the United States. One by one the fissures between the two parties were opened: revolutionary violence, totalitarianism, the Atlantic Alliance, Europe and Mitterrand's own character became subjects for public attack. Verbal violence and outrageous attacks from the PCF were, given Mitterrand's previous enthronment by the Party itself since 1965, counter productive. They confirmed Mitterrand's dominant status pointing out to anybody who would listen the leader of the left's essential moderation. After the initial surprise had passed, the Communist Party's angry tirades began to turn potential voters from the Party and even to demoralise its own activists, recruited latterly on the theme of union of the left. At the same time the public's image of the Soviet Union was deteriorating and the fate of Portugal seemed subject to hard-line Communists. When the PCF briefly changed tack at its 22nd Congress, to enable a deal to be struck for the 1977 local elections, the PCF appeared to be inconsistent and self serving. It was probably too late for the Communist Party to regain ground.

Mitterrand's strategy was not to turn his back on the attacks but to throw the responsibility for division onto the Communists so that if the break came the fault would not be his but theirs. But in the Socialist Party itself the factional balance was disturbed by the Communist Party and on the left (Chevènement's CERES) there opened a second front. Mitterrand reacted by consolidating his hold on the Party leadership, promoting his supporters and demoting the left at the Congress of Pau in 1975. CERES reacted by intensifying its attacks on Mitterrand and repeated Communist demands inside the Socialist Party; something which made dealing with it very difficult without seeming to repudiate the possibility of a rapprochement with the PCF at the same time (a dilemma not lost on Chevènement). Communist success in winning seats and city halls in the 1977 local elections may then have confirmed it in its determination not to allow its ally to marginalise it. It seemed as if the alliance of the left was unlikely to persist into 1978.

This breakup was confirmed when, in September 1977, the Communist Party decided to end the alliance by refusing to negotiate further on the updating of the Common Programme (then five years old) for the general elections of the following year (Hincker 1981, p. 186). An updating of the Common Programme was long overdue but the negotiation was not about the conditions (which had changed in between 1972 and 1978 from fast to sluggish growth) or application but about politics. There was extensive discussion about detail in what was a struggle for control of the agenda rather than economic rationality. It looked as if the Communist negotiators had been told not to take 'yes' for an answer in what was a protracted and bitter series of meetings (O. Duhamel 1980, p. 371). It was clear that the PCF could not negotiate back the power it had lost over successive elections and the renegotiation was abandoned (Hincker 1980, p. 189).

The 'Defeat' in 1978 and the Consequences

Predictably there then opened a long campaign against Mitterrand and the Socialist Party for 'betrayal' of the Common Programme alliance. It was a reckless ploy, but one in which the superior resources and discipline of the Communist Party might have been expected to prevail over the new and inexperienced Socialist Party and its leader. The continuing dispute drove floating voters away from the Socialists and the 1978 general elections were not the left-wing victory widely expected (*Le Monde* 12/3/78 and Goguel 1983, p. 91). The President's coalition won him a victory with a solid majority of 291 seats to 200 (*Le Monde* 21/3/78). The Communists with 86 seats (20.7 per cent) were clearly overtaken for the first time since the Liberation by the Socialists and their allies 114 (25 per cent), while the supporters of President Giscard won 290 seats. It was then that the Communist Party, which had retreated into confrontational hard line, began to split and fracture (Courtois and Lazar 1995, p. 381). A series of protests arose within the Party (of unknown dimensions but more public than previously – *Le Monde* 20/3/78) which rent the previous solid front to the outside world and there was protest after protest at the leadership's comportment and sabotage of the prospect for victory.

Inside the Socialist Party things were less fraught but the defeat in 1978 did lead to a *fronde* by the supporters of Michel Rocard (Hervé and Rotman 1988). This was a challenge to the strategy and ideology of the Party Mitterrand had run since joining it in 1971 and was the most serious factional confrontation of the new party until 1990. By concentrating on the strategy of alliance with the PCF (and consequent radicalisation of the Party's appeal) the Rocardians more or less forced Mitterrand into a defence of the Communist/Socialist alliance. This is perhaps what he would have done in any case after 1978, in order to minimise the Communist accusation of sell-out, but the attack from the Socialist centre deprived him of room for manoeuvre. It was a long-drawn-out argument which tied down the leadership and diverted attention from the objective of the 1981 presidential election and gave the impression that the Parti socialiste was terminally split. Mitterrand never came close to losing control of the apparatus but was forced, by Rocard's challenge at the divisive Metz Party Congress in 1979, to cede ground to the left (CERES) and to radicalise the language, in order to keep control.

That gave the impression, however, that Mitterrand was still extending a hand to the Communist Party despite significant opposition within the Parti socialiste. However, because Mitterrand controlled the apparatus and had built up the Party, filling key positions with his supporters, he was able to move into the candidacy at the time of his choice. It was the presidential strategy which again asserted itself: Mitterrand was able to slough off the more radical (not to say bizarre) commitments made by the Parti socialiste in its 1980 *Projet* and to emerge as an apparently moderate candidate but with a reform programme of substance.

In the first European Parliament elections the Communist Party ran a strongly anti-European campaign highly critical of the Socialists and the left polled badly. Communists polled 20.6 per cent and to the Socialists' 24.9 per cent while the President's UDF took 27.4 per cent and the elections seemed to confirm Giscard's tenure on the Elysée (Goguel 1982, p. 96). In 1981 the alliance of the left was conflictual and the Parti socialiste far from harmonious, but the Giscard Presidency was unpopular. Giscard had promised 'change with continuity'. There had been change (notably the deterioration of the economy) but the elements of continuity were more evident. Mitterrand was able to capture the mood for change and the exasperation with the failure of the economy to turn up after a septennate of 'austerity'.

The 1981 Elections

Rocard, after an abortive attempt to force Mitterrand to back down, declined to stand against the Party's leader (*Le Monde* 9–10/11/80). In February 1981 the Socialist Party overwhelmingly endorsed Mitterrand as their presidential candidate and accepted his platform. He had, as in his two previous presidential elections, again been given a free hand but his presidential programme (the hastily composed '110 propositions') were not given much attention (Favier and Martin-Rolland 1990, Vol. I, p. 108). The message remained the need for an alliance of the left, carefully adapted for the middle class (managers and entrepreneurs to whom the Parti socialiste had successfully appealed) although salted with appeals to the Communist voters. Communist voters were not swayed by Marchais' campaign or dissuaded from voting Socialist by Mitterrand's centrist foreign policy.

Giscard made an issue of his own record in foreign policy but it was here, in a threatening Cold War climate following the Soviet invasion of Afghanistan, that Mitterrand's Atlanticism and Europeanism proved disruptive in the President's camp. Giscard had been hampered by anti-Europeanism within the conservative coalition and had, in 1980, attempted to play the East-West go-between with Brezhnev. This initiative had badly backfired and made Giscard appear the weaker of the candidates vis-à-vis the USSR. At the same time the attacks on Mitterrand by the PCF, which were unrelenting, were the principal feature of Marchais' own campaign; that was meant to stop Communist voters drifting to Mitterrand on the first ballot, and to dissuade them from voting for him on the second (Goguel 1983, pp. 141–2). These served to concentrate attention on the PS candidate and in a backhanded way assured voters that the reviled Socialist was not a stooge of the Communists.

Splits in the conservative camp, which had been in power for a record twenty-three years, and the failure of Giscard to do enough by way of renewal to justify a second term were determinant in the end. Mitterrand had, however, run a faultless campaign (and his television appearances had been worked up to perfection) in which he held out the promise of a new direction but did not neglect the centre. Mitterrand emerged on the first round with 25.9 per cent, just behind Giscard's 28.2 per cent, but well ahead of the PCF's candidate Georges Marchais' 15.4 per cent. Giscard's position was more fragile than it appeared (he had to consolidate the entire conservative vote including those who had viscerally opposed him) and the decline of the Communist vote was a shock. Communist leaders, it is true, had 'talked up' their prospects, but there had been an expectation that the PCF would hold 'its' 20 per cent. When it did not the beneficiary was the candidate they had built up themselves since 1965 as the incarnation of left-wing unity and many must have voted for Mitterrand on the first ballot 'as usual'.

Despite some dismay in the Communist activists' ranks, and a hint that a 'revolutionary vote for the right' would be in order and attempts to dissuade Communists from working for Mitterrand on the second ballot (Courtois and Lazar 1995, p. 392). Mitterrand had no difficulty following up the dynamic of the first round by uniting the left and left-centre behind him for the second. Giscard, on the other hand, could not reassemble the conservative right's coalition which proved split beyond the immediate 1981 elections. Mitterrand was elected by 51.8 per cent to Giscard's 48.2 per cent on the second ballot and followed the capture of the Elysée with a dissolution and a general election before the conservatives could regroup (*Le Point* 11/1/82). A Socialist general election landslide was the result (helped by conservative divisions and abstention) and the Communist Party, driven back into the left-wing alliance by the fear of losing further votes, was reduced to 44 seats (16 per cent) (Ibid., p. 393). There was only one precedent for the extent of the Parti socialiste's victory (38 per cent on the first ballot and an absolute majority) and that was the Gaullists' in 1968 (Goguel 1982, p. 177).

From Campaign to Government

Yet had Mitterrand lost the election it is difficult to say how he would have been remembered, except for his reputation as a florentine strategist. Unlike Mendès France, he would have left no guiding philosophy or line of thought to his successors. What had brought Mitterrand to the Presidency in 1981 was the insight into the strategy needed and the unflagging determination to carry it through despite setbacks which would have discouraged most leaders (*Le Monde* 12/5/81). Mitterrand was not clairvoyant and did not foresee all the difficulties in the left's long march to the Elysée. It was his ability to adapt and innovate within the overall strategy which was crucial in overcoming unforeseen obstacles. He was aided in this by divisions in his opponent's ranks and the inability of the PCF to adapt. Politicians are not visionaries and Mitterrand was no more so than others. In this respect, his governing style was the continuation of this tactical virtuosity and the fluidity of response enabling him to turn the disaster of the first Mauroy governments into an eventual success in 1988. The victory of 1981 confirmed Mitterrand's dominance on the left; his ascendancy over the government was as great as any of his predecessors.

Although the victory was the product of conservative collapse, Mitterrand adroitly exploited the occasion (Goguel 1983, p. 145). In line with his long-term calculation, the new President decided to continue the strategy of consolidating the left, to hollow out the PCF, as a captive in his government. This meant offering ministerial portfolios to the Communist Party. However, unlike Portugal in 1974 or Italy, the Socialist Party was in a position of complete domination and the presidential entourage itself was untouched by a Communist presence (Courtois and Lazar 1995, p. 393). Four Communist Ministers were nominated, all secondary personalities, and in minor ministries and with limited administrative control. There was no expectation that the Communist Party would remain in government whatever the outcome of the Socialist government (especially if the economy worsened), but keeping faith with the ideal of a left-wing alliance was important for Communist voters.

Mitterrand could not expect a Socialist majority at every dissolution, Communist votes would be needed in the future. Mitterrand did, however, have five years to experiment before the next general elections, time which could be used to teach the Socialist Party the realities of government and their previous interludes of power had been few, brief and miserable. There was indeed, a fear on the left that, like the ill-fated Popular Front and every previous left-wing administration, the Mitterrand Presidency would have time for one, perhaps two big reforms, before being returned to opposition after two years (Halimi 1993, p. 351 ff.).

Mitterrand's programme for the government was more ambitious than it was extreme. Much has been written about this first septennate and the exegesis has become a sub-discipline in itself. However, the dash for growth by restimulating the internal economy was not regarded at the time as extreme. Reflation was demanded by, amongst others, conservative politicians (Chirac notably) and centrists who assumed that a world economic upturn was overdue. What went wrong was the assumption that export markets would expand. Pierre Mauroy's Socialist government found itself going counter to the trends in its major partners and as a result the balance of payments deteriorated sharply as France sucked in German and Japanese imports. This, not inflation or money supply, was the problem with which the new government had to grapple and which caused three successive devaluations. After three years it was evident that reflation in one country was not possible and a U-turn in 1983 led to a more restrained and deflationary economic policy.

The U-turn

Deflation was sold to the Socialist Party itself as a 'parenthesis', although it became, at the hands of the most ardent expansionists of 1981 (Fabius and later Bérégovoy) the main thrust of policy. It was in broad outline the policy that Rocard had urged on the Party in the long factional battle with Mitterrand after 1978, but it was adopted by Mitterrand and his supporters after the frustration of the dash-for-growth. Yet it never received full explication or justification. In 1981 it had been assumed that the 'interests of capital', as represented by the outgoing Barre government, had prevented the implementation of an expansionary job-creating policy. As a corollary it was assumed that when the left was in power, the representatives of the people, then a reflation could take place. When this proved wrong, the government returned to a Barre-like orthodoxy, but Mitterrand did not (perhaps could not) take credit for what was a successful Socialist management of the economy.

This new economic policy was successful measured in conventional terms (inflation, balance of payments, credit, and investment) but did not meet the expectations stoked up by Mitterrand's campaigns over the 1970s and particularly the reduction of unemployment. In sum, Mitterrand had placed an emphasis on an economic policy to absorb unemployment which he had then been unable to fulfil and had then changed tack. However, the new policy, while successful in other regards, brought no political dividend because it was never sold to the President's supporters, a difficult task as long as unemployment remained stubbornly resistant to treatment. In addition the U-turn in priorities (to tackling inflation) was presented as a decision for Europe and its opponents were branded as anti-European. Mitterrand's government was at odds with its partners in 1981 and the new policy enabled a concentration on European integration (Colombani and Portelli 1995, p. 235). In the main part, in 1983, the objections to deflation did come from the anti-European left of the coalition (Communists and CERES), but the argument was conducted mainly within the Presidential entourage. Europe, although an excuse and not the reason, became associated for the first time for the Socialists with a policy climbdown, albeit one they accepted.

Reforms

From 1981 to 1985, there was a flurry of measures changing French life and the domineering position of the state. TV and radio were markedly freed up and choice extended, new labour laws were passed and rent control introduced. But the two big reforms of the first septennate were the nationalisations and 'la grande affaire du septennat', decentralisation. They provided the main parliamentary business of the first two years of the Socialist government. Conservative politicians won advantages as much as the left from decentralisation and could look forward to big gains in the newly formed regional councils which they could expect to enter in numbers (Ibid., p. 67). Opposition to the reforms was placed in the peculiar situation of having to argue for the maintenance of administrative supervision of elected officials, a system inherited from the Empire. In the event, warnings about the implications were accurate but the reforms proved broadly supported and difficult to unpick.

Presented as an extension of 'self-management', the decentralisation measures were handled by the most senior of the Socialist team (and once a potential Prime Minister) the Mayor of Marseilles, Gaston Defferre. Defferre had run the Marseilles council and the city region with a rod of iron and was an unlikely champion of self-management, but he represented the local government establishment which made up the main organised base of the Party and which had enabled it to survive very lean years. Mainly concentrated in the old urban SFIO federations, by 1981 it included many newcomers elected in the 1970s, particularly in the municipal landslide of 1977. Decentralisation would give powers to the local authorities (especially the big ones) which they had wanted while national government was in conservative hands. Many local elected officials had chafed at the power of the central administration which they wanted to see substantially reduced.

By mid-1982 the nationalisation measures, although delayed by the conservatives, had been pushed through the Assembly (Ibid., p. 179). They brought nine major companies and most of the banks into the state sector to the extent that 16 per cent of GNP was then produced by public enterprise. There was, however, no clear rationale for the measures. Steel had been problematic for a decade and Barre had effectively nationalised its equity as repayment for state loans; successive governments had deemed them too sensitive to tackle directly; others were a shopping list drawn up by the PCF. They were an essential proof of the Mitterrand Presidency's left-wing credentials. But the question of how they would be run and bought up (and how the Communists could be kept at arm's length) were worked out as the bill was piloted through (Favier and Martin-Rolland 1990, Vol. I, p. 125). Some Socialists saw them as means for industrial restructuring, though that had to wait for the departure of Chevènement, whose intervention was capricious and detailed, from the

Ministry of Industry in March 1983. After 1983 it became necessary to reshape these companies to meet foreign competition involving both lay-offs and plant closures. Such a root and branch reform would not have been possible outside of the public sector. That was not, however, the original justification.

The 'Reserved Domain'

In foreign and defence policy, the new President reaffirmed the Gaullist prerogative of presidential decision making. An initial highly moralistic tone (against arms sales, for example) was not maintained and it settled into 'high politics' conducted from the Elysée early in the septennate. Mitterrand made an immediate mark on foreign policy. There was a natural emphasis on France's place in the Western alliance (calming fears of a pro-Soviet drift) that included a support for Nato's deployment of 'Euromissiles'; the more easily, since they would not be deployed in France. This support was repeated to the German Bundestag in January 1983. But at the same time the new President defied the United States over its Nicaraguan and Central American policy. Despite the dissent of its Communist ally, Mitterrand developed French nuclear policy, retaining the Gaullist 'doctrine' of independence and dissuasion. European policy failed to rally partners to the policy of reflation, but it was active and integration (through the 'Eureka' programme for example) was promoted by the President.

Things started to go wrong for the Mitterrand governments from the first, partly through rhetorical excess, partly inexperience, partly through impetuosity and partly as a result of the misjudged measures being implemented. It was not so much that France was heading for unavoidable disaster, but that Mitterrand's determination to keep control of the Parti socialiste and attract the PCF electorate had stoked up expectations that could not be met. In June 1982 balance of payments constraints provoked a wages and prices freeze and there were spending cuts accompanied by a second devaluation of the Franc. In particular, the unemployment figures remained stubbornly resistant to the quick fix of reflation and Finance Minister Jacques Delors called for a 'pause' (Ibid., Vol. I, p. 409).

As mistakes were made, policy faltered and as the right began to win by-elections and then local elections, morale on the left deteriorated. In March 1983, the left's vote slumped to 44 per cent in the local elections and there was a third devaluation followed by an austerity package (*Le Monde* 16/3/82). Prime Minister Mauroy resigned on 22 March and was immediately reappointed but with a new, smaller, Cabinet and a mission to introduce a restrictive 'austerity' package – the U-turn (Favier and Martin-Rolland 1990, p. 465ff.). A truckers' strike paralysed the country in February 1984; in March the 'restructuring' of coal and steel was announced to furious Communist opposition. In June 1984 the left's vote slumped in the European elections: Socialists took 21 per cent and the PCF only 11 per cent.

The Débâcle

It was probably the continuing inability to reanimate the left which led Mitterrand and Mauroy to embark on a delayed attempt to bring the Church schools under the state system (Pfister 1985, p. 255). Secular schooling had been a violently partisan issue on the left before the Fifth Republic; it had contributed to the sinking of an alliance between the Christian Democrats and the Socialists in the 1940s and 1950s and kept them apart in the 1960s. However in the 1980s, it served to mobilise the right more than the left. In July 1984 the proposal to change the status of Church Schools was met with massive demonstrations (the biggest since the Liberation) and the measures were dropped along with the Mauroy government and its hapless Education Minister Alain Savary (*Le Monde* 26/6/84). At a stroke the President had been deprived of the moral high ground of freedom of choice, and dropping the whole issue was his only alternative. The European elections of June were a further setback at which the PS took 20.75 per cent (20 seats); the Communists 11.2 per cent (10 seats) while the Front national made its breakthrough with 10.95 per cent (10 seats) and the combined conservative UDF-RPR took 43 per cent and 41 seats (*Le Monde* 19/6/84).

Modernisation

With the U-turn in government policy and the drive to 'modernisation' and Europeanism, Mitterrand (and the Socialists) began to reorient themselves for the general elections in 1986 and the presidential elections of 1988. A number of key appointments made the outlook clear. In the first place the nomination of Mitterrand's young protegé Laurent Fabius as Prime Minister set the technocratic and non-dogmatic tone for the new government and the reshuffled ministerial team. In the place of the traditional justifications of the left came the peace makers and the consensus managers (*Le Monde* 9/11/84). Education, the cause of the massive demonstrations, was passed to Chevènement who, with his habitual lack of nuance, reaffirmed the conservative principles in the system, disguising them as a return to 'Republican values' and in doing so made himself a 'présidentiable'. Rocard stayed with the Agricultural portfolio, where he did much to calm rural discontent thus enhancing his reputation. Industry under Cresson and Finance under Bérégovoy, meanwhile, were reshaped as market-oriented ministries with a vocation, not to socialise the economy, but to prepare France for the competition of the new world.

None of this centrism was particularly new; it was designed to reposition the Mitterrand Presidency to occupy the all-important centre ground in time for the 1986 parliamentary elections. But it had started – unacknowledged – under the Mauroy government after the U-turn of March 1983 (*Le Monde* 4/1/85). This was a crucial point because the Communist Ministers had remained in the government thus accepting the new 'modernisation' with its abandonment of the dash for growth and the 'priority of priorities' of reducing unemployment (*Le Figaro* 17/1/90). In the reshuffle to create the Fabius government, the Communists were not forced out, but took their time to turn down the offer to continue. Communist fortunes had continued to deteriorate and the Party leadership had decided there was more to be gained outside than inside (Courtois and Lazar 1995, p. 396). Withdrawal had been likely, ever since the Party leader Marchais headed the steel workers' demonstrations in April 1984, but its timing and manner plunged the Party into further turmoil. Mitterrand continued as before, appealing to the voters and deftly forcing the onus of the break onto the Communists. Mitterrand's centrism was therefore qualified by apparently (for, of course, the Communists disputed it) keeping faith with the left and its voters. Despite PCF hostility, Communist voters were no longer at the call of the Party itself; a portion of them remained the most reliable section of Mitterrand's support. Assured of their support Mitterrand was free to bid for the centre (*Le Monde* 9/10/84).

The Fabius government had what seemed like an impossible remit, but it began to climb back from the abyss of unpopularity into which the 1983 U-turn and the 1984 imbroglio had plunged the governments, the President and the PS (Colombani and Portelli 1995, p. 244ff.). Over the two years to the 1986 elections there were mistakes of implementation (notably by Fabius himself) and presentation but, broadly, the strategy worked. It had, however, insufficient time with the result that the general elections of 1986 were narrowly lost. Mitterrand had hoped the introduction of proportional representation might allow the PS to remain the largest party and to continue to govern by splitting an opposition weakened by competition from Le Pen's Front National. Notwithstanding, the

Presidency had occupied the crucial middle ground and had placed itself to win the inevitable 'cohabitation' battle with the parties of the conservative right.

In that limited sense the new strategy pursued by Mitterrand with Fabius had its justification though it was gained at the cost of bringing the FN into national politics with 35 seats in the new Assembly (Favier and Martin-Rolland 1991, Vol. II, p. 306). Previous governments of the left had left office under a cloud; Fabius' did not and left with the feeling that given a few more months the elections might have been at least drawn if not won. Socialists formed the main Opposition and dominated the left. They were held in high esteem by the public and (unlike 1993) they were untainted by scandal or tarred by incompetence. Over the five years of the legislature the Socialists had begun to move to a culture of government. This had been slow, fitful and incomplete, but it had begun. Mitterrand had, however, confirmed his position as the focus of the political structure confirming the Gaullist vision of the Presidency which was accepted by the Socialist Party and, so it transpired, by the voters of the left. Despite a change of orientation and the dashing of initial hopes, the Presidency, set up and run by the right for twenty-three years, was accepted by the left as 'their' institution.

Conclusion

Mitterrand combined a long-term strategy with a tactical flexibility in the long campaign he conducted for the Presidency. This campaign started with the intention of consolidating the left-wing coalition around his own candidacy and it continued after 1981 when he entered the Elysée at the head of a governmental alliance. It was, however, based on a rhetorical but powerful 'alternative' to the prevailing view and was contested inside the left itself. However, the suggestion that there was an alternative, that the political autonomy of the Presidency was greater than it really was, became a difficulty in itself. Mitterrand had, by 1981, established his own credentials as the representative of the left and these were enough to retain him support during the U-turn of 1983 and the move to the centre in 1984.

Mitterrand's strategy, *pedagogie par les faits* (or whatever it could be called) did leave a gap between expectations and performance. It also made it difficult to justify and claim the government's subsequent actions. Mitterrand's governments could have been presented as success stories but this was difficult to do without disparaging claims made in the run-up to 1981 (and the 1981-2 euphoric rhetoric) and suggesting that the whole campaign had been based on an illusion. Unsurprisingly the government decided to side step the issue and describe the U-turn of 1983 as a 'parenthesis' holding out the possibility of a return to 'social democracy in one country'. Mitterrand's governments after 1984 had the worst of both worlds and found themselves unable to claim their record or to repudiate the past. It was an ambiguity which remained after Mitterrand's departure in 1995 but it was a long-term disability and not a short-term impediment.

–9–

'Cohabitation'

Although the left had been defeated in the 1986 general elections, it was not a repudiation of the President and Mitterrand had been careful not to put his office at stake. At the beginning of 1986, the President's own popularity rating had moved into the positive of 'satisfied' over 'dissatisfied' and continued to climb as the year went on (Duverger 1996, p. 577). Socialists celebrated on election night almost as if they had been victorious: they had polled 32 per cent and taken 216 seats. Proportional representation, introduced for the 1986 elections, had taken the edge off the right's victory and prevented the landslide that might have made the President's position untenable. Proportional representation may have deprived the conservatives of the perhaps 60 seats that they would have won under the old system and it also cost the right seats that went instead to the Front national (*L'Express* 21/3/86). Front national pressure on the conservative right was intense. Proportional representation meant that the Socialist Party did not need to make deals with the Communist Party, still hostile to President Mitterrand (it took under 10 per cent and only 35 seats) (Courtois and Lazar 1995, p. 398).

Conservative politicians were downcast at the narrowness of their victory, with their vote only marginally improved on 1981. There was, however, a working majority of 291 of the 577 seats for the conservative parties: 151 RPR, 130 UDF and 10 Independents. Within the right, the RPR had managed to retain a slight edge but it was by no means in a hegemonic position. the cohesion of the majority could not be taken for granted. Proportional representation had also enabled Le Pen's Front national to take 35 seats (with 9.8 per cent of the vote) and it entered the Assembly in no mood to assist the conservative right (*Le Monde* 18/3/86).

Faced with a conservative majority, the President had no interest in forcing a confrontation by trying to nominate as Prime Minister any other politician than the clear leader of the conservative coalition, Jacques Chirac (*Le Monde* 19/3/86). But Mitterrand was as ever averse to appearing to be forced into a corner and encouraged speculation about other outcomes (Attali 1994, Vol. II, p. 11). Rumours were circulated about possible presidential choices (notably Chaban Delmas) and these had the first effect of impelling Chirac to consolidate his majority by giving concessions to Jean Lecanuet of the UDF and Léotard of the Parti Républicain, and then of creating a minor surprise when Mitterrand called on Jacques Chirac (Favier and Martin-Rolland 1990, p. 458). Mitterrand's reputation for deviousness was well established on the right and 'tricks' were expected. However, the most florentine strategy is sometimes to play it straight; it is possible that this directness was disarming and that the government temporarily dropped its guard (Ibid., p. 386). But Mitterrand had made clear his determination not to be a passive president (*Le Monde* 4/3/86).

Presidential Strategy

'Cohabitation' was a political trial of strength in which neither President nor Prime Minister could count on being secure in their domain (*Le Monde* 4/3/86 12/7/86 and 26/3/86). In 1986 what was ultimately at stake was the presidential election of 1988 which both President and Prime Minister meant to enter. 'Cohabitation' in 1986–8 was a master class in the presidential political arts. As with the coalition building of the 1960s and 1970s Mitterrand's strategy for the 'cohabitation' was simple and artfully direct although, as always, the tactics were sinuous. He intended to leave to the Prime Minister the prose of government and arrogate to himself the poetry of campaign. He could delay but not alter the government's programme; he even managed to associate himself with its successful measures. Allowing the conservative right to govern was, for Mitterrand, the only practical possibility, but their strength was used to unbalance them: they would be given the means to engineer their own defeat. But the Elysée had decided to camp out on the 'reserved domain' of foreign and defence policy and to reaffirm Gaullist doctrines (*Le Point* 10/12/86). Defence and foreign policy was the area which the public viewed as 'presidential' and which could not be brazenly contested by the Prime Minister although Chirac had decided not to surrender them to Mitterrand (*Le Monde* 26/4/86).

What Mitterrand had was time. An adagio pace meant that he was able to play on two registers: setting the Presidency up as the 'arbiter' above the battle and as an impartial moderating force. He went further and set out his view of the Presidency as the guardian of national unity in May 1986 (*Le Monde* 20/5/86). What could be called the 'dignified' function of the institution would enable him to maintain his representative role and to keep a presence in defence and foreign policy. At the same time as appearing to decide matters of 'high politics', he was able to disown the government's blunders. Cabinet meetings ceased to be decision-making bodies but did provide a public platform for the President to advise, encourage and to warn as well as to embarrass the government.

One danger of this route was that the non-partisan nature of the Presidency could be imperilled if the intervention was too evidently one-sided. At some point, Mitterrand would have to descend into the political arena, but he had every interest in preserving a privileged status above the battle for as long as possible. In this Mitterrand's public doubts about running for another term and the pretensions of the eternal pretender, Michel Rocard, were useful: by maintaining uncertainty and the diversion of Rocard as a possible candidate, the President was kept 'presidential' and out of a re-election campaign until 22 March 1988 (Favier and Martin-Rolland 1991, Vol. II, p. 716).

Outside the formal structure of the state, the President had the vital support of the Socialist Party. Lionel Jospin was First Secretary and in regular contact with the Elysée although the Party had to be handled carefully to avoid the President being implicated. In 1986 the Parti Socialiste was the core of a potential presidential majority and would be vital for the 1988 elections. As long as the President remained distant and above the political arena that instrument could be used. If, on the other hand, the President sided with the Opposition against 'his' government the attribute of impartiality would be lost. Socialist politicians were active in exploiting the government's many weaknesses, and in appealing to the Constitutional Council. It could be partisan where the President was not, although they were restrained by the difficulty that the 'President's party' and the 'President's government' were on opposite sides so attacks had to be carefully measured.

In addition to there being a sitting and highly regarded President, the conservative right was divided by competing 'présidentiables'. Former Prime Minister Raymond Barre had overtaken Jacques Chirac in the opinion polls as the preferred candidate of conservative UDF/RPR voters in late 1984 and had maintained that lead in 1986 (apart from the brief 'honeymoon' at the beginning of 'cohabitation') (Knapp 1994, p. 83). Barre, from the smaller centrist UDF, could see no potential in 'cohabitation' and warned that it was an experiment which endangered the Constitution (*Le Monde* 29/1/86). Jacques Chirac, on the other hand, decided to make 'cohabitation' work in the hope that it would lift his ratings to the front rank of 'présidentiables'. A crisis forcing the President to resign would have been difficult to manipulate to the RPR's advantage given the President's popularity and the Socialists' reviving strength and would likely have been to the benefit of Raymond Barre (who would vote for the government, however) (Amouroux 1986, p. 570).

Prime Ministerial Strategy

In constitutional terms the President was a hostage in the Elysée. As long as the Prime Minister was backed by a united majority, they held the formal levers of power and the substance of policy making and implementation. Chirac had more freedom of action than when he was Prime Minister in 1974-6; he was a 'happy' head of government (*Le Monde* 23/9/86). Here was an unusual inversion of normal priorities: at stake was the Presidency which held no powers and the means was the Premiership where power resided. Fifth Republic practice had accustomed people to the executive presidency and 'cohabitation' was seen then by most of the political class (and by the right in particular) as an interlude after which politics would return to 'normal'. One constraint on the Prime Minister was that neither he nor the conservative coalition had any wish to see the institution (which they hoped to occupy) demeaned and nor did public opinion.

Jacques Chirac had an almost free hand in composing the government, and without Elysée interference, although an attempt was made to save face by the Elysée on Defence and Foreign Affairs (*Le Monde* 20/3/86). Former President Giscard was isolated and Raymond Barre stood aloof. But the rising stars of the UDF needed, for their own careers to prosper, ministerial responsibility. Chirac was able to denude the Barre camp of its principal backers in a judicious distribution of ministries (which could bind them to the Prime Minister) although it led to continual tension in government. Politicians had to be appeased with posts consistent with their own evaluation of their status: Léotard, Madelin, Méhaignerie and Rossinot, all from the centre (but not devoted 'Chiraquians'), entered the Cabinet and other favours were bestowed through junior ministries (*Le Monde* 20/3/86). RPR politicians close to Chirac were also given important ministries and that consolidated the neo-Gaullist movement, but not the 'barons' (Chaban, Peyrefitte or Guichard) (*Libération* 21/3/86). Defence and Foreign Affairs were the heart of the 'reserved domain' and were points of potential conflict. Chirac's first nominees for these ministries were the result of the constraints of the conservative coalition. When Mitterrand objected, Chirac acceded but in doing so seemed to confirm presidential primacy. In fact, Defence went to the combative André Giraud (a UDF figure who was flanked by an RPR junior minister) and the Quai d'Orsay to Chirac's lieutenant J.-B. Raimond, a Gaullist career diplomat. This Cabinet mixture was not homogenous. There was thus a parallel conflictual 'cohabitation': of conservative factions in the government that had to be maintained without public clashes or messy resignations.

Moreover, Jacques Chirac had only two years to recast himself as other than a sectarian, impulsive and divisive figure (J.-L. Parodi 1988). Chirac had to outpoll the other conservative Barre and cement his own coalition. This led to an impetuosity of government action and the short-term haste undermined the long-term nature of the strategy. There were two main thrusts to the goverment's policies, economic and law and order, but the mistakes of ill-prepared reforms undermined both.

The 'Mexican Stand-Off'

The defining confrontation came in domestic policy, where the President had seemed to concede the government's domination: there were significant challenges. In fact, the first carefully prepared, but well-signalled, presidential 'coup' came in domestic policy (Balladur 1989, p. 60). It was a test of Chirac's resolution to make 'cohabitation' work and, once conceded, the President, psychologically, had the upper hand. Chirac's impatience, his narrow and fragile coalition and the presidential election due in 1988 tipped the Prime Minister into hasty measures. A whole package of controversial measures were pushed through the Assembly in its first session, invoking the confidence procedure Article 49-3 to enable the government to use time-saving decrees. Article 49-3 allowed for legislation to be deemed passed unless a vote of censure was successful (that would require a majority of all deputies to vote against the government). Decree powers were taken by the government to speed the privatisation of sixty-five state enterprises and the return to the old electoral system of single members and double ballots, but with new constituency boundaries drawn up by the government.

Mitterrand had warned in March that he would not feel obliged to sign all the decrees proposed by the government but this had not been taken as significant. On Bastille Day, against the backdrop of the French flag, the President announced that he would not sign the privatisation decrees, remarking amongst other things that this would allow them to be sold off cheaply to foreign competitors. He added that, although the route through the decrees was blocked, the parliamentary path was still open. This path was, in fact, opened by the President who signed a new decree changing the agenda for an extraordinary session (*Le Monde* 16/7/86). This was, strictly speaking, an extension of presidential power and possibly beyond its constitutional limits (*Le Monde* 18/4/86, Michel Debré in *Le Figaro* 16/7/86). Mitterrand's refusal drew attention to a policy (selling public property) about which opinion was divided, put the Prime Minister on the defensive, drew the left behind the President and asserted the Elysée's presence as a political actor. It was symbolic, but Jacques Chirac was thrown off balance.

But it was the Prime Minister's decision to back down that was the key: that meant that a show-down, an attempt at a ministerial 'strike' and the threat of general elections, would be avoided. It was a stand-off in the sense that whoever 'shot first' would lose. Jacques Chirac, with an uncertain majority and a not very popular cause (privatisations), could not risk an election (proportional representation was still in force) against a popular President. Even had Mitterrand resigned, which he could not be forced to do, Jacques Chirac could not be sure to prevail against the conservative voters' preferred 'présidentiable' Mr Barre. He had to keep his government together and had to make 'cohabitation' work to his benefit. There was also the personal difficulty that he had walked out of Matignon once before (in 1976) and had an image of impetuosity which he hoped 'cohabitation' would efface. In sum, for Chirac, it was the wrong issue at the wrong time. On 16 July, the Prime Minister conceded that the decrees would be passed as legislation and they went through the Assembly by the end of July. Government 'spin-doctors' made the best of it and vaunted the privatisation programme.

In September 1986 the President returned to the attack with a refusal to sign the decrees replacing proportional representation. Redistricting had been undertaken by the neo-Gaullist Minister of the Interior (Pasqua) who naturally gave the left (and Le Pen) no presents, but the issue was again a technical one. Hence once again the public would not have appreciated the breakdown of 'cohabitation' over such a point and the precedent, of presidential right to refuse to sign, had been established. For the second time the Prime Minister withdrew decrees and sent them through the Assembly where a bill was passed by the conservative majority.

May '68 and November '86

Chirac's main blunder was the result of one measure and not of a political or constitutional wrangle over presidential prerogatives and it was not without precedent. Difficulties with education have been a constant for French governments but the 'cohabitation' government, nothing daunted, charged into the gap. It never recovered from the blunder, it demoralised its own side, enabled the President to intervene, mobilised the left and lost its control of the political process. The sequence of events had similarities with May '68, starting with the universities and then spreading to industry.

Junior Minister Alain Devaquet was a former university teacher, well-intentioned but a relative newcomer, who was caught between his own better judgement and the firebrands in the RPR who wanted to bring the university world to heel. Liberal in outlook, the so-called 'Devaquet law' was intended to set the wind of competition blowing through the bureaucratic academic world, to create a 'Premier League' of French Universities. But it was also going to devolve to the universities the power to set admissions standards. Sixth formers would thus lose the notional right to go to whichever university they chose and students would have to pay a yearly tuition fee. Selection riled the high-school students approaching university entrance and (and as in May '68, unexpectedly) brought huge numbers onto the streets (*Le Monde* 10/12/86).

Devaquet's bill progressed uneventfully through the first reading in Parliament in August and through the special session to speed things up. Had the government been precipitate instead of just rushed it might have been passed during the summer and gone unprotested. As it was, the Opposition were given time to organise over the vacation and took it. By the second half of November the universities were in turmoil and the entire student body had been mobilised to oppose the bill. There were three big student demonstrations, the first planned for 23 November.

On 22 November the President used the commemoration of the educationalist Paul Bert to obliquely criticise the Devaquet law and to sympathise with the students ('comment voulez-vous que je me sent déphasé par rapport à eux?' (Favier and Martin-Rolland. 1991, Vol.II, p. 599). Socialist politicians were not inactive in encouraging student discontent and ensured a regular liaison between the student leaders and the Elysée as long as the crisis lasted, shielding the President's involvement with plausible deniability. His supporters' work was evident the next day when the demonstration 'spontaneously' carried placards: 'Tonton tiens bon'. A further demonstration followed and the Prime Minister used a television appearance to propose a 're-examination of the contentious parts of the law'. A climbdown appeared to be in progress and then Malik Oussekine, a student bystander, was savagely beaten by police after a demonstration and died as a result. Most in the government thought that no bill was worth that price (*Le Monde* 10/12/86). But the government's authority had already been badly undercut.

Unfortunately the RPR was celebrating its tenth anniversary over the weekend and that became the sounding board for accusations about anarchists and foreign agitators. Jacques Chirac, who was in London for a European Council meeting, cut short his meeting and returned to a disoriented government (*Le Matin* 17/1/87 and Balladur 1989, pp. 126–7). Mitterrand announced that 'national cohesion must come before everything else' and, coming dangerously close to giving the hardliners another target for their ire, called for the law to be dropped. Mitterrand also visited the bereaved family. On 8 December the Devaquet law was withdrawn along with the contentious nationality laws and the plan for private prisons (also student targets). Alain Devaquet resigned, but the real damage had been done to the government's standing and reputation as well as to its cohesion and direction. Mitterrand had, on the other hand, emerged enhanced. He was seen as in touch with young people, consensual, and open and he had both dissociated himself from the Devaquet laws and retained his position above the political arena.

Troubles come not singly, and (as in 1968) the unions had been caught up in the unrest as public service workers realised the possibilities. A strike of drivers started on the railways on 15 December and this spread to the merchant marine, job centre personnel, posts, metro, electricity, gas and Air Inter. In a nod in the direction of the burgeoning strike movement President Mitterrand refused to sign the decrees introducing 'flexitime' on 17 December and the government, still reeling from the student demonstrations, had to struggle to retain authority. Pompidou's strategy of letting the movement burn out was adopted, but the spontaneous and disorganised nature of the movement made it difficult to find anybody to negotiate with (*Le Monde* 7/1/87).

Once again the President stirred the pot. On 1 January, with the strike at its height, a delegation of strikers went to the presidential residence, the converted fort of Brégançon, to be met by the President. This meeting was denounced by the conservative politicians but the public do not seem to have been offended (*Le Figaro* 13/1/87). Meanwhile the government tried to pit the seriously inconvenienced commuters against the strike, but the movement was winding down as small concessions were made and as resolution weakened. For Jacques Chirac it was the start of an *annus horribilis* as he slipped behind in the presidential race: only a year remained.

Chirac's Main Thrusts

Jacques Chirac needed 'cohabitation' to effect a 'conservative revolution' and establish hegemony over the right; he had only two years in which to accomplish this (a constraint which added to Chirac's natural impetuousness). There were two principal fields: economics, under Edouard Balladur, and law and order, under Interior Minister Charles Pasqua. Pasqua was a Resistance Gaullist of Corsican origin with a taste for populist politics and a profound knowledge of the RPR's grass roots. These were both areas where a rapid impact was difficult. Economies take time to turn and are subject to outside conditions. Pasqua was to reassure people that the 'crime wave' was being dealt with and the means would be a crackdown. However, anti-crime measures, even if quite successful, do not alter the *perception* of insecurity widely and fast enough. In law and order things went wrong for the government and its policies were turned against it. In economics policy did not so much go wrong as never came completely right.

Chirac had a series of measures ready and intended to show how the new government would be tough on crime unlike, it claimed, the outgoing Socialists. Much of Chirac's speech introducing his programme had been devoted to the 'effective struggle against crime, delinquency, drug traffic and terrorism'. This policy was devolved to Pasqua, to 'Bob' Pandraud as Delegate Minister for Security and Albin Chalandon as Justice Minister. Pasqua and Panraud were almost self-selecting, so tied up were they with the RPR and Chirac's career and the issues of policing, and so indentified were they with the established 'hard-line' populism. Albin Chalandon was a different matter.

It was Albin Chalandon who presented the first 'law and order' measures to the Assembly as a start to the 'conservative revolution'. These were intended to reintroduce the tough 'Peyrefitte laws' which had been scrapped in 1981 and to tighten nationality laws, both changed, so it was alleged, in a Socialist ideological spasm (Hargreaves 1995, p. 171). Thus the laws reintroduced the police's right to demand proof of identity without cause; mandatory prison sentences; established an anti-terrorist bureau and anti-terrorist courts (with judges replacing juries); and an assortment of measures to crack down on delinquency and petty crime. Although many in the majority thought these too lax, in September, when Chalandon announced that drug users who refused cure for the habit would go to jail and that 1,600 prison places were to made available for that purpose, there was uproar. Government ministers broke ranks to dissociate themselves from the proposals (*Le Monde* 4/10/86). Socialists, for their part, concentrated on the police 'stop' powers which were resented by minorities as discriminatory and arbitrary.

Minister Chalandon faced a fast-rising prison population (a natural result of the sentencing policy) and decided to promote private prisons. At the time the scheme was seen as dogmatic and irrational. It was progressively watered down, although the prison building programme went ahead. Opinion was also inflamed by the new nationality laws which changed the automatic right of people born on French territory to claim French nationality ('droit du sol'). Chalandon's proposals caught the 1986 demonstrations on the upswing and gave them further impetus. These measures intensified the impression of an ideologically blinkered government and enabled the President to intervene as a moderating force. The Front national, whose thunder the measures had been intended to steal, now had a golden opportunity to criticise the conservatives' unwillingness to put through the 'necessary' laws. After the 'events' of 1986, the problem of nationality was remitted to a Nationality Commission.

It was not long before the 'tough on crime' policy caused problems for the Interior Ministry. Charles Pasqua, with his graphic lack of nuance, but keen to show that he was no pushover declared that he would be a 'supporter of the forces of order'. This, in a country where police over reaction was not unknown, was taken by some to be a carte blanche. In August there was a tragedy when police killed two young people they assumed to be joy riders and a vigorous criticism began of 'shoot first and ask later'. Damaging criticism came from the supporters of Raymond Barre who consistently dissented from the government's policing policy. Interior Minister Charles Pasqua responded by having a group of illegal immigrants from Mali deported on a government chartered flight (Friend 1998, p. 108).

New Caledonia, in the Pacific Ocean, was also defined by the new government as a law and order problem. Serious conflict had started in 1984 between the European and indigenous 'Kanak' populations and had been the subject of the Pisani plan. For Pisani, the problem was to reduce tension on the island and to give the Kanaks a better stake in a community in which they were – in economic terms – marginal. A presidential emissary, Edgard Pisani, had offered a route which might lead to independence and which did lead to a redistricting to the benefit of the Kanaks. This plan had angered the European settlers. By contrast Bernard Pons, Chirac's Minister for Overseas, wanted no concessions in Cabinet. In May, the President had warned of the need for consensus in New

Caledonia. By August Pisani's settlement had been retracted and in November 1986 rioting had started. Despite criticism by Barre's supporters, a referendum was then organised on independence which would (since the majority was European) endorse the status quo and this enraged the Kanaks who saw it as a sweeping aside of their problems. In February 1988 Kanak militants, exasperated by the government's attitude, took some hostages. In between the two ballots of the presidential elections, on 5 May, paratroops were sent to free the hostages with a loss of twenty-one lives (Plenel and Rolant 1984). Although the operation had been intended to help win the election for the Prime Minister it did not have that effect and Mitterrand, who had formally endorsed the operation, escaped the opprobrium for it.

The Economy

On the economic front, Edouard Balladur was the 'Prime Minister' to Chirac's 'President'. He was the architect of the RPR's economic strategy and had been close to Jacques Chirac since the early 1980s. It was Balladur who had provided the RPR's justification for 'cohabitation' (*Le Monde* 16/9/83). Their association continued in government; they, for example, passed mash notes to each other in Cabinet. But Balladur's strategy implied a seven-year presidential term not a two-year horizon. Secretary of State Balladur had all the authority needed to 'liberalise' the French economy, but the looming 1988 presidential poll required rapid and visible results not stolid progress building in the Socialist direction since 1983. Chirac's government concentrated on economic policy, as the Socialists had done in 1981, also mistakenly assuming that their predecessors' political dogma was the problem

Neither Balladur nor Chirac were partisans of the 'y qu'a' free market, though they sometimes affected to be, but much that went wrong here was a matter of presentation, and measures were made to seem more friendly to 'rentiers' and the rich than to ordinary people in, for example, the suppression of the wealth tax. There was a cautious aspect to Balladur's policy and certain notorious problems (like the social security deficit) were covered by classical methods of fudge; deep-rooted and fanciful reform was left for another time after the election. All the same, the expectation was that the government would tackle (or very clearly begin to tackle) the problems of sluggish growth and unemployment and that confidence would return. A new President would then be elected in 1988 on the back of the upward trend in the economy.

There were immediate reductions in expenditures, removal of price and wage and exchange controls, changes in working regulations and shifts in tax burdens. This last proved a public relations disaster because the conservative government appeared to capriciously favour the well off. Although some measures were close to what had been planned by the Socialists, the amnesty for tax evasion and the scrapping of the wealth tax enabled the Opposition to give the impression that a vindictive attack on ordinary people was underway at the behest of the powerful. If the scrapping of the wealth tax proved a barn door target for the Socialists, the devaluation of the Franc also came in for direct criticism. Cutting expenditure was not painless and was the first wedge between the spending ministries (like Culture, mainly centrist) and the (Gaullist) Treasury. Tax reforms went ahead, but their impact was dissipated.

Privatisations were then located at the frontier of left and right. Socialists had nationalised in 1981 and the conservatives intended to privatise in their turn. There were ninety-two banks, thirteen insurance companies and several large combines taken over in 1981 and on top of the banks and businesses nationalised at the Liberation. Privatisation was portrayed as a way of invigorating the economy and starting with Saint-Gobain, were pressed ahead fast (Colombani and Portelli 1995, p. 181). French opinion on both right and left was dubious about the new government's proposals. President Mitterrand caught those fears, expressed reserves about foreign control, defended de Gaulle's nationalisations and refused to sign the decrees. But there were privatisations of Paribas, CCF and Société Générale in 1987 for which there was a big share uptake. However the privatisation of the Suez conglomerate was underway in October 1987 just as the collapse of the markets wiped billions off share values. Many small investors, lured in to create a new and popular share-holding class, got their fingers burnt. Subsequent privatisations were viewed more sceptically and the government was accused of creating a 'hard core' of shareholders who were beholden to the RPR.

Privatisation was highly contentious and nowhere more so than the selling of the public television channel TF1. This project fell to the young and rising Parti républicain Minister of Culture François Léotard. He was, however, inexperienced and was caught between the 'whole hog' privatisers who exerted pressure through Matignon and more cautious deregulators like himself. Contrary to the Minister's wishes, the RPR pressed for a new High Authority to regulate broadcasting to be created and then nominated government supporters to it (undermining its purpose to keep government out). After one of the most turbulent passages of the parliamentary year the new High Authority (CNCL) was in place by

September. It started by ousting the station heads and replacing them with conservatives (mainly RPR). It then gave the franchise of Channel 5 to the pro-government Hersant newspaper group and Channel 6 was passed to the Lyonnaise des Eaux run by a leading neo-Gaullist. Fifty per cent of TF1 was sold to the Bouygues construction company. It was unedifying spoils process from which the Minister had been excluded and played out in front of a public less tolerant of 'state television' and expecting more diversity and impartiality. This the President was able to point out, and the government came in for severe criticism.

When Pasqua started what Léotard called a 'daft anti-pornography campaign' he turned on the Prime Minister accusing him of being in hock to the old reactionaries in the RPR. What was left of the 'special relationship' between the Prime Minister and 'Léo's band' was dissolved and they declined to hitch their wagon to his. Léotard's imprecations led to an ultimatum: keep quiet or quit. Léotard was sufficiently sure of his position, or exasperated enough not to care, to ripost that he would speak out and stay and demanded a communiqué from the Matignon giving him a free hand. Thus, only a year into 'cohabitation', Chirac's spiders' strategy of spooling the centre in had failed and the Republican Party (although remaining unenthusiastic about Barre) would not mobilise behind Chirac for 1988.

Unemployment, as in 1981, was the King Charles' Head for the government. As early as April 1986 the Minister of Employment Philippe Séguin, tabled measures to be passed speedily by decree and business was given a series of incentives to take on young people while the market was to be 'freed up' by reducing bureaucracy. This last was counter-intuitive. Most people assumed that requiring authorisation for lay-offs kept people in jobs they would otherwise have lost. Decrees to dispense with the state's say-so were the occasion for a parliamentary battle which drew attention to the perverse view that it was necessary to make it easier to create redundancies to save jobs. It was resolved only by the use of the Article 49-3 vote in June 1986 – after the damage had been done.

High Politics

Despite some farcical interludes, government and President were able to speak (as the cliché had it) through two mouths but with one voice. Yet the one place where the Prime Minister could forge a 'statesmanlike' profile was in the 'Presidential sector' of foreign affairs. Jacques Chirac had no intention of allowing the 'presidential domain' to remain unchallenged and sought to move onto it (*Le Monde* 26/4/86). An ardently desired presidential dimension could be gained by participation in high-level diplomacy and through a judicious choice of meetings with foreign Heads of State and Prime Ministers. Among Prime Minister Chirac's first acts was, therefore, a series of foreign visits and these punctuated the entire 'cohabitation' period (including visits to Washington and Moscow). Mitterrand had not abandoned domestic policy, but had lost control of the agenda in the eyes of public opinion although foreign policy remained for them presidential (Duverger 1996, pp. 558–9).

A radical change of direction in foreign policy was not envisaged and the careful placing of the Socialist policy on the Gaullist terrain had helped the President keep the initiative. However, the new Foreign Minister J.-B. Raimond, took his orders from the Prime Minister while using his diplomatic skills to avoid an open clash with the President (Raimond 1989, p. 222). There was a continuous dialogue with the Elysée and the Foreign Minister had weekly meetings with the President. In Matignon, the Prime Minister had set up a foreign policy unit headed by François Bujon de l'Estaing and conservative junior ministers covered all the key areas while African policy was run from the PM's office. Bit by bit the Elysée was cut out of the 'information loop' on which the exercise of real power depended and although Mitterrand had anticipated this there were times when the President was uninformed. Staff in the Matignon interpreted the President's 'need to know' restrictively and telegrams were routed through the Foreign Minister's Office the better to decide their onward transmission (or not) (Favier and Martin-Rolland 1991, pp. 541–2).

There were many examples of the Elysée being shut out and they included neglecting to pass on information on 'hot spots' in Chad, Iran, Iraq, Syria and Saudi Arabia. Foreign policy is not conducted in isolation from other ministries and that cooperation became difficult to obtain when the conservatives took charge. Significantly, information began to flow back to the Elysée in January 1987 and as the 1988 presidential elections approached, and Mitterrand looked the winner, information was almost completely restored.

Unsurprisingly, in view of what was at stake, one of the first 'cohabitation' discords had come in foreign affairs. Just as the new government was appointed the tension between the USA and Libya was reaching a climax. When the White House asked for US over-flying rights for a bombing raid on Libya both the President and Prime Minister refused the United States French airspace. However, on 23 April the Prime Minister maintained that it had been the Matignon's decision to refuse the American President's request. Elysée staff then used their contacts in the press to make it known that it was a 'presidential' decision.

More significant was the first G-7 meeting of the major industrial countries of the West and held in Tokyo on 4-6 May. This became a vigorous battle for precedence, but the struggle was an unequal one. Mitterrand had been involved in months of preparation and his attendance was expected by the Japanese as natural (for a Head of State). A long behind-the-scenes and embarrassing diplomatic wrangle could not alter Tokyo's understanding of diplomatic protocol and the President had first place. Jacques Chirac travelled separately to avoid being too obviously second rank. At the summit itself Chirac could only appear out of place although he had his revenge, explaining to the Japanese Prime Minister Mr Nakasone that he made foreign policy and not the President (it was leaked to the press). But Mitterrand easily held centre stage at Tokyo and reinforced the public perception of a unified foreign policy under the President.

It was unfortunate for the Prime Minister that the Tokyo summit came so early in 'cohabitation' but Matignon did not give up its search for pre-eminence and the incidents intended to display, or suggest, Chirac's determining role continued. Jacques Chirac would, on occasion, criticise the President and his policies and he would be rebuked. One of the most famous of these presidential put-downs came in March 1987 in Madrid after the Prime Minister had deplored the Socialist government's indulgence to Basque terrorism and (for good measure) the entry of Spain into the Community. Presidential disdain, displayed during a press conference with the Spanish Prime Minister, Gonzalez, ended the incident.

Next in line was the European 'cohabitation' battle played out within Franco-German relations. Unwilling to interfere in French internal politics, the German government wanted to appease both sides or – better still – get them to decide between themselves on who took precedence. However, the close relations with the Elysée remained intact. It was de Gaulle who had ensured that they would by making relations under the Franco-German Alliance treaty pass through the Presidency. Prime Minister Chirac could not negotiate a new treaty and was in no position to impose another outcome. Regular Franco-German meetings went ahead, as envisaged, in the presidential chateaux.

On European Community matters, where the protocol was more flexible, there was a similar 'Gaullist' legacy in the way of the Prime Minister. De Gaulle himself had set up a group, the Secrétariat général du comité interministériel pour les questions de coopération économique (SGCI), to ensure that European affairs did not escape presidential scrutiny. Just before the elections, Mitterrand nominated his Chargée de Mission for Europe, Elizabeth Guigou, to head it and that meant that the

Elysée was informed of European dossiers as well as of inter-ministerial disputes (Favier and Martin-Rolland 1991, p. 487). Jacques Chirac might want to wrestle the European dossier out of the President's hands, but he faced a position in which the technical details and the preparation of European policy were with the SGCI staff in 1986 and could not be summarily removed.

However, at the first European Council meeting dealing with economic, agricultural and social policy at the Hague on 26–27 June, two French delegations arrived at the table: one presidential and one prime-ministerial – the Foreign Minister had to wait in an ante-room. Jacques Chirac had been 'converted' from his anti-Europeanism of 1979 and piloted the European 'Single Act' through the conservative Assembly, but the President was able to play on divisions over Europe in the majority coalition. This did lead to larger differences as the President expressed more Europhile positions and these were 'corrected' by Matignon, replied to by the Elysée and so on. Before the end of the first year, however, it was the Prime Minister who was negotiating on technical detail while the President intervened only to support French positions (Pfister 1985, p. 250).

In general the struggle for the control of foreign affairs was a trench war which never quite subsided. However, Matignon had a clear victory in nominations (*Le Monde* 19/3/86). Some forty-eight Ambassadors were moved around by the Prime Minister like chess pieces and the President mostly failed to keep people in post. Mitterrand avoided unwinnable battles, in nominations as elsewhere; in addition, he did not wish to appear to be preventing Chirac from applying his policy.

Middle East policy changed under the new 'cohabitation' government but it showed the difficulty of separating out the strands of foreign policy from other ministerial responsibilities. Relations between France and Iran had reached a low point in 1986. Chirac's government tried to switch tracks and to 'normalise' relations with Iran building up goodwill and following on with informal contacts (Péan 1987). It was the government's view the regime in Iran should not be treated as an errant to be whipped into line, but as a full member of the international community, and that Teheran would respond to such treatment. Had this been followed through then Chirac's government would have had to change allies in the Middle East, not least from its long-standing preference for Iraq. That they never did seemed to Iran to be evidence that they were not serious about a fundamental shift.

In May 1986 the Iranian Deputy Prime Minister came to Paris and indicated that the rift in relations could be healed if an outstanding debt were paid off and if France ceased to harbour Iranian dissidents. Seven French hostages were being held by a pro-Iranian group in the Lebanon and this was also raised. In June two hostages were released and this was seen as a thaw by the Prime Minister (according to Raimond 1989) and the government proceeded on that assumption. Iranian dissidents were expelled and debt negotiations were started at the same time as secret contacts were kept up. None of this new policy was to the liking of the President who criticised it obliquely whiled his party attacked it quite bluntly (*Le Point* 10/10/86).

One of the government's objects was to bring the hostages home safely. The recent precedent of President Carter's inability to resolve a hostage crisis (which cost him the election) was still vivid. However, there was also the public perception of how terrorists should be dealt with. Should a firm line be maintained or should deals be made? This was the dilemma which the Socialists highlighted and the President played on, insinuating that 'something' had been surrendered. In January 1987 the left-wing daily *Le Matin* caused a storm by asserting that the conservative right had undermined the Socialist negotiations with Teheran for the release of hostages by suggesting that a better deal would be available after the 1986 election (*Le Matin* 17/1/87). This allegation was always hotly denied, but it had its effect.

In fact the bombing campaign in Paris in September 1986, which left ten dead and 161 injured, consolidated the 'cohabitation' and brought the nation together. An unknown organisation, which demanded the freeing of three prisoners, claimed responsibility and the Ministry of the Interior took on the task of negotiating with the myriad of small groups in the Middle East – not all of them were close to Iran. The President and even the Foreign Minister (to his intense irritation) were kept out of the matter. Pasqua's Interior Ministry had lighted on Wahid Gordji, a translator at the Iranian Embassy, as one of those implicated in the terrorist network and police were ordered to surround the Paris Embassy in an attempt to force Gordji before the courts (Favier and Martin-Rolland 1991, Vol. II, p. 587ff.). In Teheran the French Embassy came under siege. Once again the government had been over hasty. On 2 July it transpired that there was no effective evidence against Gordji and the Foreign Minister considered resigning (J.-B. Raimond 1989).

On 17 July, France broke off diplomatic relations with Iran. Negotiations then took place for the release of hostages and the ending of the siege of the Embassy. Two more hostages were released in November 1987 and Gordji was hustled out of France after a compliant judiciary agreed that there was no reason to detain him (*Independent* 17/12/87).

Three hostages remained and Teheran continued to play cat and mouse with the French negotiators. Wahid Gordji's case and the July 1987 crisis became a point of acrid dispute in the campaign TV debate in 1988. (It turned on who knew what and when.) On Wednesday, 4 May 1988 (before the second ballot on the 8th) the three remaining hostages were released and were met by the Prime Minister on their arrival in France on 5 May. There was no perceptible effect on the voters.

In defence, where the public was long habituated to presidential dominance, the main conflict came over the modernisation of the French nuclear force. Mitterrand set out a Gaullist doctrine at the Institut des Hautes Études de la Défence Nationale on 12 September 1986 and later filled it out: it was one of deterrence, of massive and not graduated response. Jacques Chirac, who was under attack from the supporters of Raymond Barre and Atlanticists within his own coalition, generally chose to align himself with the Elysée against his more pugnacious allies (like Giraud) (*Le Monde* 17/2/87).This deprived him of a margin for manoeuvre. For the President the priority was the upgrading of the nuclear submarines; for the Minister of Defence it was the creation of a more powerful but more mobile force of land missiles. On 25 June 1986, the Defence Minister announced, against presidential advice, the scrapping of plans for new submarine-based missiles. This, it was decided, would free funds for a system of SX mobile land missiles and was supported by the Prime Minister. President Mitterrand threatened a public dispute.

Faced with the possibility of a crisis over defence, to the benefit of Mr Barre, the Prime Minister backed down and prevailed on the Defence Minister to do likewise (*Le Monde* 7/11/86). André Giraud accepted the priority but retained the option for a mobile SX system until this too was dropped by the Prime Minister. Although somewhat perturbed, André Giraud went on to embrace the heretical doctrine (to Gaullists) of 'graduated response' (*Le Figaro* 15/10/87). But Giraud, on this arcane matter, was not supported by the prevailing Gaullo-Socialist consensus (*Le Monde* 19/3/87). Mitterrand increased pressure on the Prime Minister by asserting the traditional Gaullist doctrine of 'dissuasion' (in the autumn of 1987). Again the Defence Minister, abandoned by the government, backed down.

A second front was opened by the President who raised the problem of disarmament at the meeting of the Defence Committee, over which he presided, in mid-1987. Soviet-American arms reduction talks and a flow of unsettling proposals from Soviet President Gorbachev, produced the so-called 'zero option'. Under this all United States' missiles would be removed from Western Europe. It was a perspective which, from the government's perspective raised the spectre of American isolationism – but not the President's (Raimond 1989, pp. 173–4). This disagreement became open towards the end of 1986, when the Prime Minister addressed the WEU on the problems of 'decoupling' the USA from West Europe and proposed a security treaty for Europe (*Valeurs Actuelles* 17/11/86 and F.-O. Giesbert 1987, p. 293). Mitterrand's response was to raise the stakes by officially welcoming the 'zero option' and the Prime Minister swung behind the President to avoid further conflict. When the second 'zero option' was proposed by Gorbachev in April 1987 the battle was over and presidential predominance in strategy was conceded (except by Giraud). When the disagreement resurfaced in February 1988 the Prime Minister again avoided a confrontation.

'Cohabitation' in Political Perspective

The 'cohabitation' of 1986–8 was an 'Aronian' Cold War: peace impossible, war improbable. There were skirmishes over secondary objectives and over keeping or losing face but a potentially bruising clash was avoided, for it would have offended public opinion; in place of direct confrontation there was a continual probing for weaknesses (*Le Monde* 13/2/73). It became in practice an attempt to throw the opprobrium for mistakes onto the adversary and to appropriate the credit for success. Thus the debilitating in-fighting at the top of the state and the open disagreement and public criticism was relatively rare (though more than in 'normal' times). It was very much a war of smoke and mirrors.

Foreign policy is a good example of this effect. As the first year wore on the Prime Minister became increasingly sure in the decision making in the presidential reserved domain 'fully exercising the prime ministerial role' (*Le Monde* 12/7/86). It was the first time under the Fifth Republic that Matignon had had the means to run foreign policy, a diplomatic and military unit and its own junior ministers. Preparation, planning and execution was conducted through defence meetings (*Le Monde* 13/7/86). This did not alter the case that this was a sideshow in a battle which was being fought elsewhere. Already, in the first three months of 'cohabitation' Mitterrand had led the French delegations at Tokyo and the Hague, emphasising the pre-eminent role of the President in nuclear deterrence (*Le Monde* 17/3/86). Repeated presidential assertions of his decision-making power in foreign policy were sometimes uncontradicted by the Prime Minister and served to fix the notion of the 'reserved domain' (*Le Monde* 18/11/86).

The 1988 Elections

This background explains why the 'cohabitation' struggle of 1986–8 was an unequal one from the start. In 1986 François Mitterrand was a popular President, while Chirac led a small disunited majority. If he could retain that pole position and avoid egregious blunders the battle would be won. A rushed and easily panicked government provided further justification for Macmillan's adage that the Prime Minister's worst enemy is 'events'. President Mitterrand went on a carefully choreographed series of visits to foreign states and used diplomatic 'crises' to presidential advantage. And, if it was not inevitable, the retention of a presidential aura was possible with reduced powers. This limited objective of remaining 'presidential' was accomplished with a firm resolution which never lost sight of the target audience. Where it was varied – when Mitterrand attacked the government – it was to remobilise his own supporters in the presidential coalition. This strategy was assisted by the Parti socialiste, poised for a victory in the next general elections (party support was missing in the 'cohabitations' of 1993 and in 1997).

Despite the elaborate use of pre-cabinet meetings ('conseils du cabinet') to ensure Cabinet solidarity and other measures to keep together the Prime Minister's majority, the President was able to play on divisions in conservative ranks (*Le Monde* 12/5/86). Most important of these divisions was the cleavage between the supporters of Raymond Barre and Chirac's own neo-Gaullist party, but there were many other difficulties including the resentment of the RPR's domination, the small parties' sensibilities and personality clashes. Although the Prime Minister managed the conservatives' own 'cohabitation' relatively well, by the end of the first year mistakes were worsened by an internal feuding which led to Chirac's loss of authority.

As a result of the same internal coalition rivalry, Jacques Chirac's main problem was that he had, in Mr Barre, a more popular rival by 18 per cent in February 1987 (SOFRES 1988, p. 117). He could not risk a showdown with the President which would vindicate his rival's prediction about 'cohabitation' and would start a presidential campaign in which he was behind. Thus the Prime Minister had committed himself to making 'cohabitation' work and backed down on important challenges. This pattern, too, was established early on in the 'cohabitation' with the President's refusal on 14 July to sign decrees. This could have been challenged but was accepted: thereafter the Prime Minister was in a losing frame, having disarmed his only 'deterrent'.

Mitterrand's entry into the ring was delayed till the last moment making use of his position as President above the arena and maintaining suspense. It also meant that he did not have to campaign at length. His platform, published in the newspapers on 7 April, took the form of a billowy 'Lettre à tous les français' which set the consensus tone of a campaign intended to be all-embracing. For Mitterrand, however, there was no competition to speak of on the left and the main battle was between Chirac and Barre. In this Chirac proved the superior campaigner and had superior organisation and legitimacy as Prime Minister. He moved into the lead after his declaration of candidacy in February 1988 but lagged behind the President in the polls despite a lead (on paper) for a right which he was unable to gather under his name (SOFRES 1989, p. 96). It was not, given the constraints, a lively campaign but one which de-emphasised political differences, eschewed excess and fought for the middle ground. Only Le Pen stood out against centripetal forces.

On the first ballot the President headed the list with 34.1 per cent followed by the Prime Minister with 19.9 per cent and then Raymond Barre with 16.5 per cent. The Front National's Le Pen took a surprising 14.4 per cent while the Communist Party's decline was confirmed by its candidate Lajoinie's 6.8 per cent. Barre stood down for Chirac but Le Pen did not call for a vote for the conservative candidate. There was an easy victory for the President over his Prime Minister on the second ballot: 54 per cent to 46 per cent. Mitterrand re-elected dissolved the Assembly but a conservative France had elected a Socialist President and was not to repeat the landslide of 1981. Mitterrand's tactic for the general elections was not forceful nor did he follow up what seemed to be the promise of a centre 'opening' to the parties of the UDF, and the conservatives under Giscard reacted by organising themselves and limited the scale of defeat. After a short campaign, and a record low turnout, the voters returned a new Assembly in which the Socialists held only a relative majority: 277 seats to the conservatives' 270 (*Le Monde* 7/6/88). Although the FN had only one seat, the twenty-seven Communist Party deputies held the balance in the new Assembly.

Conclusion

Mitterrand's 'victory' in the 'cohabitation' of 1986–8 was based on a perception of the Presidency which had been established by de Gaulle and followed up by Pompidou, Giscard and Mitterrand himself. It was a curious 'looking-glass war' in which the symbolism of the institution was more important than substance, but in politics symbols confer their own power. Mitterrand's coalition was maintained by moving to the centre and that suited a defence of the Presidency itself as a consensus and 'arbitrating' institution representing the middle consensus ground. This had been made possible by an adroit exploitation of political advantages and a skilful out-manoeuvring of the Prime Minister.

Thus the defence of the Presidency in 1986, as with the building of the Gaullist Presidency, was a political process which took advantage of the circumstances of 'cohabitation'. These were a conservative government which had to make 'cohabitation' work and a division in the conservative camp to the disadvantage of the Prime Minister who also had to face a challenge from the extreme right. It was, however, a personal victory for a moderate and moderating President which was not easily transformed into a victory for the President's party in the general elections.

-10-

Fin de Règne

With Mitterrand's re-election in 1988, the Fifth Republic Presidency entered a difficult phase. His re-election was rightly celebrated as an achievement for the leader of a modern state, but it posed difficulties not the least of which was that a third term was not a possibility. This period is well known in the United States as the 'lame duck presidency' after re-election in which the President's authority dwindles and can pass, in some cases, to the likely successor. De Gaulle had faced this problem after 1965 and particularly 1968 when Pompidou emerged as the 'dauphin', but Mitterrand had no clear successor. In President Mitterrand's case there was no May '68 crisis and the Presidency continued in apparent stability despite the undertow of weakening authority. In the seven years which followed Mitterrand struggled to retain a failing authority and mistakes which would have been surmounted in the first septennate, cost the Presidency dear.

As the presidential election approached, PS First Secretary Lionel Jospin made it clear that he would not continue in that post into the second septennate. It was a decision which revealed the slippage of presidential power. Jospin's move left open the key position in the Party, important because control of the Party indicated who would control the nomination for the next presidential election. Mitterrand wanted the post to go to Laurent Fabius who was widely seen as the 'dauphin', a choice that united all the other 'présidentiables' in the Parti socialiste and particularly displeased Jospin who had been his rival within the Mitterrand faction since 1986. On 16 May, a week before the general elections, the Party refused to accept Fabius and instead chose a compromise candidate – the reassuring former Prime Minister Pierre Mauroy. Mauroy was in place thanks only to the backing of an unstable and negative anti-Fabius coalition. The Mitterrand supporters were left enduringly split into 'Fabiusians' and 'Jospinians'. Fabius did not accept the rebuff, the 'Jospinians' did not forget the threat, and the factionalism intensified over the next five years.

Mitterrand had, after 1983, moved onto the centre ground. This had enabled him to win the presidential elections and he needed a general election to confirm his authority by returning a supportive Assembly. Yet Mitterrand's 1988 second ballot poll of 54 per cent, higher and a more 'national' vote than any President since de Gaulle, had been a highly personal one, going beyond the support the left normally received and to some extent confirming the slogan 'la France unie'. A Prime Minister who could help in the victory and who could capitalise on the presidential result was needed. It was in this way that Mitterrand turned to Michel Rocard, his long-time rival and nominated him to the Matignon before dissolving the Assembly. He also had supported the 1988 Mitterrand campaign and in addition he had developed the credentials of a 'centrist'. He was also better qualified than any Socialist (other than Jacques Delors) to build bridges to the UDF. Rocard was the second ranking politician on the left after the President himself and looked to be the next in line.

Ending the 'Rocard Mortgage'

From Mitterrand's point of view the nomination of Rocard might well remove a rival; in the normal course of things (following the 'Parodi curve' of popularity) the Prime Minister would pose no challenge and would be 'worn out' after one or two years, particularly since Mitterrand anticipated a recession. Rocard could then be thanked for his services and replaced with a more amenable nominee (Schneider 1992). Rocard, for his part, had no illusions about the nature of the task. Rocard's entry as Prime Minister seemed proof of the new direction (Favier and Martin-Rolland 1996, Vol. III, p. 15) Yet, although there were some individual centrists who moved to the Socialist side to join the government (24 of 48 Ministers were non-Socialists), the centrist parties in the UDF remained unseduced by the prospect of a place in the Mitterrand system (and Mitterrand did not try that hard to woo them) (Attali 1995, Vol. III, p. 13). They remained in the Opposition. Lack of centre support became potentially dangerous when the June general elections returned an Assembly lacking 14 needed for an overall socialist majority. Rocard, and his associate Guy Carcassonne, would have to navigate between the centrist and Communist sensibilities and they proved adept at finding majorities and avoiding votes of censure in the Assembly. The Communist Party was both falling apart and in no mood to be cooperative (Courtois and Lazar 1995, p. 406).

Hence Mitterrand's second septennate started on a centre-leaning note with Rocard as Prime Minister. But it also continued a 'cohabitation' tactic in which the President distanced himself from the government, playing the role of a 'quasi opposition' handing out plaudits and blame and intervening where it was politically opportune, for Mitterrand had no tenderness for Rocard (Attali 1995, Vol. III, p. 175). It was an opportunity which Rocard was initially able to exploit because he took the responsibility. In 1988, the most fraught situation was in New Caledonia and it became a practical exercise in 'Rocardian' politics (Colombani and Portelli 1995, pp. 81–2). Because of the events in New Caledonia and the armed intervention on 5 May, the two sides had moved to extremes and the Prime Minister's problem was to bring them together durably (*Le Monde* 28/6/88). Exhaustive negotiation was the means to a compromise on 20 August assisted by a small number of highly regarded people and promoted by the Prime Minister. It was a compromise backed by the President, but it was the Prime Minister's work.

In New Caledonia as in other issues, Rocard did not so much go counter to the President's will as provide a concrete shape to the vague aspirations which had been provided in the 'Lettre à tous les français' written for the 1988 presidential campaign. From this Rocard drew the principle lines of action: to maintain balanced public finances, modernise the economy, promote equal opportunities and make education a priority (Favier and Martin-Rolland 1990, p. 93). But the novelty was in the method of working to find a consensus which would base reforms in society and make their undoing the more difficult later; Rocard sought to prepare fundamental change without drama.

In this way Rocard gave substance to two proposals. The first was the guaranteed minimum income for the young, long-term unemployed (revenue minimum d'insertion – RMI) (*Le Monde* 16/7/88). The second was to introduce a direct new tax (the cotisation sociale généralisée – CSG), a low flat-rate tax paid by everyone on all sources of income and which enabled the reform of social security finance. These were considerable achievements for a government without a secure majority; there were enough opponents of these schemes in the PS to have torpedoed them, but Mitterrand was not yet ready to dispense with Rocard. Rocard brought credit to the premiership: as the reforms went ahead they largely increased his and the President's popularity.

During 1988 there was a degree of 'voter fatigue' as the public were called to the polls on six occasions but the Socialist Party held its ground well. After a year of government, the Parti Socialiste performed well at the 1989 local elections (where abstention was lower) and won an additional thirty city halls (*Le Monde* 14/3/89). However, Rocard's government was not unchallenged. The conservative right also remained a force and there was a rise in the vote for marginal lists at the local elections. There were strikes, some of them nurses, and they hit Socialist Party sensibilities (*Le Monde* 18/10/88). The 'unofficial' strikes, with no effective union to negotiate with, but supported by socialist and extreme left activists in many cases were indirectly supported by Mitterrand himself (in December 1988) (*Le Monde* 20/10/88). In the autumn of 1990 the plans for education reforms, developed by the new Minister of Education, Lionel Jospin, provoked demonstrations as did the proposals to reform social security tax.

The 'Reserved Domain'

If the government was handed the responsibility for domestic politics in the main part, the so-called 'presidential sector' of foreign affairs remained under the Elysée's control. After a year, and helped a great deal by the Bicentenary of the Great Revolution, this presidential domination was summed up by the journal *Le Point* as 'Mitterrand at the steering wheel' (Northcutt 1992, p. 306). Mitterrand marked his authority over the Prime Minister with a series of initiatives in the 'reserved domain' of diplomacy. This possibility came almost immediately with the June European summit where the President decided to launch the idea of rebalancing the Single Act with a Community social dimension. Workers were insufficiently regarded in the integration process, it was argued, and a degree of protection from the depredations of the market was overdue. He also undertook a publicised visit to the United States and there followed visits by the Soviet Foreign Minister to Paris as well as other prestigious and well-known diplomatic envoys.

A Franco-German summit in Bonn in November developed plans for strengthening the relations between them. Franco-German relations were becoming more intense as a result of rapidly unfolding events in Eastern Europe in which the Eastern bloc countries one-by-one overthrew their Communist regimes. As that happened consideration of the German commitment to the security of the continent and the French position in it became urgent. Once again the President found himself at odds with the Gaullist assumptions of French foreign policy, which could no longer apply in a deteriorating situation. With the Soviet leader Gorbachev apparently trying to remove the United States from European politics, the French President found himself indirectly supporting the continuation of Nato. When, soon after the Wall came down in November 1989, the reunification of Germany became inevitable despite temporary French and continuing British opposition it seemed more than ever imperative to tie the united country to the West. A united Germany should not be neutral. A reinforced Nato would, as the President saw it, counter the temptation offered by Gorbachev to create a neutral Europe 'decoupled' from the USA.

German reunification was much more rapid than anybody had foreseen but the attitude of the rest of Europe would be determinant and the modalities and the implications were not worked out. Mitterrand's own view, like the rest of France, was one of disquiet (Védrine 1996, p. 445). Mitterrand made demands for the guarantee of the Oder-Neisse frontier but was, like others, discountenanced by the new world (Ibid., p. 433 and Colombani and Portelli 1995, p. 106). Events in Germany were part of the collapse of Soviet power that year which saw the nations of the East cast off the Communist system. Mitterrand envisaged the division of Germany continuing with Russia as a counterbalance in the East, an old idea dating back to the Third Republic (Attali 1995, Vol. III, p. 501). Gorbachev's USSR, we now know, was in a pitiful state, in no measure able to play that balance of power role and in fact looked to Germany for assistance (Favier and Rolland 1996, pp. 195–9). Nobody, not the Russians (as the President discovered in a face-to-face meeting in Kiev on 6 December) nor the United States, was going to stop the reunification of Germany which had been official Nato policy for a long time – though nobody expected it to happen in the near future (Giesbert 1993, p.106). Mitterrand accepted reunification, more rapidly than some, but taking the GDR to be a force likely to continue for some years, visited Eastern Germany after the Wall came down on 20 December 1989. This untimely visit to the fossil Communist system was not appreciated in the FRG, but the President was able to bounce back from the miscalculation. Mitterrand's pressure on Chancellor Kohl to recognise the Oder-Neisse line between Poland and Germany (which meant renouncing a quarter of the territory of the old Reich) was determinant. Other Western leaders were no more prescient about the collapse of the Soviet system than was the President of France, but with Mitterrand there was a strange failure to bring public opinion along with developments, as if unable to accommodate the new system.

It is more than likely that the first French reaction to the coup against Gorbachev on 19 August 1991 was governed by considerations of this sort. France's reaction to the army coup by hardliners was a very muted disapproval. A strong Soviet Union would, as before, exert pressure on Germany and the President, unlike other Western leaders, initially took the coup as successful and expected to have to live with the new leaders. On the evening of 21 August, the putschists were dismissed as 'unreal' by the President, but an impression of ambivalence lingered (*Le Monde* 23/8/91). However, the putsch only hastened the disintegration of the USSR and the rise of Boris Yeltsin. Despite the rebalancing of Europe, the French President had some leeway in European policy. As a counterpart to the reunification of Germany and the decline of the USSR, the President used the integration of Europe to assure France's position. This meant the continuation of integration through 'deepening' and the creation of a single currency as well as the enlargement of the Union, in other words leading to the Maastricht Treaty negotiations of 1991. This was a Franco-German accomplishment against the recalcitrants and worked mainly through the understanding between Kohl and Mitterrand (who personally committed themselves to it) (Védrine 1996, p. 476).

The Balkanisation of Yugoslavia

Even as France and Germany agreed on further integration, they disagreed on the situation in Yugoslavia (which had begun to fissure badly after the election of Franjo Tudjman as President of Croatia in April 1990). By 1990 Yugoslavia was entering a further phase of disintegration. France had pro-Serbian sympathies dating back to the First World War which continued in the Second (shared by Mitterrand himself) while Germany had Croatian links (Ibid. 1996, p. 615). On 17 May 1991, the internal settlement in Yugoslavia finally came apart and the federation disintegrated. In May 1991 Croatia declared its independence and that in turn led to a Serbian offensive. Croatia was recognised by Germany at the end of 1991. Yugoslavian Federal forces under Serbian control then started warring with Croatia, Bosnia and Slovenia to prevent secession. Mitterrand and the other Europeans somewhat reluctantly recognised Croatia and Slovenia (Ibid., p. 620).

Despite their own splits, the European view (where it struggled to emerge through the new European Political Cooperation mechanism) was of hope for an internal settlement which would guarantee the rights of minorities and a desire not to be caught between opposing forces (or worse, to become embroiled in a guerrilla war). There were a differences between Kohl and Mitterrand, which the French President did try to bridge and ideas were floated for a peace keeping force before the UN's intervention. But Mitterrand's studied neutrality and the refusal to lift the arms embargo on Bosnia were criticised by the intellectual left as an encouragement for Serbia. Serbian action moved public opinion against the old ally over 1991-2. In 1992 French troops formed the biggest component of the peacekeeping force in former Yugoslavia.

At the end of June 1992 President Mitterrand undertook, with some physical courage, a gruelling visit to the besieged Serbian capital. It was undertaken as a 'coup de théatre' while the European Heads met in Lisbon and without their knowledge (a slap to a common policy). This, at a time when the Bosnian crisis was acute, enabled an increased humanitarian effort and was a change in the President's appreciation of the situation in the former Yugoslavia. But the main effort went through the United Nations. Shortly before the Balladur government took over in 1993 the Vance-Owen peace plan was proposed, only to be rejected. France was accused of standing by while the 'ethnic cleansing' took place and the Presidency suffered from its powerlessness in confronting a civil war. In this the President was handicapped by the Gaullist legacy of presidential power in foreign policy: the assumption encouraged by successive Presidents that France could impose its will. On the left the 'gauche morale' was pleading for 'humanitarian' action to prevent continuing slaughter and criticised the President for lack of resolution (*Le Nouvel Observateur* 18/5/95). In 1993, the election of Balladur brought a new policy and then the victory of Jacques Chirac in 1995 was followed by a reappraisal of Belgrade policy.

'Dauphins'

Problems for Rocard in 1988–92 also came from the Elysée. Mitterrand encouraged Fabius (serving as Speaker of the Assembly as a consolation prize) to lead the PS European slate for the 1989 Parliamentary elections to counterbalance the Prime Minister (these proved a setback for the PS and a confirmation of the fragmentation of the system) (*Le Monde* 20/6/89). There were also the affairs implicating Mitterrand's Elysée entourage and the Socialist Party finances were becoming rather gamey. In April 1989 documents were sequestered from the PS headquarters by the judicial authorities and the revelations grew (Favier and Martin-Rolland 1996, Vol. III, p. 307). Affairs had burgeoned in the first septennate but became almost quotidian in the second (Colombani and Portelli 1995, p. 11). The abuse of power and funding scandals were not new in the Presidency, nor was the placing of 'pals'. Cronyism has long been a feature of Republican politics; Gaullists took an interest in jobs and pay-offs which would have done credit to any ward heeler (see Foccart 1999), but de Gaulle had maintained an unstained reputation (Jeanneney 1981).

Mitterrand, on the other hand, had to live down a reputation as 'devious' and had, as well, made a great deal of the Gaullist abuse of power as an Opposition leader. There was his criticism of corruption and of the *Coup d'état permanent,* his view of the Gaullist Presidency. Yet his own tenure of the Elysée was revealed to be every bit as regal – and as paranoid – as the General's and 'his' police as careless of rights as previous administrations. When it came to the 'argent facile', as Mitterrand had put it, Socialists were no better than their opponents were (Gaetner 1992). French political competition had engendered an 'arms race' of electoral spending in which all sides used what resources they could find. Mitterrand was not one to be beaten at this game and a Socialist system had been developed after his takeover in 1971 to organise the collection of money not only for party purposes, but also to finance the factions in the divided Party. It was the unremitting revelation of scandals to set against the declarations of 'clean handedness' which began to tarnish the President and to sap his authority.

Part of the system of placement and money was caused by factional competition and the factional battle spun out of control even as the President sought to impose his authority on it (and keep it out of Rocard's hands). He only provoked resentments. This factionalism tore the Party apart at the Rennes Congress of 1990, in a merciless confrontation between the partisans of Fabius and those of Jospin with the 'Rocardians' and others (Favier and Martin-Rolland 1996, Vol. III, p. 339). Fabius was not strong enough to take over the Party, but was able to prevent others establish effective control even if Jospin was persistent enough to keep together a coalition behind the outgoing First Secretary Pierre Mauroy (Dupin 1991, p. 258).

It was an unedifying spectacle, from which nobody emerged well, the Party's image was badly damaged and Fabius' rebuff was also the President's (Attali 1995, Vol. III, p. 438). Pierre Mauroy was re-elected First Secretary in the week after bruising Congress at which no resolution could be found despite the President's indirect but determined intervention. Presidential authority had been defied and the President had had his grip on the essential instrument of the party further loosened. Mitterrand was not a bystander in this factionalism: he had used it to divide his opponents and maintain his position at least to veto a successor and thus maintained control of the Party. From Mitterrand's perspective, so long as Rocard was kept out, a quarrel between the two 'Mitterrandists' did at least prevent either gaining the upper hand and a President in waiting emerging. Rocard, as Prime Minister, was discreet in the factional game but was also the object of suspicion from the Elysée which had blocked off his route to power in the Party.

The Gulf War

What changed the political situation temporarily was the Gulf War in 1991 and the diplomatic activity preceding it. On 2 August 1990, Iraq invaded Kuwait and the Western allies supported by the Soviet Union mounted a concerted operation to free the sheikdom from the invader. President Mitterrand immediately took centre stage making the main declarations and decisions – while Rocard was on vacation (Attali 1995, Vol. III, p.551). Under the Fifth Republic, France had developed a distinctive position in the Middle East and had attempted to make Iraq – now threatening stability and supplies – an ally and client (July 1997, p. 190). Mitterrand's choice in this instance was informed by the Gaullist concern for France's rank in the world and thus played a role of solid dependability. Although the alliance was led by the United States, French interests were at stake and the end of the Soviet bloc had meant that there was only one superpower in the world. France's place in the new post-Wall world was as a main part of the Western coalition – though not without marking out its own diplomatic positions by insisting on a United Nations operation (backed by its veto on the Security Council) maintaining pressure to negotiate if possible (Alia and Clerc 1991).

'Desert Storm' gave Mitterrand the high ground always conceded to the President in time of war and guaranteed Rocard's tenure as Prime Minister for as long as the hostilities continued. Presidential domination reasserted itself in the 'reserved domain': the war was run from the Elysée with an active foreign policy. In its outcome, the Gulf War revealed the importance of the United States in any operation of this nature and the inadequacy of the European institutions including WEU. Once again the Gaullist legacy was a problem. A conscript army was no substitute for professionals in this sort of operation. Conscription was, however, a Republican tradition and the Socialists had not hurried to end the system during Mitterrand's septennates. It was President Jacques Chirac who scrapped the conscript system and professionalised an army which had proved barely adequate for 'Desert Storm'.

There were disagreements as well within the presidential coalition as a result of the reorientation of the policy away from Gaullist bases. After the President committed French troops to the operation public opinion was not solidly in support of a war so there was a reason for caution on the domestic front (*Le Point* 7/1/91 and SOFRES 1990). In the government Defence Minister Jean-Pierre Chevènement's position was distinctly odd. A long-time holder of 'third worldist' positions, a proponent of a pro-

Iraq French Middle-Eastern policy, his views were no secret and he had been thrust to the margins of the Socialist Party; he also had Gaullist doubts about joining an American-led coalition. He resigned from the Ministry on 29 January 1991. Mitterrand kept him in the Cabinet despite his leaking to the press (it was probably better to have him in than out) and Chevènement's support was some indication of a French independence (*Le Monde* 17/5/91).

These were not enfeebling desertions. What the President lost on the left was made up on the centre and right and public opinion was unperturbed by either the Communist opposition or the resignation of Chevènement (Alia and Clerc 1991, p. 218). President Mitterrand used press conferences and a special session of the Assembly as well as a series of meetings with the principal politicians of the conservative right to engineer a consensus. A show of independence had been made by France, opposition leaders had been 'squared' and efforts to secure a negotiated peace had been visible. Thus public opinion was led cautiously into support for the war and the dissidents were isolated. In January 1992 the Assembly voted 523 to 43 for military action. National Front leaders, who opposed the war from pro-Iraqi positions, found themselves a self-proclaimed patriotic party, not supporting French troops' action. In the event the fighting was relatively brief and (for the allies) costless, and the public stayed confident in the President. As a result of a short and relatively bloodless victory, the dividend anticipated by the anti-war parties did not materialise and the President's poll ratings rose (Colombani and Portelli 1995, p. 248).

But war was an abnormal situation. As ever people rallied round the flag but the problem was to turn that into an enduring political support. Neither Prime Minister Thatcher nor President Bush found a way to do this and Mitterrand also missed an opportunity, partially because he used the occasion of the end of the war to sack a popular Prime Minister (Ibid., p. 257). In the normal pattern of Fifth Republic politics the Prime Minister was due, in any case, to be replaced with a more 'presidential' appointment, reflecting the President's own authority and ascendancy over the majority coalition. Elysée staff had encouraged attacks on the Prime Minister and Rocard had no illusions about his ability to stay at Matignon indefinitely. The summary 'sacking' of Rocard for no evident reason was inelegant and clumsy, though it had the effect of destabilising Rocard. There were, however, many possible prime ministers amongst the party's 'Mitterrandists' and they all had their attributes.

The Cresson Premiership

Mitterrand's coup d'éclat was to nominate Mme Edith Cresson, the first woman French Prime Minister. The new government was much more Mitterrand's and the 'Rocardians' and centrists were removed (*Le Monde* 19/5/91). Edith Cresson was not a conciliator and her abilities as a team manager were unknown, but she had been a supporter of Mitterrand when he was still outside the Socialist Party, heading the CIR (*Le Monde* 17/5/91). She had business training and had had a long ministerial experience (though of mixed success) starting as a combative Minister of Agriculture (1981–3), Trade Minister (1983–4) and Industry Minister, restructuring and relaunching the failing nationalised companies (1984–6). She had been Minister for Europe in Rocard's government but had resigned in protest at the government's insufficiently active industrial policy. Mrs Cresson had the fighting spirit and the left-wing credentials as well as a reputation for understanding business. Mrs Cresson's mission was to re-energise industry and prepare for the competition of the Single Market while giving priority to job creation and closing the gap between rich and poor (the 'social deficit'). Public opinion at first appreciated the surprise nomination: she started on 15 May 1991 with a very good poll rating (Colombani and Portelli 1995, p. 249).

Mme Cresson did not have the right approach or the backing to make an impact as Prime Minister; unlike Rocard, who wooed the centrists and encountered demoralised conservatives, the right was back in full cry by 1991. Not surprisingly, the new Prime Minister found the Rocardians hostile and Fabius' supporters dubious, while Bérégovoy at the Finance Ministry (who sought to become Premier) consolidated his own position at the expense of the Matignon. Socialist Party factions continued to square up and the main party figures in the government were subject neither to the Prime Minister's authority nor to that of a failing President. As was usual with Mitterrand, the Cabinet was composed of representatives of the party 'baronies' while Finance Minister Bérégovoy with no independent base in the Party was put in charge of a 'super-ministry' regrouping finance, trade and industry.

Mrs Cresson's position was not eased by a tendency to outspoken comment (Schemla 1993, p. 165ff.). In addition the 'social deficit' was slow in closing. In a month, social security contributions ('cotisation') were increased by 0.9 per cent and VAT was increased despite a declared disdain for regressive indirect taxes. Her lack of grip over policy and authority over the Cabinet led the Elysée to intervene more frequently and aligned the President with the Prime Minister. Opinion poll ratings quickly began to plummet and, the appointment being so markedly Mitterrand's, brought down the President's as well. In April the Socialist Party headquarters were again raided by the police who took away documents in an investigation which unearthed extensive corruption. The Party's popularity was no help to the Prime Minister for, reflecting the discredit the Socialists had fallen into, it also sank in the public's estimation. Before two months were up the government's popularity was negative and after a year it was the most unpopular in the Fifth Republic.

As the government continued to wrestle with unemployment and the problems of coalition management, the presidential system constructed by Mitterrand was hit by the revelations about an overzealous police unit run from the Elysée. In January, the PFLP leader George Habbach was secretly hospitalised in Paris. Habbach was held responsible for numerous terrorist incidents in France and it was unclear who had given the authorisation for this treatment (Health Minister Georgina Dufoix was dismissed) (*Le Monde* 6/2/92). Then Laurent Fabius and former Health ministers Hervé and Dufoix were accused of having allowed AIDS-contaminated blood to be used for haemophiliac transfusions in 1985 (*Le Monde* 25–26/10/92). There began to be a time-serving, fatigued appearance to the septennate.

At the end of 1991 First Secretary Mauroy of the PS tired of trying to keep the factions apart, escaping the foreseeable election disasters, and announced his forthcoming resignation despite a near unanimous rewriting of the Party's documents to bring its thinking into line with the post-marxist socialism then in practice. Laurent Fabius at last took over from Pierre Mauroy as PS First Secretary, a result of a deal with the Rocardians which gave him the Party in exchange for the promise of a presidential candidacy for Rocard. From the President's point of view this put Rocard in pole position for the next presidential elections and could not be considered a victory. In January 1992 the PS was raided again by the judicial authorities; the local and regional elections in March and April promised to be a rout for the left and the PS. Here again, the Prime Minister was left to carry the can for the predictably bad results.

In March, the PS polled only 18 per cent in the regional elections (on a high turnout) and kept the presidency of only one regional council (*Le Monde* 23/3/92). In April the cantonal elections confirmed the setback and the left lost control of six general councils. Mitterrand was accused of having failed to support his beleaguered Prime Minister (Schemla 1993, p. 306 ff.). Mrs Cresson's remit was large and ambitious and would have required very extensive powers on the best estimate (*Le Monde* 19/3/92).

Yet Mitterrand seems to have overestimated the residual authority of the Presidency in the second septennate, as he had no means of helping Mrs Cresson to overcome her own mistakes even though her failure brought him down as well. He was, by 1992, in no position to call subordinates into line or to restore order. Lionel Jospin, then Education Minister, criticised the Mitterrand method of factional jockeying and deals while complaining of a lack of direction from the top (Jospin 1991) Mitterrandism, although it was not much noticed at the time, was being rejected by its successor.

Bérégovoy's Year

Desperate times, desperate measures: Mrs Cresson was replaced on 2 April 1992 after the local elections. For the President there was only a restricted choice. Finance Minister Pierre Bérégovoy ('Béré') was at last appointed Prime Minister (*Le Monde* 19/3/93). Pierre Bérégovoy was the dominant figure in the Cresson government: his appointment had been canvassed before, but characteristically Mitterrand had kept him waiting. Bérégovoy was a loner, however, and not a part of the factional landscape or a 'player' in intra-party politics; a Mendésiste who supported Mitterrand in the PS, he was not one of the President's inner circle (*L'Express* 6/5/ 93). Elysée secretary-general in 1981–2 and then Minister for Social Affairs, Bérégovoy was at first opposed to the U-turn of 1983 to impose a deflation on the economy, but then became one of the enthusiasts for the 'prudent' and fiscally conservative 'franc fort' policy of competitive deflation which the party then adopted (*Le Monde* 19/3/93).

Bérégovoy had very little time in which to make an impact, could not afford to make mistakes and had to deal with the problem of unemployment which had remained intractable over his entire time as a government minister when, it is true, inflation had been the main enemy. Of modest origin himself, he set himself up, rather theatrically, as 'père la morale'. His Cabinet rang in the changes, but not always the right ones and it was the Elysée which had had the final say. Lionel Jospin left the government and Jack Lang became Education Minister. Bernard Tapie, not a Socialist but a flamboyant business enterpreneur (later jailed), became Minister for Cities. This was the beginning of the misfortunes, confirming the impression of 'sleaze' which the press was beginning to play up. An amnesty had been declared for those involved in political party funding, and the public was suspicious of the motives of politicians. Six weeks later Tapie, under investigation, had to resign, but rejoined the government in December when the charges were dropped. In July the Socialist Party

Congress in Bordeaux was disrupted by the issue of a summons to one of the leaders (former Treasurer Henri Emmanuelli) and the First Secretary Fabius was later indicted over the 'AIDS-contaminated blood affair'. These were in line with a whole series of 'affairs' amongst which were: Irlandais de Vincennes, Lucet, Knobelspeiss, Greenpeace, Luchaire, Nucci, Orta, Urba, Sormae, Trager and so on. It was, it seemed, the confirmation of endemic corruption over the septennate, and Bérégovoy had made it a priority to eliminate these practices.

Within a very short time, therefore, Bérégovoy and the government were in trouble. When Mitterrand's cancer deteriorated and he underwent surgery on 16 September 1992, a more than ordinary burden of leadership fell on the Prime Minister. Had he been given time, perhaps the PM would have developed the missing persuasiveness and sureness of touch: as it was he was thrust into a worsening situation which presidential political intervention considerably aggravated. It was in these circumstances that the President decided to hold a referendum on the Maastricht Treaty of European Union (amongst other things for a common currency), confident of a victory which would redound to his benefit and split the conservative right. In September the Maastricht Treaty was only just ratified, the President's unpopularity bringing down the 'yes' vote and the campaign gave the leaders of the pro-European right an opportunity to intervene and claim to have saved the day. It was a divisive referendum which moved Jean-Pierre Chevènement to opposition and partially out of the PS. It split the PCF from the Socialists and separated the Socialist Party from its own support more than it divided the Opposition (*Le Monde* 22/9/92). It completed the demoralisation of the Socialist Party and confirmed the isolation of the President. Unlike 1986, the 1993 general election looked likely to be a catastrophe for the Party. The worst continued to worsen.

On 2 February 1993 the satirical journal, the *Canard enchaîné,* revealed that Bérégovoy had been given a one million Franc interest-free loan from the President's crony Roger-Patrice Pelat who had been implicated in insider trading and preferential treatment (in the Pechiney takeover of American Can, Vibrachoc and Société Générale) (*Le Monde* 4/5/93). This loan was not in itself illegal, but the revelations about Pelat, the 'cronyism' and the return of the 'service rendu' which a loan of that size implied were enough to discredit the PM. Bérégovoy never recovered. His reputation as a man of probity was ruined ('Mr 0 per cent'), he did not rebut rumours and he was unable to give a convincing account of repayment. On 1 May, after the general election disaster for the PS, cut off by the Elysée and in a fit of depression, he committed suicide (*Le Monde* 4/5/93). In a funeral oration, the President criticised the press for hounding the Prime Minister to death to distract attention from Mitterrand's way of running his own personal court (Montaldo 1993).

Bérégovoy's loan did play its part in the general election campaign of 1993 and his popularity had dropped (not as low as Cresson's or the President's), but the Socialist defeat was foreseeable already in 1992. In effect it was the end of the Mitterrand era and Bérégovoy was the last Prime Minister he was free to chose. With 17.5 per cent of the vote the 1993 general elections were the worst setback for the socialist party since 1967. Of their 282 seats they retained only 67 in an Assembly of 577. Although on the left the Greens had promised to poll well they did not win a single seat and the Communist Party (hostile to the PS) won only 24. On the conservative right the UDF won 207 seats and the RPR took 242, an enormous majority which reflected more the collapse of the Socialist Party than the popularity of the Opposition. With a majority of such size, and a Prime Minister in waiting before the general elections, there was no 'wiggle room' and the President's hand was forced: a 'cohabitation' with the 'Chambre introuvable' was unavoidable, and on much less favourable terms than in 1986 (Habert et al. 1993, p. 283ff.).

Last Things

Mitterrand was ill and his party had been repudiated at the polls but he was determined to continue until the end of the presidential term in 1995 (*Libération* 9/6/96). Within the conservative parties a substantial victory had been anticipated, but the Presidency was still seen as the real prize. Jacques Chirac had chosen not to go to Matignon for a third time, reckoning it to be the graveyard of presidential ambitions, and had delegated that task (thankless, it was assumed) to his close colleague Edouard Balladur who was premier in waiting (Balladur 1995, p. 64). Balladur was one of the chief theorists of 'cohabitation', he had been scrupulously correct to the President in the last 'cohabitation' and had determined to make the next one work to his own advantage (*Le Monde* 31/3/93). He had agreed with his party leader Jacques Chirac that he would become Prime Minister and the RPR had assumed that Balladur would prepare the way for the 1995 presidential elections but he started preparing a presidential campaign almost as soon as he was nominated (Hausser 1995, p. 183).

As most senior politicians – including Charles Pasqua but not Chirac – anticipated, Balladur became a 'présidentiable' at Matignon. As Balladur's status grew the President's authority was undercut but so too was that of the conservative 'présidentiable' Jacques Chirac. Once again the conservative right was divided, yet this time less between the RPR and UDF (most major figures in the UDF supported Balladur) but within the RPR.

But Edouard Balladur, champion of 'cohabitation douce', had every reason to make the system work. If it did it would launch him as a 'présidentiable'. He had the advantage of having thought out the first 'cohabitation' of 1986–8 and worked through it as Minister of Economics, indeed (given Chirac's presidential deportment and ambitions) almost as 'Prime Minister'. He had learnt lessons and avoided the obvious traps (like the use of ordinances), but had also discovered how to back into the limelight – appropriating the government's achievements to himself (*Le Monde* 19/1/95). (In the first 'cohabitation' it was the President who had managed this public relations feat with dexterity.) As Prime Minister, Balladur dominated the government and had also quickly mastered the Assembly which, unlike 1986, had a very big conservative majority (Colombani and Portelli 1995, p. 281). In the process as the Prime Minister could, but as only Pompidou had previously done, he became the real leader of the majority (*Le Monde* 19/4/93).

Balladur's Presidential Premiership

Balladur's strategy for the 'second cohabitation' was presidential: it was to move to the centre the better to place himself in a 'moderate' position as a conciliator and consensus-minded politician capable of constructing a wide coalition (*Le Monde* 1/4/93). Balladur's coalition was clear in his very carefully balanced Cabinet which included the major majority figures and was heavily centrist. That ambition also meant avoiding an open battle with the President even though Mitterrand was both ill and deprived of party support; presidential weakness meant that Mitterrand was in less of a position to thwart the Prime Minister, so there were few confrontations. Balladur knew of the President's illness, which became debilitating in 1994 (Balladur 1995, p. 190ff.). There was no countervailing power to the Prime Minister and the battle for succession would be fought on the conservative right.

Balladur had to contest presidential authority while remaining respectful of an institution he hoped to win himself (*Le Monde* 11/5/95). While publicly respectful of the President, the Prime Minister centralised power and made clear who had the authority while leaving nothing untouched (even the 'reserved domain') (See for example Balladur's interview in *Le Monde* 18/5/93.) Although Mitterrand asserted that he had a special authority in foreign affairs, there was not even the pretence of Presidential control over the nominations to the Defence and Foreign Ministries (*Le Monde* 16/7/93). Cabinet Council meetings were held twice weekly under the Prime Minister to prepare government business as were interministerial committees of ministers and civil servants (*Pouvoirs* No 71, 1994, p. 195). President Mitterrand was, as in 1986, progressively deprived of information.

President Mitterrand had some means with which to prevent the undercutting of his authority. At a declaratory level, advising, encouraging and warning, the President announced his 'defence' of the marginal and the 'little people' and of social cohesion (*Le Monde* 25/10/93). There was little direct intervention on these issues and the government was not constrained to listen to the President, but his statements were made on specific issues and helped slightly to rebuild popularity, although Mitterrand's poll ratings remained negative from 1993 to 1995 (Colombani and Portelli 1995, p.245). There was only one constitutional clash and that came over the referendum to ratify a change to the Constitution under Article 89. President Mitterrand's refusal to endorse the referendum was probably unconstitutional, but the Prime Minister, wanting to avoid a breakdown in the 'cohabitation' harmony accepted the 'veto' (Ardant 1992, p. 82 and Cohendet 1993, p. 212). In November 1993, the amendment was voted by the Parliament, meeting in Versailles. In July 1993 the President, again interpreting the Constitution in a highly presidential sense, refused to allow the law changing Church School statutes ('Bourg-Broc' law) on the agenda of the extraordinary session of Parliament. Once again the Prime Minister backed down and preferred harmony rather than constitutional conflict. Moreover, when the Assembly did debate the revision of the secular settlement, in January 1994, there were big demonstrations and the government dropped the new law (*Le Monde* 18/1/94). The President had made clear his criticism of the government's action and that no doubt encouraged opposition to it; it was the widespread political opposition to the new law by the state-school teacher unions that caused a backdown.

The 'Reserved Domain'

It was in the 'reserved domain', where public opinion expected presidential activism, that the skirmishes were frequent. Both Edouard Balladur and President Mitterrand claimed authority in foreign affairs but, as a clash was not desired, it was rebaptised by the Prime Minister a 'shared domain' (*Pouvoirs* No 68, p. 179). While Balladur emphasised that the Prime Minister had the right to control policy, the President maintained that the Presidency was the representative of France to the world (*Pouvoirs* No. 66, p. 189). Balladur's tactic was to allow the President to take centre stage, but strictly as the representative of the Premier's policy (Giesbert 1994, p. 241) For example, the G7 meeting in Tokyo in July (which had caused such trouble for Chirac) was left to the President and Foreign Minister Juppé. Balladur declined to go and gave Alain Juppé detailed instructions. Much the same procedure was applied for the GATT negotiations which were also left to the President to front – and to take the opprobrium. By 1994 the government's superior resources and its information circuit led to the Prime Minister increasingly conducting foreign affairs. In the negotiation of the international economic treaty GATT in December 1993, it was the Matignon and the Ministries which were the pacemakers with the Elysée 'informed' of decisions – although the President and Prime Minister did agree on the issue (*Le Monde* 16/12/93). In the event the GATT treaty was voted by 466 to 90 in the Assembly, the Prime Minister had overcome the reservations in his majority and had advanced his own claim to the Elysée (*Le Monde* 16/12/93).

Edouard Balladur needed success in foreign policy to make his 'presidential profile' and this led to his audaciously claiming the reward for diplomatic action and playing an active role (*Pouvoirs* No. 72, pp. 173–4). Apart from the commercial matters where technical expertise was at a premium, the Prime Minister took the lead in African affairs, in relations with Algeria and in the European stability pact. Balladur devalued the Central African Franc and integrated the former colonies into the world market, cutting the old links (Colombani and Portelli 1995, p. 333). At the end of August 1994, he had the boldness to claim the 'reserved domain' as his and was called into line by the President (*Le Figaro* 30/8/94). President Mitterrand's 'response' came in *Le Monde* (3/9/94) and the Prime Minister prudently retreated. On two occasions the President was disavowed by the government (*Le Monde* 7/2/95 and 23/2/95). A semblance of harmony was maintained (better than in 1986–8) and a duality of representation was established at major meetings. This disguised the slippage of authority to the Prime Minister, a victory for the President, because Edouard Balladur required 'cohabitation' to work as part of his campaign to become President himself.

In defence matters the President was able to assert supremacy and to threaten a dissolution to retain recognition of his role. Decisions were taken in collaboration with the Prime Minister, the Defence Minister and the Foreign Minister. Where they agreed they could take action as they did in Bosnia (in November 1994) and in Rwanda (in June 1994). Balladur acceded to the continued moratorium on nuclear testing, despite RPR complaints. In nuclear defence the President proclaimed his sovereign 'powers' (*Le Monde* 7/5/94). These were thin, but the power of the nuclear button was conceded to the President and there was a reprise of Gaullist defence doctrine. This logic of 'deterrence' put the President at the centre of defence policy and led (as in 1986–8) to the rejection of mobile missiles (*Le Monde* 12/5/94). These decisions, taken in 1994, did have consequences for the future, and they were not the object of conflict with a Prime Minister who aspired to the Presidency himself and (like Chirac in 1986) backed down in face of a threat to cause a crisis (*Le Monde* 12/5/94)

Socialist Party 'Meltdown'

Mitterrand's presidential vehicle, the PS, finally shattered in 1993. Hardly was the election over than, on 3 April, there was another coup in the Socialist Party. Michel Rocard and his supporters allied with those disenchanted with 'Mitterrandism' to depose the First Secretary Fabius. For the first time since Epinay in 1971, the Mitterrand faction was wholly displaced. The defenestration of the President's dauphin and the capture of the Parti Socialiste by Mitterrand's long-time rival was a dramatic repudiation of presidential authority. Rocard's coup was unexpected and brutal and it was a measure of desperation: it was a last chance action by the 'virtual presidential candidate' of the PS who could see no future unless the Party were renovated for the 1995 elections. The coup was widely denounced and it placed Rocard in the ring with the other party leaders swapping insults and cutting deals. His position above the squabbles had been the making of Rocard and he had (reluctantly and as a last throw, it is true) undone it at a stroke.

Rocard had called an 'Estates General' of the left for July. At this meeting the fragmented components of the left were to be brought together around the Socialist Party once again in view to a mutually beneficial cooperation and succesful presidential campaign. It was a necessity for a presidential strategy given the decomposition of the Parti socialiste. However, the Socialist activists saw themselves being sidelined (or written out of the process) and the newcomers (ecologists and others) being brought in. 'Outsiders', on the other hand, were not impressed with being 'consulted' and given no institutional part of a failing party which they were to help revive. At the same time the Elysée, marginalised in the Parti socialiste by Rocard, began to support the pretensions of the former Minister Bernard Tapie now in the left-wing Radical Party. Bernard Tapie's populist instincts had been appreciated by the Elysée and he was seen as capable of rivalling Rocard for the socialist vote. From the President's point of view (irrespective of his dislike for Rocard) he needed a more credible Socialist Party to enable him regain some authority. It was, as a party, now almost hostile to Mitterrand.

The Party Rocard inherited showed some signs of revival but continued to haemorrhage members (*Le Monde* 29/3/94). Jean-Pierre Chevènement quit to found a new party and Lionel Jospin left the political field. Rocard was elected leader by the Party at its October Congress and a more 'Rocardian' leadership was installed. But Rocard's position was slipping as he fell behind in the polls. Socialist Party fortunes had not markedly revived under the new First Secretary and there were the European elections of 1994 made more difficult by the competition from Chevène-ment's anti-Maastricht list and from Radical's Bernard Tapie, none too subtly encouraged by the Elysée. Rocard, by contrast, chose the dangerous option of leading the PS list feeling he could do no other. 'Europe' had never been a favourite theme of Rocard's, he was exhausted and was markedly uncomfortable as leader of a campaign which failed to take off.

When Rocard polled only 14 per cent in the European elections in June, the First Secretary resigned and his career as eternal 'présidentiable' was over (*Le Monde* 26/6/94). Tapie had brought out the voters and polled 12 per cent. However, the investigating authorities caught up with Tapie in July and he was out of the political reckoning by the end of the year. Rocard's resignation left the Socialist Party without an obvious leader of presidential timber for the April presidential elections next year. Henri Emmanuelli, a limited sectarian Socialist, took over as First Secretary and moved the Party sharply leftward. Placing a non-credible presidential candidate at the head of the Party and moving to the left suggested that for the moment the Party had given up on the presidential election and would look to the good repair of their municipal alliances (local elections would follow the Presidentials in 1995) and live out the next septennate in their local government bunkers.

Mitterrand's System Ends

In April 1994 a Presidential aide committed suicide and then Mitterrand's reputation was dealt further blows by the revelations that he had a 'second' family and a daughter (*Paris-Match* 10/11/94). More seriously, his Vichy past, though not new was spelt out, along with his friendship with the Vichy Police Chief René Bousquet, in meticulous detail in Pierre Péan's book on the future President's war years (Péan 1994), raising questions of probity and his wartime record which were deeply troubling (*Le Monde* 2/9/94). In November 1994, the Socialist Party held its last Congress before the elections in Liévin, a small mining town in the North of France and the commemoration of a mining disaster was the pretext for a visit from the President. It was a gloomy Congress which confirmed the Party's decline and its lack of leadership.

Socialist politicians had not entirely given up hope of finding a presidential candidate. It was to the 'King over the Water', to the President of the European Commission, Jacques Delors, that the Party now looked. Jacques Delors had been making his substantial reputation as a statesman in Brussels while the Mitterrand Presidency became bogged down in its internal difficulties. Jacques Delors had not been nominated as Prime Minister, perhaps because he had no experience or taste for the internal politics of the Socialist Party and perhaps because he had little taste for (or experience of) the rough and tumble of French electoral politics. Delors looked on the state of the Party in its lurch to the left and on 11 December declared he would rather not stand. This left a vacuum. On 4 January, Lionel Jospin announced his candidacy for the nomination. In a hastily organised internal party election, Jospin easily won the nomination and was, rather late in the day, the Socialist Party candidate (candidates were already campaigning) (*Le Monde* 5–6/2/95). A second ballot duel between the candidates of the right looked possible.

Jospin's main task was not to win an election which was thought unwinnable given the state of the party, but to put the pieces back together and get to the second ballot (Perrineau and Ysmal 1995, p. 70). In this he started with the advantage of legitimacy in the Parti socialiste (of which he had been First Secretary for seven years) and of having once been a potential 'dauphin' and Mitterrand's right hand. Jospin had, however, broken with the President and had never been a 'lap dog' (*Le Monde* 16/5/95). He was thus in a position to repudiate the worst parts of the heritage and to make a new start for the Party. He had started to do so in 1991-2 and had placed himself in contrast to the President's style of politics. To avoid an internal party war, he claimed the 'right of inventory' over the double septennate; a right which he prudently never exercised.

'Jospinism' was a readoption of the 'Mendésisme' incarnated by Rocard. What Jospin chose to highlight was the rejection of the instrumentalism of Mitterrand's 'florentine' side: his flexibility and ambiguity were seen as having fired up factionalism. There had been a slide into scepticism and then to distrust and this in turn caused a disenchantment with the lack of direction. In addition Mitterrand's 'court politics', the favourites, hangers-on and fixers would go. Jospin, having seen this close to, decided that President Mitterrand's system, its 'affairs' and its 'little Spanish customs' could no longer be tolerated. It did not look at first sight that Jospin was the candidate to incarnate the renewal, but his rigidity and lack of pretension, his unpretentious persona, his refusal to sway with the breezes and his determination to stick to long-term objectives were reversals of Mitterrand's outlook, and ultimately telling.

Jospin's 'Triumph'

Mitterrand's supporters did not appreciate these oblique criticisms of the outgoing President and this was made clear on at least one occasion during the campaign. Mitterrand could not resist muddying the waters on the right and encouraged Jacques Chirac to enter the fray when the polls showed his cause as a lost one. Jospin was supported by the main personalities in the Party who rallied round. In the first ballot Jospin emerged as the principal politician on the left by topping the poll: he took 23 per cent to Chirac's 20.47 per cent and Balladur's 18 per cent. It was a victory more over the left than over the conservative right (which, when united, had a majority) but like Mitterrand's showing in 1965, it got him on to the second ballot and enabled Jospin to dominate the Socialists more or less without contest and to continue the modernisation of the Party.

Jospin in some ways entered where Mitterrand had come in. In 1971 the Socialist Party was at a low point and the coup at Epinay was made possible by Mitterrand's status as the only 'présidentiable' on the left. Jospin had in 1995 the same position and used it to pick a new Socialist leadership in the autumn, putting the Old Guard of Mitterrand's supporters in the shade. At the same time the Party's programme was renovated on a modernist – or 'Rocardian – basis and made 'realistic'. This rewriting was itself paced slowly and the process was not allowed to be distracted by the intrusion of events. Jospin also had to refashion the left-wing coalition. This had to be carefully negotiated, but it was undertaken from the left, as in 1971. Jospin had been one of the principal go-betweens discussing the possibilities of coalition with the groups on the left in 1992. He put this to good use and bit by bit started to piece together the coalition. It was more difficult than in 1971 but the painstaking and concrete style once again showed the Rocard-Mendès method of consensus-building and detail. This Jospin adapted and was both effective and a contrast with Mitterrand's mercurial politics.

When Mitterrand had left office he had explored many of the previously theoretical possibilities of presidential politics and had established the possibility of a working 'cohabitation' (something which had been doubted – see Zorgbibe 1986). Mitterrand's second septennate confirmed the necessity of keeping a coalition of support and of public confidence; without those the Presidency has no authority. It was Mitterrand's reconciliation of the left to the Presidency and his working of the institution in the absence of a presidential majority which were his legacy to the institution. If his own reputation was badly tarnished, he set the pattern for presidential politics in 'cohabitation' and with a narrow majority. However, the double septennate ended with a determination in the presidential party (the Socialists) and amongst the public to turn the page on the Mitterrand years. In many respects this 'new start' was represented by Jospin as much as by the conservative candidates and Jospin, by establishing a distinct identity, had changed course for the Socialist Party and for government. Moreover, Jospin, who took over from the dying and discredited leader, did not have to outshine the Sun King.

–11–

'Chirac président'

Jacques Chirac's campaign for the Elysée had been underway for at least twenty years before he was eventually elected: nobody could doubt Chirac's ambition or indeed his Nixonian ability to pull himself off the canvas after an apparently knockout blow and start another round. What was more in question was Chirac's strategic vision and his understanding of the difficulties of presidential politics. It was the campaign of 1995 which was to reveal the weakness of his presidential politics. In particular Chirac's loss of power in 1997 underlines more than two previous 'cohabitations', the fragility of presidential dominance and the difficulty of maintaining an institution as the repository of supreme power.

Jacques Chirac

Chirac is certainly an enigma for an apparently simple man. To a distinguishing feature of sheer application (or 'agitation' in Giscard's dismissive words), must be added the approach which owes more to Corrèze's famous son, the old-style Radical Dr Henri Queuille than to de Gaulle. Chirac, it is true has a vigour which is at the opposite pole from the 'Bon Docteur' who would drift with the political stream, from time to time putting out a boathook to prevent bumping into the banks. However, the agglomerating of support groups, like a Radical 'arrondissementier' of the Third Republic is more Fourth Republic than Fifth. Chirac has an elephantine memory for 'friends' and for the 'service rendu' (but is equally capable of giving some unfortunate a twenty-minute dressing down in rich, not to say fruity, language) (Colombani 1995, p. 16). Yet Henri Queuille's influence is not just in the speech making, the sympathetic man-of-the-people, chain-smoking, beer-drinking, sport-loving 'ordinary Joe,' but the whole political approach.

What emerges from Chirac's record before 1995 is an inconsistency unrelieved by a 'Chiraquian' message. Jacques Chirac had been a Gaullist, Pompidolian, Giscardian, anti-Giscard, nationalist, European, social-democrat ('travailliste'), liberal free-marketeer, anti-cohabitation, 'cohabitationist' and so on. Impulsive (supporting Chief Buthelezi and, in 1975, Saddam Hussein), protean, precipitate and transparent to an exceptional degree: in the brutal words of Séguin, 'Chirac first acts, then consults and then thinks.' By 1988 a substantial part of Chirac's original close supporters, including Balladur and Pasqua, had begun to have doubts. He was followed through the 'desert years' of 1988–95 only by a few close compagnons such as Alain Juppé, Jacques Toubon, Jean Tiberi, Bernard Pons and Jean-Louis Debré.

The Campaign and Balladur's Challenge

Chirac's third try for the Presidency in 1995 was marked by an initial loss of initiative. When the right won a landslide victory in the 1993 general elections, the RPR leader decided not to endure a second 'cohabitation' ('Matignon, non merci, j'ai déjà donné') with the author of his 1988 defeat. Chirac allowed 'his friend of thirty years standing' Edouard Balladur to become Prime Minister (*L'Express* 20/1/94). Balladur quickly became the favourite of conservative voters in the opinion polls and to adapt Rabelais, 'L'appétit vient en mangeant' (see Balladur 1995, p.227). Edouard Balladur was not a political novice, but his appearance at the Matignon in 1993 was a novelty and he appeared from the ranks as a new man in a political elite still dominated by figures from the 1970s (and before). His reserved and careful manner made him appear to be distant and disdainful and was ridiculed as 'sa suffisance' but gave an impression of competence and solidity. Publicly making no pronouncement, but privately preparing a campaign team in autumn 1994, Balladur had the advantage of incumbency which he used to the full. It was the unanticipated entry of Balladur as a 'présidentiable' thanks to his tenure at the Matignon in 1993 which also destabilised Chirac.

Balladur's government followed a conservative and European strategy which strengthened France's position in view of the impending monetary union and the 'convergence criteria' for the single European currency worked out with the EU. It also endeared him to the centrists of the UDF. Thus, the natural ground for the Gaullist and UDF candidate for the Elysée had been occupied, at Chirac's behest, by the Prime Minister whose supporters relentlessly hammered the line that 'there is no alternative', the conservative right's argument in the run-up to the general elections of 1993. Chirac, on the other hand, could not run for election on the programme being applied with success by his rival. He was thus placed in the position of having to produce a new policy but not one which was so eccentric that he would be unelectable or reduced to the ranks of an also-ran.

Allies began to desert the Chirac camp: Interior Minister Charles Pasqua, who had brought Chirac to the leadership of the RPR, and in the autumn of 1993, Budget Minister Nicolas Sarkozy, ambitious Mayor of Neuilly, in particular were both firmly in the Balladur camp. 'Sarko', whose defection devastated the Chiraquians, employed his talents on Balladur's behalf and devoted himself to enticing deputies into the Balladur camp or keeping them neutral. One deputy with whom he had no success was the Assembly Speaker Philippe Séguin and another was the Foreign Minister and President of the RPR, Alain Juppé.

Chirac's Response

Chirac was in danger of being sidelined and announced his candidature from the Nord very early in the election cycle on 4 November 1994. By making this declaration, Chirac had avoided being pushed offstage or forced into 'primaries' which would have been to the advantage of the Prime Minister but the problem remained of how to find a message suitable for a 'présidentiable'. Chirac had faced this dilemma before in the 1970s: of being loyal to his own side but needing to demark himself with a distinctive, attractive and credible message.

As a 'présidentiable' Chirac needed a plausible European policy but not a Eurosceptic one, but a slight opening had been created by the Maastricht referendum for an appeal to Eurosceptics. He impulsively sought a margin over the Prime Minister by looking for the Eurosceptic vote. As a Gaullist Chirac had to contend with a substantial anti-Maastricht pressure: he suggested the holding of a referendum before the 'third phase' of monetary union moving to a single currency in 1997–9. This suggestion destabilised the markets, caused near panic in the pro-European ranks and was rapidly retracted. Still, the Prime Minster was camped on the European high ground, and Chirac, who had no reason as a Gaullist to throw himself into the role of a Europhile, had differentiated himself from Balladur. He contradicted himself within days and began criticising the Balladur government for not adhering strictly enough to the budget limits necessary to make the Maastricht criteria and supporting the Franc's alignment with the Deutschmark.

Yet Chirac still sought the edge his campaign needed and without which he would be rejected as a carbon copy of the gradualist and prudent Balladur in preference for the real thing. Bit by bit the physiognomy of

Chirac's programme emerged and it began to increasingly resemble the 'alternative politics' promoted by the maverick neo-Gaullist Philippe Séguin. Séguin was also inclined to retreat to his town hall ('Epinal les deux Eglises') if frozen out of the RPR mainstream – which was often. Séguin envisaged a volunteristic neo-Keynesian policy, determined to end the passive acceptance of unemployment and to set things on a new course. Keynesian themes of deficit of demand (against Balladur's emphasis on the supply side) began to be hammered in the speeches and economic growth became a commonplace. As Chirac put it: 'la politique n'est pas l'art de faire ce qui est possible, mais celui de rendre possible ce qui est nécessaire'. In particular a new policy would place employment at the heart of the government programme and cause severe difficulties for France's European partners. Rather than getting the main indicators of inflation right and then allowing the economy to solve the unemployment problem there would be government action. That Chirac's tilt to the left went unanswered by the Socialists was as a result of their collapse, thus there was in 1994 a gap which might be exploited.

Starting with a speech in Lyons on 16 December, Chirac took up this theme promising to change priorities by introducing a 'pacte républicain'. This 'pacte' would be intended to overcome the 'social fracture' which had opened up in France and would close the gap which he said existed between the people and the technocratic elite. Balladur, he implied, was in the grip of an orthodoxy, the 'pensée unique', and had a strictly unimaginative view of public finances ('gestion notariale') in which all expenditure was a cost to the community. Chirac tried to pit the technocratic elite against the ordinary people and to stress the elite origin of the Balladur supporters as well as to lash out at 'intellectuals'. Chirac played the populist card in response to Balladur's patrician style.

To this 'alternative politics' was, rather confusingly, added a dash of free-market liberalism, tax reductions and the slimming down of the welfare state. Chirac's add-on of Reaganite liberalism, à la Madelin, had been promoted by Balladur's former Minister for Business who had 'come over' from the Prime Minister's camp. Alain Madelin, who had not found Balladur receptive to his proselytism of free-market policies, had joined the Chirac camp as others were leaving and played the outside chance. This introduced a contradiction, between the herald of the minimal state (Madelin) and the proponent of Gaullist state action (Séguin) which was present throughout the Chirac campaign – and never resolved. On the one hand Madelin, the apostle of the free markets and 'flexible' employment, argued that 'trop d'impôt tue l'impôt' (a French translation of the 'Laffer curve') and gave the campaign the theme of tax reforms. On the other hand the Séguiniste 'pacte républicain' went in another direction proposing to increase purchasing power and altogether condemning the market forces which made France the plaything of financiers and the *'pensée unique'* which made the principal task the reduction of the budget deficit. But the ambiguity came from the candidate's speeches which used the language of the Séguin-style break with the past while retaining the essence of Madelin's 'market-friendly' reforms. Chirac decided to keep both themes running. However, with Chirac two promises seemed to be clear: there would be lower taxes and wages would increase ('la feuille de paie n'est pas l'ennemi de l'emploi'): 'le renouveau du pacte républicain passe par une mobilisation générale contre le chomage'. When challenged Chirac would refer to the 'cohabitation' government of 1986–8 which had accomplished both (*Le Monde* 8/4/95).

Chirac's Lead

In January 1995, Balladur still led, but Chirac still dominated the RPR. Then Balladur's campaign launch on 18 January and his manifesto presentation on 12 February went badly and the Prime Minister began to sink in the polls. Balladur was personally attacked for his business links. Worse, the government faced social problems with students and strikers and, despite its declaration of intent, the Minister of the Interior was enmeshed in a scandal and with the Prime Minister in a phone-tapping 'affair' (Balladur 1995, p. 238). This was very serious and the Prime Minister was dragged down. With Balladur flagging, Chirac's campaign began to take off marking a difference with the Balladur rally on 17 February. Balladur did not have the backing of a political party and refused (or appeared to disdain) the campaign circuit, a disrespect for the usages of Republican debate, which had damaged de Gaulle and Giscard before.

Chirac, nothing if not a strong campaigner, had seemed to be headed for a good first round lead and expected a vote of at least 23 per cent and perhaps 26 per cent (Bacqué and Saverot 1995, p. 193). In the event, the first ballot on 23 April was a revelation of Chirac's inability to enlarge his camp's audience with 20.8 per cent, and he came behind Jospin (23.2 per cent). This was a near triumph for Jospin (Perrineau and Ysmal 1995, p. 198). Balladur had recovered from the disastrous start to poll a creditable but insufficient 18.58 per cent (2 per cent more than Barre in 1988) but the real shock was the 15.1 per cent for Le Pen, who had no love for Chirac (dismissed as 'Jospin en pire'). Chirac had won in his traditional fiefs, took most of the RPR vote and increased the Gaullist audience amongst the working class and unemployed. Balladur, on the election result, made a declaration of full support for Chirac who went on to an unexpectedly close fight with the Socialist Jospin for the second round. (Le Pen had called for everything but call for a vote against Chirac.) In the run-off on 7 May 1995, Jacques Chirac was elected fifth President of the Fifth Republic with 52.64 per cent. His election was a personal achievement but he was elected with the lowest first round vote of any Fifth Republic President, an indication that he needed to enlarge and consolidate his support.

However, the victory needed the support of the Balladurians and the minor parties of the right who contributed to the further ambiguity and contradictions of the Chiraquian programme. Yet for the close circle of Chiraquians the victory was euphoric. It was a highly Parisian 'Chiraco-Chiraquian' government of politicians from local and regional positions, with few consoling positions for the Balladurians. Chirac had been stung by the desertion of former supporters and depended excessively on a few close associates (Juppé, Pons, Debré and his staff) and even put his RPR party under the Prime Minister. Rewarding the faithful had the politically dangerous effect of keeping out many of the conservative right's most popular and reliable 'ministrables'. On 17 May Alain Juppé ('le meilleur d'entre nous') was nominated Prime Minister charged with effecting the new President's 'fire and water' programme (Biffaud and Maudit 1996, p. 147ff.).

The Juppé Government

Juppé's nomination was intended to reassure the commercial and European circles that the administration would be solid and reliable, giving ballast to a new regime suspected of lacking what the Victorians called 'bottom' (Jarreau 1997, p. 115). Juppé, a bit like Fabius, had a stack of degrees and certificates which marked him as one of the new generation of meritocrats: Normalien (classical literature), Enarque, agrégé and Inspecteur des Finances in 1972. Juppé, or 'Amstrad', reputed for his intelligence had, however, been educated out of his wits. Unfortunately, Juppé, according to Frédéric Pagès, 'a le malheur d'incarner tout ce que déteste le militant de base RPR: le parisianisme, le technocratisme, le manque de rondeur': a typical product of the 'technocratic Parisian elite' Chirac had campaigned against. The choice of Juppé also had the unfortunate effect of tying President and Prime Minister together in a 'three-legged race'. Very quickly the couple of President and Prime Minister came to be judged together and when the Prime Minister's popularity began to fall the President's followed it.

Juppé's first government was large and unwieldy: composed of 26 ministers, 2 delegate ministers, and 14 secretaries of state, involving difficulties of coordination between departments (Brisard and Pinard 1996, p. 97). It was a 'feminised' government with 4 ministers and 8 ministers of state ('jupettes'); 11 ministers had been on the Paris council whereas 28 had never been ministers previously. RPR loyalists were rewarded: Toubon (Justice), Debré (Interior), Pons (Transport). Madelin of the Parti républicain, a supporter in time of need, went to the Economics Ministry. Giscard's supporters, de Charette (Foreign Affairs) and Millon (Defence) were rewarded for their patron's timely 'Chiraquism' in the presidentials. There were two prominent centrists: Bayrou was given the Education Ministry and Douste Blazy Culture and only two neo-Gaullist 'Balladurians'. Séguin, the incarnation of the 'alternative politics' was marginalised as the Speaker of the Assembly and the government looked in towards the small world of the RPR rather than out to the wider French society (Ottenheimer 1996).

The 'Unreadable' Policy Shifts

Previous Presidents had marked their inauguration with a 'first hundred days' of reform. Perhaps with the Gaullist heritage in mind, or perhaps because opportunities presented themselves, President Chirac started by making a mark in foreign affairs (Coudurier 1998, p. 83). Yet President Chirac's first attempts to construct a diplomatic presence were not popular. Restarting the atomic tests in the Pacific on the fiftieth anniversary of Hiroshima was a mistake (Chirac had changed his opinion on the need for them) and neglecting to tell the Pacific rim or European partner countries was insensitive (*Le Figaro* 12/10/95 – Giscard's criticism). Meetings with the Italian and Belgian Prime Ministers were cancelled after they criticised the tests (Moïsi 1998). By the same token the new President's tone at the G7 and European summits which came fast on the heels of the victory was far from conciliatory (dressing down the Netherlands on the drug problem and of Greece for its treatment of Macedonia, for example) and disquieted allies – especially Germany – who sought assurance on European policy (Menon 1996). Chirac's policy in the former Yugoslavia did, however, meet with approbation, particularly in America, where decisive action by a European ally was appreciated (*Le Figaro* 31/5/95).

Juppé's government had to somehow apply the contradictory presidential policy and started seek a way out. As an excuse, the outgoing Balladur administration was accused of leaving a financial black hole, but this was resented by the 'Ballaurians' who immediately hit back (*Le Figaro* 8/6/95). Policy making waited on the municipal elections in June. At those there were no presidential 'coat-tails' and the Front National took several large towns in the South. After the local elections in June, Juppé rushed through a mini-budget which had the impossible task of increasing expenditure and reducing receipts and for a few weeks the campaign promises were held: the minimum wage was put up by 4 per cent on 1 July and money was found for job creation (39 billion Francs, an increase of 6.7 per cent). Yet no sooner were the local elections over than in June the new government increased taxes on a variety of fronts (CSG, VAT, corporate tax, wealth taxes etc.) and continued to put them up through the year (September and November) to a record 44.7 per cent of GDP. Most of this tax increase negated the effects of the measures for the worst off and taxes went up in line with the fiscal orthodoxy and out of line with the specific campaign promises (not to tax savings, for example). Juppé's mini-budget opened up the credibility gap which grew from that time on. Juppé admitted that the burden of these 'provisional taxes' was not reduced over the two years. On 25 August, Alain Madelin the 'liberal' Economics Minister resigned. Madelin, who wanted to lighten the tax load had been frozen out by Juppé and decided to leave to set up his 'think tank', and the Franc began to slip on the exchanges.

On 4 September the government announced that there would be a wages freeze in the public sector for the next year. This was followed up by the Presidential support for the wage freeze: 'the [state sector] pay slip', the President now declared, 'was the tax bill'. By way of explanation the recession and the state of the budget (worse than foreseen, it was said) were invoked but the new policy was a U-turn which provoked the unions (which, for once united, organised a strike) and, because Juppé's abrupt freeze was unprepared, the government did not prepare public opinion. It was nothing less than a return to the 'stringent finances' criticised in the campaign by Chirac himself but the impression was one of indirection (*Le Monde* 9/9/95).

The following month the reform of the costly social welfare system was mooted. Juppé's budget, announced on 20 September, planned new taxes for 1996, admitted that there was no prospect of cuts, but allowed spending to rise only slightly so that the budget deficit would not get out of hand (it was projected to fall from 5 per cent in 1995 to 3 per cent in time for the Maastricht criteria to be met in 1998). Barre was one of the first to attack the lack of determination to reduce the deficits and the Balladurian Philippe Auberger (chair of the Assembly finance committee) led the attack in October (*Le Monde* 20/10/95). The most intractable of public deficits was the 60 billion franc deficit in the social welfare budget. Juppé's next U-turn was to propose a reform of the social security system once again contrary to what, as candidate, Chirac had promised. By the autumn the polls showed that more people had a bad than a good opinion of the President's start as Head of State.

The Continuing 'Affairs'

Juppé meanwhile also had other problems. Hardly a sympathetic figure, he was initially seen, nevertheless, as being a disinterested public servant. This advantage was eliminated by the revelation in the *Canard enchaîné* that members of the Juppé family were the beneficiaries of luxurious Paris city flats (Habitation à loyer modéré) notionally reserved for the less well off or homeless. Juppé's HLM was a luxury flat in the best area and at a peppercorn rent. As the affair wound on the existence of a Gaullist 'nomenklatura' in Paris was revealed as was the extent and nature of RPR funding. Juppé's reaction was to regard any questions on the subject as 'insulting': 'Je suis droit dans mes bottes.' It was not illegal but it was not legitimate. Juppé's disdainful defence drew attention to that gap between the political elite and the public which Chirac had proposed to close: in the 'République des copins et des coquins' there was one law for the politicians and another for the ordinary person (Clamecy 1997, p. 19).

The franc slipped again on the exchanges and a worried Chancellor Kohl came to Paris to urge the implementation of the Maastricht criteria on an embattled President. In the President's key speech on 26 October confirming the U-turn, the 'priority of priorities' had become the reduction of the budget deficits and the campaign promises were sidelined or made dependent on the balancing of the account. Riots broke out in the city of Bordeaux (where Juppé was mayor) as the welfare system's reform was prepared. Before the unveiling of the new plan, the government was suddenly reshuffled on 7 November. Juppé, immediately reappointed despite his unpopularity, was brutal to the point of insensitivity. A more compact and experienced team, now reduced to 32, was put together as those who had not shown their mettle were removed, but 8 'jupettes' were dismissed and only 4 women ministers remained. Out went the 'Chiraquians' R.-M. Aubert and François Baroin as well as the centrist Claude Goasguen and the Séguiniste Jean de Boishue while others were abruptly downgraded. Brought in were Franck Borotra and four Balladur supporters: Alain Lamassoure (Budget), Dominique Perben (Civil Service), J.-C. Gaudin (Urban Affairs) and Jacques Barrot

(Employment and Welfare). Still none of the heavyweights were given portfolios; the main ministers were confirmed in place: it was a government formed to impose the austerity programme precipitately announced in September.

Return to 'Balladurism'

On 15 November Juppé revealed his plan which was intended to control expenses and which had the target of reducing the social security deficit by half in 1996, eliminating it in 1997 and, more importantly, changing its structure to eliminate the constant overspends. In particular the joint control by workers and employers' elected representatives was to be replaced by parliamentary control (in other words by government) which would set spending caps and determine policy and public sector workers' privileges were to be reduced. All of which was brusquely announced with no consultation or attempt to swing public opinion behind the measures. At the same time as controlling expenditure the Juppé plan proposed to increase income by increasing health charges on the unemployed and the old and by introducing a new flat rate tax (remboursement de la dette sociale) to pay off the accumulated deficit while the CSG was to be widened to increase the numbers of those taxed. Government reforms had created enemies on a very wide front by bundling together policies which could have been kept separate (welfare, pensions, tax changes). By the time the social welfare taxes were proposed, the government had lost the trust of many of its former supporters who no longer believed it would keep its promises.

Juppé's plan, prepared without consultation in Matignon (Pasqua noted that you don't run the country like an 'administrative committee'), was applauded in the Assembly but inspired a general discontent and crystallised anti-government feeling in the country. Juppé appeared to be repeating the history of 1986–7: there were general strikes which started with the rail workers on 23 November and paralysed transport over a month as well as spreading to schools, power stations, PTT and the students. Government response to the strikes was maladroit. A 'comité d'usagers' was created along with a petition ('laissez-nous travailler') in a rather too obvious way by the RPR to counter the sympathy the strikers had (and held) in public opinion – and then dropped when it became counter-productive. Séguin, unable to contain his schadenfreude at Juppé's misfortune, met SNCF strikers in the town hall at Epinal; the President declined to enter the arena to back his own administration ('social disorder is the Prime Minister's problem'); with ministers taking cover it looked as if the government had lost its grip (*L'Express* 7/12/95).

Juppé's response, when it came (on 5 December) was to offer talks and to make a few minor concessions clearing up, in passing, some 'minor misunderstandings'. It dropped proposals to privatise the railways, and instead took on SNCF debts and guaranteed rail workers' pensions; promised more money to the universities; postponed the tax reforms and set up a committee to look at public sector pensions. But the main lesson was that the 'alternative politics' was off the agenda and Balladur's balanced budget was back on. Michel Crozier commented: 'Nous avons les élites les plus bêtes du monde' (*Le Figaro* 20/12/95).

Neither the President nor the government recovered from the climb-down of autumn 1995 and his already narrow electoral base had been diminished and fractured. For the next eighteen months they sought for a new élan (with the occasional éclat) but the polls and by-elections showed that the public remained reticent. What followed the strikes of the winter were a series of measures designed to show the Presidency in a Gaullist light and to pull Juppé out of the mire.

However, problems intruded. Debré, Minister of the Interior in Juppé's Cabinet, went to Corsica at the beginning of 1996 to open talks with all currents of opinion including the clandestine groups involved in the bombing campaign (*Le Monde* 13/1/96). Cloak and dagger meetings with FLNC (Canal historique) were not new, but candidate Chirac had announced that he 'never' talked to terrorists and Debré's visit to the island had been anticipated by a midnight press conference of hooded terrorists declaring a truce. The 'press conference' was followed by Debré's offer to engage in talks. Lacking any strategy and unable (or unwilling) to prevent the terrorism in the island, negotiations continued, however, even after the recommencement of the bombing campaigns and terrorist impunity became flagrant. Only when the Corsican terrorists bombed the City Hall in Bordeaux did the government seem to move onto a more active footing.

President Chirac's 'Reserved Domain'

Chirac's reform of the Army announced on 22 February 1996 was to be the 'measure of the septennate'. In an Army of 409,000 some 240,000 were conscripts. On the one hand the French Republican tradition valued the 'nation in arms' and the citizen army of which national service was the symbol. On the other hand the need for a 'professional army' which could carry out the intricate and specialist services required of a contemporary European army, and on which resources could be concentrated, was a necessity. Chirac had not always seemed set on ending military service, although it had been raised as a possibility in the campaign, but his Defence Minister, Charles Millon was opposed to the change. President Chirac met with the Gaullist compagnons (Messmer) and took his decisions on the matter often leaving the Defence Minister 'out of the loop' (*Economist* 10/2/96). At the same time the arms industry, facing difficulties in the post-Wall world, was to be restructured to move onto the world stage and to collaborate effectively with partners. These were significant and, given the French context, difficult reforms and the President's determination showed what a dextrous Elysée could still accomplish.

Part of President Chirac's French defence policy was a further reconciliation with Nato: it took a Gaullist to take the final step and rejoin Nato's military committee sending the Defence Minister to Nato meetings. A move back into the Nato machine was eased by the concession that the alliance could develop joint missions within a European context and not necessarily involving the USA. Before any such missions could be undertaken a European defence identity would have to take shape and a WEU chain of command developed that could take over the Nato structure for limited purposes (peacekeeping). Presidential policy sought an EU role in foreign and defence matters through a new mechanism.

French policy in Nato did not accord with either the British or the Germans, but the view that the American presence in Europe was unwelcome was revised and portrayed in a more positive light as the new Presidency developed. But Chirac's reintegration of France back into Nato was not without conditions, one being the French control of the Mediterranean command (based in Sicily and American). Other European powers and the Americans resisted Chirac's demand. France's demand for the control of the so-called 'Southern Command' could not possibly have been conceded and looked like a case of inadequate diplomatic preparation. Likewise the attempt by the President to keep Boutros-Ghali as UN Secretary General against the American preference for Kofi Annan was hopeless without maximal European support. France, the proponent of a united European foreign policy, neglected to ensure unity when vital and preferred freelance campaigns in sensitive areas (Coudurier 1998).

Chirac was not free of the anti-American reflex as these several incidents showed and the reflex of French exceptionalism in foreign policy was not lost. Without undue care for American susceptibilities, the French President made clear France's differences on Middle Eastern policy with the USA in a series of meetings, reactivating the critical stance of the Gaullists to Israel and visiting the capitals of the Gulf States demanding a Euro-Arab dialogue (keeping contacts with Iran). Chirac called for more determined financial assistance to the Palestinian state; in Egypt, he supported the regime while criticising American policy; and then sent Hervé de Charette on a regional peace shuttle (*Le Figaro* 3/3/96). President Chirac's visit to Israel in October 1996 was not a success even if it served to raise France's presence in the region as a distinctive actor.

While this was happening, the situation in Algeria deteriorated with the taking hostage and execution of seven French monks in the Atlas mountains. France's Algerian policy had drawn closer to General Zéroual's regime under Chirac's aegis and even appeared to support an anti-Islamic front although the Elysée made demands on Algerian policy and disclaimed any intention to take sides (Angeli and Mesnier 1997, Ch. 5). But the implications of a proposed meeting with General Zéroual (which the General, draping himself in the flag, cancelled) were not lost on the internal Algerian opposition and on the regime. President Chirac, caught between a desire not to be seen to interfere and a desire to demand evidence of good conduct was ultimately caught in the quarrel: Zéroual had himself re-elected. Islamic groups restarted a campaign in France with a murderous bomb in the Port-Royal underground station on 3 December 1996.

'L'Affair des sans Papiers' and Juppé's Continuing Weakness

During the summer of 1996 some 220 clandestine immigrants ('sans papiers') who were in a strictly illegal position demanded sanctuary from the authorities in a church (Saint-Bernard), in effect drawing attention to the plight of illegal immigrants. The government appeared unable to find a compromise and hesitated for a month until, abandoning negotiation, it decided to use main force to empty the church. This action was not censured by public opinion (though it was not approved by the intellectual community) and may have misled the government into thinking that a hard line could swing part of the National Front vote behind the conservative coalition. This incorrect assumption possibly led to the introduction of new 'Debré laws' in the 1996-7 session to curb illegal immigration. Juppé's popularity did not, as a result of further mistakes, revive in the summer of 1996 (*Le Figaro* 24/10/96).

During the year there were many occasions on which the President could have, without obvious political damage, dispensed with the Prime

Minister. It might have made one kind of sense to remove Juppé in mid-1996 or even as late as mid-1997 to prepare for the general elections due in 1998. Pompidou, Chirac's patron, had performed a similar operation in July 1972 when Chaban Delmas, mired in scandals, had been removed to make way for Pierre Messmer who had won the subsequent general elections for the President in March 1973. Juppé, loyal to a fault but without independent political weight, had the profile of a second premier of the septennate. Other figures (Séguin, notably, but also Pasqua or a Balladurian) might have brought support for the Presidency but, by the same token, they would have been a challenge to the weakened Jacques Chirac. President Chirac, therefore, chose to keep Juppé. Chirac's loyalty to Juppé, and his refusal to use the Prime Minister as a scapegoat, identified the President with him and created a 'tandem' in which the falling popularity of the Premier dragged down the President. Juppé worried an increasing number of conservative deputies in a bloated majority elected in 1993 on the back of a Socialist collapse, many of whom were highly sensitive to changes in opinion as they were unlikely, even in the best circumstances, to find themselves back in the Assembly (Mano and Birnbaum 1997, p.49).

Amongst right-wing voters a majority were critical of the Prime Minister and deputies reflected this disquiet. At the RPR's meeting in Le Havre in September 1996, Juppé's welcome was so hostile that he threatened not to deliver a planned speech. In response the President delivered a message to the deputies through Michel Péricard that the RPR could not claim to support him if it did not back the government. Juppé's reaction was to demand a vote of confidence in the Assembly but, as that had a built-in conservative majority, the victory was a foregone conclusion and was meaningless. Criticism of the Prime Minister continued. Many in the conservative majority openly demanded the Prime Minister's removal but presidential confidence in Juppé was publicly renewed again in November 1996 and Juppé, for his part, did not hesitate to announce his intention to lead the election campaign due in 1998.

Juppé's repeated assertion that the economic upturn was near did not restore confidence in either the policy or the administration. But unemployment was continuing to rise and the Franc was not helped by the President's attack on the Governor of the Bank of France Jean-Claude Trichet. On 5 September, Juppé announced that certain taxes would fall (though not to the pre-1995 level), but the more visible indirect duties on alcohol, petrol and cigarettes went up. Wealth tax, on the other hand, concerning only a few thousand people, was reduced, a change badly received by some conservative deputies and the public. In addition to an incoherence of policy and giving the impression given of rewarding 'fat cats', the overall effect was not of prudently lowering taxes when the time was right, but of giving with one hand and taking back with another. Further accusations of serious incompetence or worse were fired at the government after it announced, at the beginning of 1996, its intention to sell the public arms/electronics group Thomson. Initially the Elysée seemed to think that Alcatel was the appropriate purchaser before ceding it to Matra and the Korean Daewoo for a 'symbolic franc'. Juppé's argument, that Thomson had nothing but debts, went down badly not just with the company's employees but with the conservative defenders of the state's property. In late November the sell-off was cancelled on the insistence of the Committee on Privatisations. Other privatisations were slowed by an unseemly wrangle about who should head the proposed private firm, rather than the terms of sell-off. Disarray in the conservative ranks was intensified and the rumours of a government reshuffle circulated in the 'Tout Paris'. Giscard, using the occasion to add to the President's discomfort, openly questioned the government's strategy and the policy of linking the Franc to the D-mark. Juppé launched a media campaign intended to put him in a sympathetic light and published a book (*Entre Nous*, written, the public was assured, at the height of the truckers' strike) which had a small impact on the polls and raised his popularity slightly.

Stoppages had been the order since the teachers strike of September which had been followed by hospital employees (and doctors) and banking staff as well as a day in defence of jobs in October. The unrest was mounting again for another winter of discontent. In mid-November 1996 the country was paralysed by a truckers' strike which blocked the main routes in and around France; the government, again surprised and unable to gain public understanding, backed down. Chirac's response was to deliver a lacklustre presidential message on 12 December. What was remembered from it was his regret that 'le pays est profondement conservateur', that it was therefore extremely difficult to change anything at all with the implication that the government might not have been right to capitulate. These complaints were partially withdrawn in subsequent days (when French entrepreneurship was praised). The President also promised a reform of the judicial system to give the judges independence from political interference but this message was partially vitiated by a criticism of the judges (who were flushing out the scandals) and by Chirac's nomination of partisan public prosecutors against the advice of the High Council of the Judiciary. (Giscard, marking his continuing position as 'elder' of the right criticised Juppé's, and implicitly, Chirac's incompetence (*L'Express* 21/11/96).

Dissolution

New Year 1997 started with a flurry of rumours about a government reshuffle (published on 27 January in *Libération*, then officially denied). These 'Chinese whispers' may have been promoted by the Elysée but few people anticipated a dissolution. A reshuffle, it was assumed, was more likely and would bring into the government major figures such as the Balladurian Nicolas Sarkozy and the UDF's François Léotard in a way which would capture the diversity of the conservative coalition and bring a vital competence to ministerial portfolios. With nearly eighteen months to go to the scheduled general elections of March 1998, normally that would have allowed time for a government to turn the situation and to win back the margin required to save the conservatives' majority. On the other hand a reshuffle, given Chirac's obstinacy in standing by the Prime Minister, would be unlikely to replace Juppé, the weakest link in the right's electoral chain (Perrinau and Ysmal 1998, p. 51).

However as the year progressed the right began to take heart. There were, to start with, problems in the Socialist Party. Revelations about Mitterrand's bulimious appetite for phone taps undermined the image of the previous President (Juppé, by claiming that they came under national security and refusing to investigate, wasted this issue to some extent). Worse, the Socialist programme had entirely failed to 'catch fire' and no mobilising issue or theme had emerged. In addition the left remained divided and the pieces had not yet been stuck together again (probably this 'balkanisation' impressed the President). Greens, Chevènementistes and the PCF were hostile to Maastricht and these divisions appeared to make the assemblage of a winning coalition of the left more difficult than it had been in 1988. It may have been feared that the implementation of the Maastricht criteria (imposing limits on budget deficits) meant austerity in 1997–8 and not the liberal spending régime which a general election campaign required.

In addition, the Debré laws on illegal immigration caught the Socialist leadership unprepared. The intellectual left (and others) inside and outside the Parti socialiste protested against the first article which obliged people who employed temporary immigrants to guarantee their return to their country of origin at the end of their employment. This outcry contributed to the impression that the Party had lost touch with its grass roots, for Debré's law (replacing the 'Pasqua laws') on immigration were popular. Debré may have impressed the conservative right with the ability of the law to bring the popular vote back the mainstream right from the National Front as well as with its divisive effect on the left. As the polls began to look a little better for the right, suggesting an early election might be won (narrowly) despite the events of 1996 with the economy hesitatingly beginning to grow again, while waiting until 1998 seemed to promise only further difficulties with the right's Assembly majority and the prospect of a credible left-wing challenge (July 1997, p. 51).

The General Elections

It was either a foolhardy, desperate or courageous decision to dissolve the Assembly in 1997, a year before the end of its normal term (Goldey 1998). A short campaign would be followed by elections on 25 May and 1 June. On the right opinion was divided. Prime Minister Juppé favoured the move as did the UDF leader Léotard, but others were not so sure. Giscard d'Estaing warned against the move as did a number of other leaders and Séguin, who (unlike Juppé) had not been involved in the preparation of the coup, was hostile and retired to his tent, in the Epinal Town Hall, for most of the early campaign. But it was better, perhaps, to tempt fate now when there was a hope of victory than to wait another eleven months: 'quand la grêle. . .'

President Chirac's dissolution address to the nation did not, however, explain why there was to be a snap election. A dissolution is exceptional and exceptional circumstances had occasioned the four previous presidential dissolutions: the Assembly overturning Pompidou's government in 1962; the student crisis of May 1968; and Mitterrand's victories in 1981 and 1988 which left him with Assemblies of the right (Perrineau and Ysmal 1998, p. 18). Chirac declared the need for a new 'élan partagé' to give impetus to change and for a majority with the strength to meet the challenges. However, the President already had a massive majority and opposition had come from the streets not the Assembly. Because it was a dissolution undertaken on the President's authority the elections put the President into the front line and not, as would normally be, the Prime Minister (Jeambar 1997, p. 129).

However, there was also a feeling that the haste hid an austerity plan to be introduced in 1998 to comply with the Maastricht criteria for the single currency; this prevented the right from using the European issue against the PS. 'Liberalism' as an issue had already been rejected, trying to run the scare 'gare aux archéos de gauche' made little headway. Prime Minister Alain Juppé, unpopular as ever, was still deputed to lead the right's campaign, nevertheless his response to the jibe that a vote for the right meant five more years of Juppé was the riposte that 'five years of Jospin would be worse' (*Libération* 17/7/97). On 27 April Juppé, the prime target of the left and the Front national, announced that he was not 'a candidate for my own succession'. President Chirac intervened on two occasions: on 7 May he published a letter in fourteen regional papers but found little response and then on 20 May he used the occasion of the German Chancellor Kohl's visit to remind the voters that France needed to be able to speak with a single voice if it was to defend its interests in Europe. 'Cohabitation', which had worked well as recently as 1995, no longer worried the voters.

For President Chirac and Prime Minister Juppé it was a devastating first round. Jospin's coalition of the 'plural left' polled 42.1 per cent and the National Front had its best legislative result with 15.09 per cent giving it the role of second round arbiter in many constituencies for, combined, the conservative allies UDF/RPR polled only 36.1 per cent. Faced with the débâcle neither the Elysée nor the Matignon knew how to react to bring the missing élan back to the right's campaign. Juppé, the Elysée was still slow to realise, would have to stand down as Prime Minister, but he was left in charge of the campaign with the 'impossible couple' of Séguin and Madelin (hitherto ignored) intending to turn the general election as they had the presidentials (though over six months). However the time was too limited and the Elysée had sidestepped any promise of promotion to the Matignon (*Libération* 12/8/97) At their joint meeting, Séguin defended the 'enabling' and 'protective' role of the state whilst Madelin appealed to the free market, competition and low taxes (Perrineau and Ysmal 1998 p. 305)

The Third 'Cohabitation'

Defeat, on the second round, was a body blow (*Libération* 10/7/97). A demoralised Elysée had no alternative but to appoint the socialist leader Jospin as Prime Minister and the 'plural left' took power (Perrineau and Ysmal 1998, p. 285 ff.). But, more than that, the President and his intermediaries (most of them defeated), lost control of the RPR. Séguins' supporters went into action and rallied support for the former Speaker to head the neo-Gaullist movement while, Juppé, in a brief attempt to prevent that outcome, sought an alliance with Balladurians (despite having refused any accommodation for two years). These 'marchandages' by a discredited Juppé and a beaten President were not a success: the 'stop Séguin' desperation was evident in the proposal to nominate Debré as RPR secretary general and Pons (a popular 'Chiraquian' and the only personality to rival Séguin) as party president. As Séguin launched an appeal to save the movement, the Balladurians threatened a schism (*Libération*

10/7/97) and on 10 June Séguin was elected, with Balladurian assistance, to lead the RPR in the Assembly and Sarkozy joined its committee. Meanwhile the leadership of the Parti Républicain was passed from Léotard to Madelin and the rivalry for dominance within the UDF between its main components sharply intensified. That President Chirac had lost control was confirmed in the RPR's Congress on 6 July when Séguin took the RPR presidency and nominated Sarkozy as secretary general. Séguin's collegiate leadership was ratified by a Congress in 1998 but in the meantime the Chiraquian hold was further loosened, but not entirely broken, for he still had his supporters and was popular with activists while the new leadership was factionalised by competition among the newly promoted. Chirac was no longer an Executive President and had lost control of the Assembly opposition. His position was more like Mitterrand's in 1993 than the President in 1986, but this time the 'cohabitation' would not end after two years and could last for five.

Over the first year of the Jospin government the Prime Minister's position was consolidated. President Chirac marked out the 'reserved domain', but as in previous 'cohabitations' this was slowly taken over by the government. To retain control of the 'reserved domain', President Chirac presented the incoming Socialists with an ultimatum: either accept the 'stability pact' (which the left had denounced) or face a constitutional crisis (*Libération* 10/6/95). Jospin chose to avoid an immediate crisis at the Amsterdam summit where the President's line prevailed. In the week after his election, Jospin reaffirmed a commitment to employment policies, in lieu of a more substantial change in European monetary policy. This manoeuvre caused no immediate difficulties for the coalition of the left, which was still basking it its surprise victory, and policy began to slip from the Elysée.

President Chirac's problems lay with his own conservative coalition which was shattered by its defeat in 1997. Gaullist politics became irremediably factional. Chirac's close associates even fell out over who was to be Mayor of Paris. Jacques Toubon challenged the sitting Mayor and Chirac's chosen successor, Jean Tiberi, who was tarred by scandals dating back to before he took the Mayor's post. President Chirac retained enough support amongst activists to block a complete takeover by the new team of Sarkozy and Séguin. Séguin wanted to use the RPR in a guerrilla war against the Socialist government, but this ran counter to the President's need for a workable 'cohabitation'. Séguin, who saw the Chiraquian Debré win the presidency of the RPR Assembly group (a sign that the Elysée was going to fight to regain control of the RPR), was also tempted to develop the attacks on Europe and the 'social fracture' which he had used in the 1995 presidential campaign on Chirac's behalf. These also ran foul of presidential needs for restraint under 'cohabitation'.

Regional elections in 1998 proved a moderate success for the government but the President's supporters disputed their attitude to take to the National Front, whose support would be needed to govern some regions (Perrineau and Ysmal 1999, pp. 125ff.). In this dispute the main damage was to the UDF which split. Madelin's party (PR, renamed 'Démocratie Libérale') broke from the UDF which left François Bayrou who had transformed the CDS into Force démocrate in charge. The conservative right was saved from the worst consequences of its fragmentation by a split, in the autumn of 1998, in the Front national itself, between followers of Le Pen and the ambitious Bruno Mégret. There were disputes about how to respond to the Front national's break up, and Chirac remained adamant that the Front national had to be isolated, while some UDF regional barons and some RPR figures, took the opposite view (Perrineau and Ysmal 1999, p. 163ff.).

Conclusion

President Chirac was not, personally, damaged by the disputes amongst conservative politicians nor by the criticisms of the government. On the contrary, his popularity climbed and his 'cohabitation' status was confirmed as the apolitical 'arbitrator' of French political life, criticising the government on occasion, and as he was doing what he did best, visiting the country – effectively campaigning for re-election. The Prime Minister also intended to run again for the Presidency when the opportunity arose (in 2002 if the timetable held), and a five-year legislative term implied a five-year presidential campaign. Polls in 1998, if anything could be made of them so far ahead of the elections themselves, indicated a possible second term for President Chirac (CSA *Le Parisien* 27/7/98). But in undertaking a second septennate Chirac risked the 'renécotisation' of the institution, the ending of the sovereign Presidency. There have been three Gaullists in the Elysée under the Fifth Republic. General de Gaulle constructed an heroic Presidency; Georges Pompidou showed how it could be made to work for an ordinary man; and Jacques Chirac showed that France could survive without an Executive President.

Conclusion

Fifth Republic politics is the politics of leadership. It is through creative leadership that the Presidency emerged as the focus of authority in the Fifth Republic. The Presidency has been able to provide the elusive ingredient of contemporary leadership, which (with the notable exception of Pierre Mendès France) the Fourth Republic had been unable to find. The 1997 'cohabitation' provides a good vantage point for making a preliminary assessment of the factors involved in presidential leadership. 'Cohabitation' in the first of the instances from 1986 to 1988 was necessarily conflictual and was a battle but it was not destructive of the institutions (Cohendet 1993). If it was not quite 'business as usual', the affairs of state were conducted in main part with firmness and decision, 'cohabitation' did not prevent initiative or movement. However, the initiative passed, by and large, to the Prime Minister and leadership was maintained.

Politics at the Top

There is in all politics a tension between the long-term and the short-term. 'Short-termism' is a continuing political temptation and its neglect may lead to long- or medium-term defeat. Long-term interests may sometimes be protected by short-term sacrifice but the politician who makes concessions may be open to attacks for 'selling out'. Presidential leadership has enabled the long-term view to be taken (though that depends on the President's capacity to do so) but that reflected the relative stability of presidential coalitions. However, there is no reason why setting long-term strategy has to be the President's role and it is not one ascribed to the institution of the Presidency. In other Western European systems this role would be exercised by the Prime Minister with a disciplined majority. However, the French Presidency does give politicians an advantageous position and they can use it to persuade the public that the national interest is served by seemingly unpopular or novel policies (Zorgbibe 1986).

But Presidents have also been tempted to favour outlooks and to adopt policies that entrench their leadership; consideration of personal power is an inevitable element of politics. Thus, the active foreign policy of the Fifth Republic and the European politics have centred on the institution of the Presidency and have enhanced its power, whatever the other 'national interest' calculations behind them. This does not mean that the Presidency made no mistakes or was always all-powerful; it means that the political balance almost always fell in the Presidency's favour until 'cohabitation' in 1986. But whereas that was not automatic, it was also a question of leadership and that is contingent. Because of the personal factor involved in the popular nature of the Presidency, it is difficult to separate the institutional from other influences. The first two 'cohabitations' were interludes (not termini) in presidential leadership; the outcome of the third remains uncertain.

The Leadership Factor

De Gaulle created the presidential régime and subsequent Presidents preserved or invigorated it. In this process the unavoidable key variable was leadership. A régime was instituted by the General and sustained by the use of political craft. Presidentialism is, to use an earlier distinction, a leadership by 'authority' depending on persuasion and not on command. Authority and power (the application of rules) are different and this distinction has to be kept in mind. This lack of power entails the continual establishment of authority through organising and maintaining political support and by using issues to throw opponents off balance. A whole repertoire of political manoeuvres is involved running from party politics, placements and campaigning to the manipulation of people and events. None of these in themselves is unique to French politics, or the Fifth Republic Presidency.

Presidents, like all politicians, work within a milieu which they do not control; although they can influence, they do not make the context which they find themselves in. However, politicians are not dependent variables. French presidential politics is a creative process and, in the Fifth Republic, is not simply reactive but is a shaping and ambitious agency. French Presidents have been 'transformational', leaders changing the situation and the outlook rather than reactive and they move society and their followers (Burns 1978, p. 19). De Gaulle can be recognised as the founding spirit in this sense, for he took a Presidency lacking in formal powers and made its own resources of power in a short time and changed the paradigm. Presidents Pompidou, Giscard d'Estaing and Mitterrand all built their own coalitions of support which they then maintained, or mended, and which gave them authority when they succeeded. Once again, the means were the political skills of the high-level politician. In turning to the problem of strategy and skills it is useful to use the comparative model of political leadership as developed by Erwin C. Hargrove for the study of the US Presidency; this model uses political categories and places individual characteristics within that larger context (Hargrove 1998 p. 36 ff.).

Context and Skill

Perhaps this relationship between the position in which leaders found themselves and creativity can be illustrated with the image of a billiard table (McCall and Lombardo 1978). A configuration on a billard table is the given: players have to work with what they find. That does not mean that every player will play the same configuration in the same way. Riker gives a preliminary exposition of how preferences, agendas and new policy dimensions can be discovered and used by the politician (Riker 1986). Players have different skills and different abilities to the extent that apparently hopeless positions can be transformed by skill and imagination. In 1958 de Gaulle inherited a situation of near civil war which even the most talented Fourth Republic politicians had been unable to resolve. De Gaulle transformed this situation of military uprising and despair into a personal triumph and established a new régime on the back of this unpromising beginning. It would be difficult to argue that any other politician could have effected the same transformation. Much the same could be said about de Gaulle's foreign and defence, policies which were stamped with his unique manner.

Politicians who move up the ladder thus find themselves in circumstances which they then use as they can. Presidents will exploit the opportunities available to them, but they may misjudge the situation, and they may not have the appropriate skills. They can also transform politics where they can intervene and exercise leadership. In the Fifth Republic, where thanks to de Gaulle, the Presidency is the dynamic institution, presidential skill is the principal lever on the political system. Where Presidents understand the context in which they find themselves and are able to work within it, they can engage in their politics and make their mark. This is not inevitable and can fail. An individual role therefore has to be mapped out and its components have to be understood. In other words the dimensions of political skill have to be compared to enable an appreciation of the President's role.

Personality and 'Persona'

Turning first to skill and strategy in context, this includes bargaining, manoeuvre and rhetoric, but also character. Character is not often thought of as a political skill, but it is a conscious construct, built around more profound personal resources. Of course, politicians in general have to have (or develop) certain psychological traits and the French Presidents have these in abundance. Thus they need to be able to withstand personal and injurious attacks and to persist despite counter campaigns (not, it is true, as unscrupulous as in the past) and they need to be able to overcome setbacks. They need reserves of nerve and stamina.

All the five Presidents of the Fifth Republic have shown this political character. De Gaulle was the original illustration of a presidential capacity for persistence. His political career was sidelined in the 1950s in conditions that lesser figures would have regarded as terminal. Although Giscard d'Estaing's career appears to be an exception, it was a golden one, he was evicted from government by de Gaulle in 1965 (accused of engineering an election-losing deflation) and found himself in the wilderness until the General was defeated in the 1969 referendum. Giscard never made it back to the Elysée after the defeat of 1981, but continued to work for a comeback when others might have been forced to retire. Other 'présidentiables' were even more greatly tested. Georges Pompidou's career was also one of steady ascension and a learning of the political ropes so that by the mid-1960s he was the next in line. However, he was brutally discarded after the Gaullist victory in the June 1968 general elections. While deprived of access to the Elysée, and the General's favour, he was subject to a whispering campaign and an 'affair' was used to implicate him (by association). Of Mitterrand it need only be noted that his career was almost destroyed by scandals on two occasions and before winning in 1981 his career seemed to be finished at least three times. Jacques Chirac faced a Dark Night of the Soul after the election defeat of 1988, a time when many politicians might well have renounced ambition.

But 'character' is a political advantage to the 'présidentiable' as well as being part of an 'image' which is designed for political purposes. Personality traits are developed by leaders for political purpose: individuality is emphasised. Where they are purely presentational they tend to be unconvincing. De Gaulle, as Lacouture makes clear, had a long apprenticeship for leadership in which he combined elements of political theory from a variety of French sources (Lacouture 1984, Vol. I). One small example is that de Gaulle gave up smoking because it did not fit with his notion of what leadership comportment should be like.

In the case of Georges Pompidou the self-presentation was of a practical person called to assume the destiny of the Republic. Georges Pompidou's unassuming but commanding personality had some success before he fell ill. The oil crisis caused economic turbulence in the mid-1970s but Giscard d'Estaing had more 'modernistic' ambitions. He, perhaps like President Kennedy in the USA, sought to embody the new France of the technocratic middle class in power. Giscard's reputation for economic competence (and 'a head for figures') was a feature of the 1974 campaign as was his youthful family. Giscard at first made great play of his meritocratic credentials and did seem to embody the new class in the Fifth Republic despite his aristocratic demeanour. However, as the septennate progressed, the demotic gave way to the aristocratic (at least in public perception) and the style was resented (Martinet 1973).

François Mitterrand is the most ambiguous of the five Presidents. His political persona was difficult to identify and crossed categories. President Mitterrand was not, by the end of his political career, regarded in a good light by the public and contributed to the difficulties of maintaining standards of public life. There were several incidents in his past which he found it difficult to explain, and at the end of the double septennate, the suicides of former Prime Minister Bérégovoy and of aide François de Grossouvre as well as other revelations tarnished his image. Giscard's septennate ended on a sour note with the 'affair of the diamonds' presented to the first family by the Dictator Bokassa for which the President never found a convincing *public* explanation. Probity in political leaders is demanded by public opinion.

'Corruption, conspiracy and treason are seen everywhere and is exploited by oppositions (including, and especially, the extreme right) (Williams 1970, p. 3). In 1980–1 it was the Socialist Party's candidate, Mitterrand, railing against the 'argent facile'. He presented himself as unsullied and attacked the President (as did some Gaullists) and declared himself adamantly opposed to the 'Etat-RPR' (Gaetner 1992). In 1988 it was the conservative parties which exploited scandals but these only began to bite effectively after they had lost power in 1988. A succession of scandals has dogged 'présidentiables': including the neo-Gaullist Jacques Chirac and then in the first years of the Juppé government other ministers were touched (including Juppé himself) (Clamecy 1997). Lionel Jospin marked, by his personality and demeanour, a contrast to the 'affairisme' of the recent past but it may be too soon to say that the 'breach opened in people's confidence has been repaired'.

Personal integrity is a political resource. Personality is part of strategic leadership, which gives society and parties their sense of direction. Personality is part of the communication of strategic leadership. This factor in the modern Republic has an impact on personnel, party members and the voters. 'Présidentiables' in the Fifth Republic attract an entourage, or group of associates. This entourage is important to the style of the Fifth Republic as they are located (characteristically) outside the party network, although overlapping with it, and they are often then staff of the private office. Here, however, is the importance of what McAlpine calls 'the Idea', the philosophy on which actions of the leader are based. It is the power of the Idea which attracts followers (McAlpine 1992).

Political Culture

It is in 'cultural leadership' where the politician comes into their own. Tucker refers to this as endowing a set of circumstances with meaning in a way which relates to other peoples' aims and concerns (Tucker 1981, p. 16). This is the heart of presidential politics as understood. A 'présidentiable' is a politician who can define problems, or formulate solutions and convince people of their applicability. This is difficult and the two sides are rarely brought together. Technical solutions developed by policy makers, think tanks, charities, freelancers and so on, are widely touted, but they can remain in ivory towers if they are not given political effect. On the other hand the ability to pilot solutions through pressure groups, parties, legislators, committees, bureaucrats and public opinion is rarely joined to the invention of solutions. Joined together, the politician's talent is to bring solutions to attention and see them through into action. This end result will rarely be perfect (or an ideal type), but the approximation to the solution with the support of the public is the political aspect. Politics is about engineering consent, but in an active not passive way: listening to problems and proposing and promoting appropriate solutions.

This 'cultural leadership' is not superficial, short-term, 'quick fix' politics or the easy way out. French politicians have been made 'présidentiables' by showing the route. In 1958 de Gaulle moved the country to the acceptance of Algerian independence and took the Army with him on the changed course. More prosaically, perhaps, Raymond Barre introduced the economics of deflation and the strong Franc in 1976 and kept to that course until the 1981 elections. In 1981 Mitterrand won the presidential and general elections on the promise of an 'alternative' economic strategy, but in 1983 the government realigned itself on the policy lines the Barre government had tried. After that U-turn, President

Mitterrand and the government sought to persuade the public (and the left) that the route was the right one. In this they were largely successful.

Culture also provides the basis for the development of the presidential purpose. De Gaulle's invoking of the millennial tradition of 'France' in the first page of the memoirs and then situating himself in that, is exemplary. De Gaulle's careful identification of himself with France and the Republic is well known and widely accepted in its implications (even today) in most parts of the political scene. 'Cultural stories', to use E.C. Hargrove's term, make sense of the society and its contemporary situation in terms of the past and point ways to the future. A nice balance is required. Political leaders must find a way of reconciling decisive action with calculation and caution. Mistakes can be made, and leaders are never infallible, but the art is to recognise the attainable.

Hence cultural leadership is the defining of purpose for the society and the Fifth Republic Presidency has provided that direction in an effective way. French political culture is one of the richest and most contradictory in Western Europe and there are many sources a President can draw on. Where the Fourth Republic had purpose (notably in Europe) but seemed to drift, the Fifth Republic's achievement through the Presidency has been to provide leadership direction. As President Bush might say, the 'vision thing' is characteristic of Fifth Republic France. This has failed on two occasions. When President Georges Pompidou was ill, in 1973-4, the Republic seemed to drift in the face of immense problems. To some extent Pomidou's foreign policy closed the gap but drift remained a problem until Giscard d'Estaing was elected in 1974. In 1995, as mentioned, Jacques Chirac was elected but then turned on the campaign promises and ditched the 'alternative' policy in favour of a return to austerity. This was badly explained and poorly managed. As a result his Presidency never recovered and his party suffered defeat in the general elections of 1997. Jacques Chirac's setback in 1997 is a reminder of how delicate this judgement is and how leadership depends on a successful communication of political direction.

Teaching Reality

Politicians must try to 'teach reality': they need to explicate problems to a discerning public alive to chicane. Presidential politics has, from the outset, brought a message and the public has listened when the President speaks with authority. Presidents are expected to give some account of France and of its place in the world. Presidents of the Fifth Republic have tried to make this 'bully pulpit' work for them in foreign policy. All

President's have 'taught' but the most famous of these is de Gaulle who also started the concentration on the international role of the Presidency. De Gaulle, however, used his own position to present France to itself as a rival to the superpowers (or at least in the same league) writing out the Vichy period in French history. Neither of these were 'teaching reality' as outsiders saw it. Keeping the Vichy period out of the public debates enabled a short-term reconciliation (and accorded with what Communists and others wanted) but left problems of collaboration unsolved.

President Pompidou's well-known caution was employed in returning France to the more mainstream positions of the Fourth Republic: European integration politics and the Atlantic Alliance. There is no way of knowing how this would have evolved had Pompidou's life not been cut short by illness. President Giscard, however, continued this evolution and promoted both the integration process with Chancellor Schmidt of Germany and the solidity of the Atlantic Alliance (in promoting, along with James Callaghan and Helmut Schmidt) the deployment of 'Euromissiles'. President Giscard was held back by the electoral weight of the Gaullist Party from proceeding as far as he might have desired and placed excessive emphasis on the 'special relationship' with the Eastern Soviet bloc. Giscard was punished at the polls in 1981 for both of these miscalculations. As President, Giscard did, however, begin to turn France away from the idea that it had a privileged status as an economy and towards a free market approach. This, at a time when the oil crisis was causing the first hardships in Western Europe, was courageous and was initially supported by the public at the polls.

President Mitterrand inherited the domestic crisis which Giscard's France had undergone and promised an alternative route to the 'competitive deflation' which Giscard had practised. This reflation was in tatters after two years and abandoned after three. In foreign policy the left's President was more prescient and brought the Socialist Party behind the French deterrent (the Communists already supported it) and the cause of European integration was already theirs. President Mitterrand's ideas on foreign politics were mainly conservative. Thus perhaps the Presidency could have brought the new situation of post-Wall Europe to public attention and explicated it. As it was the President concentrated action on the Western part of the continent, to keeping Germany in the same framework and bind it to the West. Nobody had their bearings in Europe newly liberated from Communism and Mitterrand was, in this, like others.

There is one other place where President Mitterrand could be said to have practised a historic pedagogy in action: showing the problems of the reflation as a simple antidote to French economic problems. The left espoused reflation for the first two years of the septennate. It had, it could be argued (though not by the Rocardians), to be tried and found wanting rather than not tried at all. There is a long socialist tradition on the French left which, as candidate Mitterrand chose to use rather than to challenge and it was a squatting presence during the early years of the septennate. On the left, the coalition never really recovered from the abandonment of the policy and the President's party, the Parti socialiste, was not wholly convinced of the new direction. It could be put to the President's credit that the left's old nostrums had been abandoned by the time he finished the double septennate. On the other hand it would have been better never to have encouraged them to pursue a chimera (Halimi 1993).

Of President Chirac's style of 'teaching reality' much has been said. As candidate, Jacques Chirac adopted a bewildering number of positions and outlooks. There were 'neo-Labourism', 'Reaganism', anti-Europeanism, reflation, deflation, regulation, deregulation, welfare reform and conservatism about the welfare state. Contradictions were evident in the presidential election which he won in 1995. During the campaign contrary messages were sent out: tax cuts and wage rises. One message was of a free market drive and the other held out promises of a 'Republican' (welfare/Keynesian) and Eurosceptical policy. It was through the contradictory policies that candidate Chirac became President. In the main, expectations were of a more left-leaning policy under the new President. However, hopes were dashed within weeks of his election and the Chirac Presidency never recovered from this volte face (comparable in effect to George Bush's election promise that there would be 'no new taxes'). No explanation was given, and possibly it could not have been. Jacques Chirac's Presidency failed the test of 'teaching reality' for most voters before the end of the first year. The fifth President suffered from being unable to indicate a clear route. This is not the same thing as 'demagogic' politics (teaching 'voodoo economics', for example), but in its inability to relate politics to life it was not 'presidential'

Continuation of Leadership

The Fifth Republic remained the 'leadership Republic' after the 1997 general elections and the rout of the President's supporters. Leadership, the prerogative of the right in the early years and then of Mitterrand, again changed hands: the President presided and the Prime Minister led. French politics was not, however, returned to the *immobilisme* or chaotic lack of authority of the Fourth Republic. However by 1997, the Fifth Republic, resembled Mendès France's 'modern Republic' more than it did the Gaullist enterprise. Fifth Republic politics has shown from both the left and the right that determined and resourceful leadership can build strong political positions for the Prime Minister. Mendès France, as Prime Minister of the Fourth Republic (in more dramatic and difficult circumstances) showed that a leadership position could be built. In 1997, this task fell to Prime Minister Jospin. Teaching reality, of which Mendès France was the master, was a skill learnt by the left and, over the years, lost by the right.

Bibliography

Books:

Alia, J. and Clerc C., *La Guerre de Mitterrand*, Paris: Orban, 1991.

Alexandre, P., *Le Duel Pompidou-de Gaulle*, Paris: Grasset, 1970.

Amouroux, H., *Monsieur Barre*, Paris: R. Laffont, 1986.

Amson, D., *La cohabitation politique en France: la règle des deux*, Paris: Presses Universitaires de France, 1985.

Anderson, M., *Government in France*, Oxford: Pergamon, 1970.

Andrews, W.G., *Presidential Government in Gaullist France*, Albany: SUNY Press, 1992.

Angeli, C. and Mesnier S., *Sale temps pour la République: 1995–1997*, Paris: Grasset, 1997.

Ardant, P., *Le Premier Ministre en France*, Paris: Monchrestien, 1991.

Aron, R., *L'Algérie et la République*, Paris: Plon, 1958.

Aron, R., *The Great Debate: Theories of Nuclear Strategy*, New York: Doubleday, 1965.

Aron, R., *La Révolution introuvable*, Paris: Fayard, 1968.

Aron, R., *Memoirs: Fifty Years of Political Reflection*, London: Holmes and Meier, 1990.

Arter, D., *The Politics of European Integration in the Twentieth Century*, Aldershot: Gower, 1993.

Attali, J., *Verbatim*, Paris: Fayard, Vol I, 1993, Vol II, 1994, Vol III, 1995 and Vol IV, 1995.

Auriol, V., *Journal du septennat, 1947–1954*, Paris: A. Colin, 1970.

de Bacque, F., *Qui gouverne la France?*, Paris: Flammarion, 1986.

Bacqué, R. and Saverot, D., *Chirac président*, Paris: du Rocher, 1995.

Balladur, E., *L'Arbre de mai*, Paris: Marcel Jullian, 1979.

Balladur, E., *Passion et longueur du temps*, Paris: Fayard, 1989.

Balladur, E., *Deux ans à Matignon*, Paris: Plon, 1995.

Baudoin, D., *Dans les allées du pouvoir*, Paris: J.-C. Lattès, 1990.

Bartoli, M., et alia *Giscard: le destin de la crise*, Grenoble: Presses Universitaires de Grenoble, 1981.

Bell, J.S., *French Constitutional Law,* Oxford: Oxford University Press, 1992.

Beloff, N., *The General Says No,* London: Penguin, 1963

Benamou, G.-M., *Le dernier Mitterrand,* Paris: Plon, 1997.

Biffaud, O. and Maudit, L., *La Grande Méprise,* Paris: Grasset, 1996.

Blondel, J., *Comparative Government,* London: Macmillan, 1970.

Bothorel, J., *Le Pharaon: Histoire du septennat giscardien,* Paris: Grasset, 1983.

Bothorel, J., *Un si jeune président,* Paris: Grasset, 1997.

Braudel, F. and Labrousse, E., *Histoire économique et sociale de la France,* Vol. 3, Paris: PUF, 1982.

Brisard, J.-C. and Pinard P., *Enquête au cœur du RPR,* Paris: Trancher, 1996.

Bruno, P., *La Saga de Giscard,* Paris: Ramsay, 1980.

Burns, J.M., *Leadership,* New York: Harper and Row, 1978.

Buron, R., *Carnets politiques de la guerre d'Algérie,* Paris: Plon, 1975.

Butler, D. and Ranney, A. (eds), *Referendums,* Washington DC AEI, 1978.

Capdevielle, J. and Moriaux, R., *Mai 68. L'entre-deux de la modernité. Histoire de trente ans,* Paris: Fondation nationale de sciences politiques, 1988.

Carcassonne, G., *La Constitution,* Paris: Seuil, 1996.

Cazenave, M. and Germain-Thomas, O. (eds), *Charles de Gaulle,* Paris: L'Herne, 1973.

Cerny, P.G., *The Politics of Grandeur,* Cambridge CUP, 1980.

Chaban-Delmas, J., *L'ardeur,* Paris: Stock, 1975.

Chaban-Delmas, J., *Mémoirs pour demain,* Paris: Flammarion, 1997.

Chagnollaud, D. (ed.), *La vie politique en France,* Paris: Seuil, 1993.

Chagnollaud, D. and Quermonne, J.-L., *Le gouvernement de la France sous la Ve République,* Paris: Fayard, 1996.

Chantebout, B., *La Constitution française,* Paris: Dalloz, 1992.

Charbonnel, J., *L'Aventure de la fidélité,* Paris: Seuil, 1976.

Charlot, J., *The Gaullist Phenomenon,* London: Allen and Unwin, 1971.

Charlot, J., *Pourquoi Jacques Chirac,* Paris: de Fallois, 1995.

Clamecy, C., *"Cher Alain",* Paris: Plon, 1997.

Cohen, P., *Le Bluff républicain,* Paris: Arléa, 1997.

Cohen, S. and Smouts, M.-C., *La Politique Extérieur de Valéry Giscard d'Estaing,* Paris: Fondation nationale de science politiques, 1985.

Cohen, S., *La monarchie nucléaire,* Paris: Hachette, 1986.

Cohendet, M.-A., *La cohabitation: leçons d'une expérience,* Paris: Presses universitaires de France, 1993.

Cole, A., *François Mitterrand,* London: Routledge, 1994.

Colliard, S., *La Campagne présidentielle de François Mitterrand en 1974,* Paris: PUF, 1975.

Colombani, J.-M., *Le Marriage blanc,* Paris: Grasset, 1986.

Colombani, J.-M. and Portelli, H., *Le Double septennat de François Mitterrand,* Paris: Grasset, 1995.

Colombani, J.-M., *Portrait du Président,* Paris: Gallimard, 1995.

Conac, G. and Luchaire, F., *La Consitution de la République Française,* Paris: Economica, 1987.

Conan, E. and Rousso, H., *Vichy, un passé qui ne passe pas,* Paris: Gallimard, 1994.

Constitutional Consultative Committee, *Travaux préparatoires de la Constitution, Avis et débats du comité consultatif constitutionnel* Paris: La Documentation française, 1960.

Cotteret, J.-M. and Moreau, R., *Récherche sur le vocabulaire du général de Gaulle,* Paris: Armand Colin, 1969.

Cotteret, J.-M., *Gouverner c'est paraître,* Paris: Presses universitaires de France, 1991.

Coudurier, H., *Le Monde selon Chirac: Les coulisses de la diplomatie française,* Paris: Calmann-Levy, 1998.

Courtois, S. and Lazar, M., *Histoire du Parti communiste français,* Paris: PUF, 1995.

Couste, P.-B. and Visine, F., *Pompidou et l'Europe,* Paris: Librairies techniques, 1974.

Dansette, A., *Histoire des Présidents de la République,* Paris: Le Livre contemporain, 1960.

Dansette, A., *Mai 1968,* Paris: Plon, 1971.

Debbasch, C., *La France de Pompidou,* Paris: Presses Universitaires de France, 1974.

Debré, M., *Entretiens avec Georges Pompidou,* Paris: A. Michel, 1996.

Decaumont, F., *La Présidence de Georges Pompidou,* Paris: Economia, 1979.

DePorte, A.W., *Europe between the Super-powers,* London: Yale, 1979.

Derfler, L., *President and Parliament,* Boca Raton: Florida Atlantic University Press, 1983.

De Tarr, F., *The French Radical Party from Herriot to Mendès France,* Oxford: OUP, 1993.

Domenach, N. and Szafran, M., *De si bons amis,* Paris: Plon, 1994.

Dreyfus, F.-G., *De Gaulle et le Gaullisme,* Paris: PUF, 1982.

Droz, B. and Lever, E., *Historie de la guerre d'Algérie,* Paris: Seuil, 1982.

Duhamel, A., *La République giscardienne: Anatomie politique de la France,* Paris: Grasset, 1980.

Duhamel, A., *De Gaulle-Mitterrand. la Marque et la Trace,* Paris: Flammarion, 1991.

Duhamel, O., *La Gauche et La Ve République,* Paris: PUF, 1980.

Duhamel, O. and Parodi, J.-L., (eds), *La Constitution de la Cinquième République,* Paris: Fondation nationale de science politiques, 1985.

Duhamel, O. and Jaffré, J., (eds), *SOFRES. L'Etat de l'opinion 1991,* Paris: Seuil, 1992.

Dupin, E., *L'Après Mitterrand,* Paris: Calmann-Lévy, 1991.

Duroselle, J.-B., *Clemenceau,* Paris: Fayard, 1988.

Duverger, M. (ed.), *Les régimes semi-présidentiels,* Paris: Presses universitaires de France, 1986.

Duverger, M., *Le système politique français,* Paris: Presses universitaires de France, 1996.

Elgie, R., *Political Leadership in Western Democracies,* London: Macmillan, 1995.

Esembert, B., *Pompidou, Capitaine des industries,* Paris: Odile Jacob, 1994.

Fabre-Luce, A., *Les cent premiers jours de Giscard,* Paris: Laffont, 1974

Fauvet, J., *La IVe République,* Paris: Poche, 1971.

Favier, P. and Martin-Rolland, M., *La décennie Mitterrand,* Paris: Fayard, Vol I 1981–1984,

1990; Vol II, 1984–1988, 1991; and Vol. III, 1988–1991, 1996.

Flohic, F., *Souvenirs d'outre de Gaulle,* Paris: Plon, 1979.

Foccart, J., *Journal de l'Elysée III, 1969–71,* Paris: Fayard, 1999.

Fontaine, F., *Un seul lit pour deux rêves,* Paris: Fayard, 1982.

François, B., *Naissance d'une constitution,* Paris: Fondation nationale de science politiques, 1996.

Frears, J., *Parties and Voters in France,* London: Hurst, 1991.

Frears, J., *France in the Giscard Presidency,* London: Unwin, 1981.

Friend, J. W., *The Long Presidency,* Oxford: Westview, 1998

Gaetner, G., *L'Argent facile,* Paris: Stock, 1992.

Gaffney, J., *The French Left and the Fifth Republic,* London: Macmillan, 1989.

Gaïti, B., *De Gaulle, prophète de la Ve République,* Paris: Presses de Sciences-politiques, 1998.

de Gaulle, Ch., *Le fil de l'épée et autres écrits,* Paris: Plon, 1990.

de Gaulle, Ch., *Discours et Messages,* Paris: Plon, 1970 Five Volumes,.

Gerth, H. H. and Wright Mills, C., *From Max Weber,* London: Routledge, 1947.

Giesbert, F.-O., *Jacques Chirac,* Paris: Seuil, 1987.

Giesbert, F.-O., *François Mitterrand, une vie,* Paris: Seuil, 1996.

Bibliography

Giscard d'Estaing, V., *Démocratie française*, Paris: Fayard, 1976.

Giscard d'Estaing, V., *Deux Français sur trois*, Paris: Flammarion, 1984.

Giscard d'Estaing, V., *Le Pouvoir et la vie*, Volume One: *La Rencontre* 1988; Volume Two *L'Affrontement*, 1991; Paris: Hachette.

Gladwyn, Lord, *De Gaulle's Europe or why the General says No*, London: Secker, 1969.

Goguel, F., *Chroniques électorales*, Vol III Paris: FNSP, 1983.

Gordon, P.H., *A Certain Idea of France: French Security Policy and the Gaullist Legacy*, Princeton NJ: Princeton University Press, 1993.

Grimal, H., *La décolonisation*, Paris: A. Colin, 1965.

Grimaud, M., *En mai fais ce qu'il te plaît*, Paris: Stock, 1977.

Grosser, A., *Affaires Extérieures*, Paris: Flammarion, 1984.

Guichard, O., *Mon Général*, Paris: Grasset, 1980.

Guillemin, H., *Le Général clair-obscur*, Paris: Le Seuil, 1984.

Habert, P., Perrineau, P. and Ysmal, C. (eds), *Le vote Sanction* Paris: FNSP, 1993.

Halimi, S., *Sisyphe est fatigué*, Paris: Laffont, 1993.

Hanley, D. and Kerr, A.P. *May '68*, London: Macmillan, 1989.

Hargreaves, A.G., *Immigration, 'race' and ethnicity in contemporary France*, London: Routledge, 1995.

Hargrove, E.C., *The President as Leader: Appealing to the Better Angels of Our Nature*, Lawrence: University of Kansas Press, 1998.

Hargrove, E.C. *Presidential Leadership, Personality and Political Style*, New York: Macmillan, 1966.

Harrison, M. (ed.), *French Politics*, Lexington: D.C. Heath, 1969.

Hartley, A., *Gaullisme*, London: Routledge, 1972.

Hausser, A., *Sarkozy*, Paris: Belfond, 1995.

Hayward, J. (ed.), *De Gaulle to Mitterrand*, London: Hurst, 1993.

Hervé, H. and Rotman, P., *L'Effet Rocard*, Paris: Stock, 1988.

Hincker, F., *Le Parti communiste au carrefour*, Paris: Albin Michel, 1981.

Hoffmann, S. and Ross, G., *L'Expérience Mitterrand*, Paris: Presses Universitaires de France, 1988.

Hollifield, J.F. and Ross, G., *Searching for the New France*, London: Routledge, 1991.

Horne, A., *A Savage War of Peace: Algeria 1954–1962*, London: Macmillan, 1977.

IFOP, *Les français et de Gaulle*, Paris: Plon, 1970.

Jarreau, P., *Chirac, la malédiction*, Paris: Stock, 1997.

Jeambar, D., *Un secret d'Etat*, Paris: O. Jacob, 1997.

Jeanneney, J.-M., *Pour un nouveau protectionisme*, Paris: Le Seuil, 1978.

Jeanneney, J.-N., *L'Arget caché*, Paris: Fayard, 1981.

Jobert, M., *Mémoirs d'avenir*, Paris: Grasset, 1974.

Joly, D., *The French Communist Party and the Algerian War*, London: Macmillan, 1991.

Jospin, L., *Invention du Possible*, Paris: Flammarion, 1991.

July, S. (ed.), *Histoire secrèt de la dissolution*, Paris: Plon, 1997.

Keohane, R.O. and Nye, J.S., *France After the Cold War*, Cambridge Ma: Harvard University Press, 1993.

Kitzinger, U., *Diplomacy and Persuasion*, London: Thames and Hudson, 1973.

Knapp, A.F., *Gaullism since de Gaulle*, Aldershot: Dartmouth, 1994.

Lacouture, J., *De Gaulle* Vol. 1 *Le rebelle*, 1984; Vol. 2 *Le politique*, 1985; Vol. 3. *Le souverain*, 1986; Paris: Le Seuil,.

Lacouture, J., *Mitterrand: Une Histoire de Français*, Two Volumes, Paris: Seuil, 1998.

Lagroye, J. and Lacroix, B. (eds), *Le Président de la République*, Paris: Fondation nationale de science politiques, 1992.

LeGall, J., *Les institutions de la Ve République à l'épreuve de l'alternance*, Paris: LGDS, 1997.

Lequesne, C., *Paris-Bruxelles: Comment se fait la politique européenne de la France*, Paris: Fondation nationale de science politiques,1994.

Liégeois, P. and Bédéi J.-P., *Le feu et l'eau, Mitterrand-Rocard*, Paris: Grasset, 1990.

Machiavelli, N., *The Prince*, Harmondsworth: Penguin, 1961.

Maillard, P., *De Gaulle et l'Europe entre la nation et Maastricht*, Paris: Tallandier, 1995.

Mano, G. and Birnbaum G., *La défaite impossible*, Paris: Ramsay, 1997.

Marchesin, P., *Mitterrand et l'Afrique*, Paris: Karthala, 1995.

Martinet, G., *Le Système Pompidou*, Paris: Seuil, 1973.

Massot, J., *Chef d'Etat et chef du gouvernment*, Paris: La Documentation française, 1993.

Massot, J., *L'arbitre et le capitaine*, Paris: Flammarion, 1987.

Massu, J., *Baden '68*, Paris: Plon, 1983.

Maus, D., *Les grands textes de la pratique institutionelle de la Ve République*, Paris : La Documentation française, 1985.

McAlpine, A., *The Servant*, London: Faber, 1992.

McCall, M.W. and Lombardo, M.M. (eds), *Leadership*, Durham NC: Duke University, 1978.

Mény, Y., *Le Système politique français*, Paris: Montchrestien, 1991.

Bibliography

Mény, Y., *La Corruption de la République*, Paris: Fayard, 1992.

Milward, A., *The Reconstruction of Western Europe 1945–51*, London: Methuen, 1984.

Mitterrand, F., *Le coup d'etat permanent*, Paris: Plon, 1964.

Mitterrand, F., *Politique I*, 1977; and *Politique II*, 1981; Paris: Fayard,.

Mitterrand, F., *De l'Allemagne et la France*, Paris: O. Jacob, 1996.

Mollet, G., *Quinze ans après . . .*, Paris: Albin Michel, 1973.

Montaldo, J., *Lettre ouverte*, Paris: Albin Michel, 1993.

Montaldo, J., *Lettre ouverte . . .*, Paris: Albin Michel, 1993.

Muron, L., *Pompidou*, Paris: Flammarion, 1994.

Nay, C., *Les sept Mitterrand*, Paris: Grasset, 1988.

Nay, C., *La double méprise*, Paris: Grasset, 1980.

Neustadt, R. E., *Presidential Power*, New York: Signet, 1964.

Newhouse, J., *Collision in Brussels: The Common Market Crisis of 30 June 1965*, London: Faber, 1967.

Newhouse, J., *De Gaulle and the Anglo-Saxons*, London: Deutsch, 1970.

Northcutt, W., *Mitterrand: A Political Biography*, London: Holmes and Meier, 1992.

O'Ballance, E., *The Algerian Insurrection, 1954–1962*, London: Faber, 1967.

Ottenheimer, G., *Le Fiasco*, Paris: Albin Michel, 1996.

Pac, H., *Le droit de la défence nucléaire*, Paris: Presses universitaires de France, 1989.

Paxton, R.O., *De Gaulle and the United States: A Centennial Reappraisal*, Oxford: Berg, 1994.

Péan, P., *La Menace*, Paris: Fayard, 1987.

Péan, P., *Une jeunesse française*, Paris: Fayard, 1994.

Pearce, E., *Machiavelli's Children*, London: Gollancz, 1993.

Perrineau, P. and Ysmal, C. (eds), *Le Vote de crise*, Paris: FNSP, 1995.

Perrineau, P. and Ysmal, C. (eds), *Le vote surprise*, Paris: FNSP, 1998.

Perrineau, P. and Ysmal, C. (eds), *Le vote incertain*, Paris: FNSP, 1999.

Petitfils, J.C., *La Démocratie giscardienne*, Paris: PUF, 1981.

Petitfils, J.C., *Le gaullisme*, Paris: PUF, 1986.

Peyrefitte, A., *Le mal français*, Paris: Plon, 1976.

Peyrefitte, A., *C'était de Gaulle*, Paris: Fayard, 1994 Vol I 1994 and Vol 2 1997.

Pfister, T., *La vie quotidienne* à *Matignon au temps de l'Union de la gauche*, Paris: Hachette, 1985.

Pickles, D., *Problems in Contemporary French Politics*, London: Methuen, 1982.

Pisani-Ferry, F., *Le coup d'état manqué du 16 mai 1877*, Paris: Robert Laffont, 1965.

Plenel, E. and Rolant, A., *L'effet Le Pen* Paris: La Découvert, 1984.

Poincaré, R., *How France is Governed*, London: T. Fisher Unwin, 1919.

Pompidou, G., *Pour rétablir une vérité*, Paris: Flammarion, 1982.

Pompidou, G., *Le Nœud gordien*, Paris: Plon, 1982.

Poniatowski, M., *Cartes sur table*, Paris: Fayard, 1972.

Posner, C., *Reflections on the Revolution in France: 1968*, London: Penguin, 1970.

Posner, T.R., *Current French Security Policy*, Westport Conn.: Greenwood, 1991.

Quermonne, J.-L., *L'Alternance au pouvoir*, Paris: Presses Universitaires de France, 1995.

Raimond, J.-B., *Le Quai d'Orsay à l'Epreuve de la cohabitation*, Paris: Flammarion, 1989.

Revel, J.-F., *Le Style du Général*, Paris: Julliard, 1959.

Rials, S., *Les idées politiques de Georges Pompidou*, Paris: Presses Universitaires de France, 1977.

Rials, S., *Le Premier Ministre*, Paris: PUF, 1985.

Riker, W.H., *The Art of Political Manipulation*, London: Harvard University Press, 1986.

Rousseau, D., *Droit Constitutionnel et Institutions Politiques de la Ve République*, Eyrolles: Unité, 1991.

Roussel, E., *Georges Pompidou*, Paris: J.-C. Lattès, 1984.

Rudelle, O., *Mai 58: De Gaulle et la République*, Paris: Plon, 1988.

Rustow, D., *A World of Nations*, Washington: Brookings, 1967.

Sadoun, M. et alia (eds), *La Politique sociale du Général de Gaulle*, Lille: Centre d'Histoire, 1989.

Schemla, E., *Edith Cresson*, Paris: Flammarion, 1993.

Schneider, R., *La Haine tranquille*, Paris: Seuil, 1992.

Servent, J.P., *Oedipe à Matignon: le complexe du Premier Ministre*, Paris: Balland, 1988.

Shawcross, W., *Sideshow*, London: André Deutsch, 1979.

Sidey, H., *A Very Personal Presidency*, New York: Atheneum, 1968.

Simonian, H., *The Privileged Partnership*, Oxford: OUP, 1985.

Skowronek, S., *The Politics Presidents make, Leadership from John Adams to George Bush*, Cambridge Mass.: Belknap Press of Harvard University Press, 1993.

SOFRES, *L'Etat de l'opinion 1988*, Paris: Seuil, 1988.

SOFRES, *L'Etat de l'opinion 1992*, Paris: Seuil, 1992.

Soutra, G.-H., *L'Alliance incertaine: Les rapports politico-stratégique franco-allemands, 1954–1996*, Paris: Plon, 1997.

Stoleru, L., *L'impératif industriel*, Paris: Seuil, 1969.

Bibliography

Suleiman, E.N. (ed.), *Presidents and Prime Ministers,* Washington: American Enterprise Institute, 1980.

Taber, R., *The War of the Flea,* London: Palladin, 1970.

Tanzer, N., *La face cachée du gaullisme,* Paris: Hachette, 1998.

Touchard, J., *Le Gaullisme 1940–1969,* Paris: Le Seuil, 1978.

Tournoux, J.-R., *Le mois de mai du Général,* Paris: Plon, 1969.

Tucker, R.C., *Politics as Leadership,* Columbia : University of Missouri, 1981.

Vainsson-Ponté, P., *Historie de la République gaulienne,* Paris: Fayard, 1970.

Vainsson-Ponté, P., *The King and his Court,* New York: Houghton Mifflin, 1964.

Vaisse, M., *La Grandeur,* Paris: Fayard, 1998.

Vedel, G. et alia (eds), *La contribution à la présidence de Georges Pompidou à la Ve République,* Paris: Montchrestien, 1994.

Védrine, H., *Les Mondes de François Mitterrand. A l'Elysée 1981–95,* Paris: Fayard, 1996.

Vidal-Naquet, P., *La Torture dans la République*, Paris: Minuit, 1958.

Wahl, N. and Quermonne, J.-L., *La France Présidentielle,* Paris: Fondation national des sciences politiques, 1995.

Wauthier, C., *Quatre Présidents et l'Afrique,* Paris: Seuil, 1995.

Williams, C., *The Last Great Frenchman,* London: Little, Brown and Co., 1993.

Williams, P.M., *Crisis and Compromise,* London: Longman, 1964.

Williams, P.M., *The French Parliament, 1958–1967*, London: Allen and Unwin, 1968.

Williams, P.M., a, *Wars, Plots and Scandals in Post-War France,* Cambridge: CUP, 1970.

Williams, P.M., b, *French Politicians and Elections 1951–1969,* Cambridge: CUP, 1970.

Williams, P.M. and Harrison, M., *Politics and Society in de Gaulle's Republic,* London: Longman, 1971.

Willis, F.R., *France, Germany and the New Europe,* London: OUP, 1968.

Wolf-Phillips, L., *Comparative Constitutions,* London: Macmillan, 1972.

Young, J. W., *Britain and European Unity, 1945–1992* London: Macmillan, 1993.

Zarka, J.-C., *Fonction présidentielle et problématique majorité présidentielle/ majorité parlementaire sous la Ve République*, Paris: LGDS, 1992.

Zorgbibe, C., *De Gaulle, Mitterrand et l'Esprit de la Constitution,* Paris: Hachette, 1993.

Zorgbibe, C., *Le Chef d'Etat en question,* Paris: Economia, 1986.

Articles:

Ardant, P., 'Le contenu des Constitutions: variables et constantes', *Pouvoirs* No. 50 1989 pp. 31–43.

Ardant, P., 'L'Article 5 et la fonction présidentielle', *Pouvoirs* No 41 1987 May, pp. 37–52.

Aron, R., 'L'Etat et les partis, sur le discours du général de Gaulle à Bayeux', *Commentaire* No. 41 1988 Spring, pp. 200–2.

Aron, R., 'Murrassisme et gaullisme', *Commentaire* No. 68 1994–95 Winter, pp. 927–8.

Avril, P., 'Fin de la constitution gaulliste?', *Esprit* Vol. 12 3/4, 1988 March–April, pp. 39–49.

Badache, D., 'Les positions institutionnelles des gaullistes depuis 1959', *Revue française de science politique* Vol. 34 4–5, 1984 July–August, pp. 544–62.

Barman, T., 'Behind the Brussels Breakdown', *International Affairs* Vol. 39 3, 1963 July, pp. 360–71.

Bénéton, P. and Touchard, J., 'Les interprétations de la crise de mai–juin 1968', *Revue française de science politique* Vol. 20 3, 1970 June, pp. 503–44.

Birnbaum, G., 'L'échec du système d'action barriste', *Revue française de science politique* Vol. 40 6, 1990 December, pp. 777–92.

Bon, F., 'Le référendum du 27 avril 1969: suicide politique ou nécessité stratégique?', *Revue française science politique* Vol. 20 2, 1970 April, pp. 205–23.

Bouthillon, F., 'Les schèmes qu'on abat', Pt I. *Commentaire* No. 63 1993 Autumn, pp. 467–75. and Pt. II *Commentaire* No. 64 1993–94 Winter, pp. 781–7.

Braud, P., 'Etre le parti du président –délices et maléfices', *Projet* No. 209 1988 January–February, pp. 24–32.

Carothers, T., 'Mitterrand and the Middle East', *The World Today* Vol. 38 10, 1982 October, pp. 381–6.

Chantebout, B., 'La dissuasion nucléaire et le pouvoir présidentiel', *Pouvoirs* 1986 No. 38 pp. 21–32.

Chantebout. B., 'De la cohabitation', in *Pouvoirs* 1989 No. 49 pp. 69–79.

Charlot, J., 'Tactique et stratégie du RPR dans l'opposition', *Pouvoirs* No. 20 1981 pp. 37–44.

Charlot, J., 'Le Président et le parti majoritaire', *Revue politique et parlementaire* No. 1983 July–August, pp. 27–42.

Charlot, J., 'Les mutations du système des partis français', *Pouvoirs* Vol. 49 1989, pp. 27–35.

Bibliography

Charlot, J. and Charlot, M., 'Persuasion et politique: les campagnes de Georges Pompidou et Alain Poher', *Revue française de science politique* Vol. 36 1, 1986 February, 1986 pp. 30–45.

Charlot, M., 'L'Emergence du Front National', *Revue française de science politique* Vol. 36 1, 1986 February, pp. 30–45.

Cohen, S., 'François le gaullien et Mitterrand l'Européen', *L'Histoire* No. 143 1991 April, pp. 30–6.

Cohen, S., 'Diplomatie: le syndrome de la présidence omnisciente', *Esprit* No. 164 1990 September, pp. 55–64.

Cohen, S., 'La politique étrangère entre l'Elysée et Matignon', *Politique Etrangère* 1989 pp. 487–502.

Colliard, J.-C., 'Que peut le président?', *Pouvoirs* No. 68 1994 pp. 15 30.

Criddle, B., 'The French Referendum and the Maastricht Treaty', *Parliamentary Affairs* Vol 46 2, 1993 April, pp. 228–38.

Debbasch, C., 'Président de la République et Premier Ministre dans le système politique de la Ve République. Duel ou Duo?', *Revue de Droit Public et de la Science Administratif* 1982 September–October, pp. 1175–84.

Drain, M., 'La France et la construction européenne', *Rélations Internationales et stratégiques* Vol. 9 1993 Spring, pp. 135–46.

Drefus, F., 'Letter from France. After the Referendum of 20 September', *Government and Opposition* Vol 28 1, 1993 pp. 82–7.

Duhamel, O., 'Sur la monarchie présidentielle', *Le Débat* No. 55 1989 May–August, pp. 23–6.

Duroselle, J.-B., 'General de Gaulle's Europe and Jean Monnet's Europe', *World Today* Vol 22 1966 pp. 1–13.

Eatwell, R., 'Plus ça change?: The French Presidential and National Assembly Elections, April–June 1988', *Political Quarterly* Vol. 59 1988 pp. 462–72.

Elgie, R., 'The French Presidency: Conceptualising Presidential Power in the Fifth Republic', *Public Administration* Vol. 76 2, 1996 summer, pp. 275–91.

Feigenbaum, H.B., 'Recent Evolution of the French executive', *Governance* Vol. 3 3, 1990 pp. 264–78.

Ferry, L., 'Interpréter mai 68', *Pouvoirs* No. 39 1986 pp. 5–14.

Fournier, J., 'Politique gouvernmentale: les trois leviers du Président', *Pouvoirs* No. 41 1987 pp. 63–74.

Georgel, J., 'Le talisman constitutionnel', *Revue Administrative* No. 265 1982 January–February, pp. 89–92.

Georgel, J., 'La pratique institutionnelle de la gauche', *Revue politique et parlementaire* No. 955, 1991 September–October, 1991 pp. 13–21.

Gicquel, J., 'De la cohabitation', *Pouvoirs* No. 49 1989 pp. 69–79.

Goguel, F., 'Les élections législatives des 23 et 30 juin 1968', *Revue française de science politique* Vol. 18 5, 1968 pp. 837–58.

Goldey, D.B., 'The French Presidential Elections of 1st and 15th June 1968', *Parliamentary Affairs* Vol. 21 4, 1968 Autumn, pp. 307–37.

Goldey, D.B., 'The French General Election of 21–28 March 1993', *Electoral Studies* Vol. 12 4, 1993 December, pp. 291–314.

Goldey, D.B., 'The French General Election of 25 May–1 June 1997', *Electoral Studies* Vol. 17 4, 1998 December, pp. 536–55.

Goldey, D.B. and Johnson R.W., 'The French General Election of March 1973', *Political Studies* Vol. 21 3, 1973 September, pp. 321–44.

Goldey, D.B. and Johnson R.W., 'The French General Election of 1978', *Parliamentary Affairs* Vol 31 3, 1978 Summer, pp. 294–313.

Goldey, D.B. and Johnson R.W., 'The French General Election of 16 March 1986', in *Electoral Studies* Vol. 5 3, 1986 December, pp. 229–52.

Goldey, D.B. and Johnson R.W., 'The French Presidential Elections of 24 April–8 May and the General Election of 5–12 June 1988', *Electoral Studies* Vol. 7 3, 1988 December, pp. 195–223.

Goldey, D.B. and Knapp, A., 'Time for a Change: The French Elections of 1981', *Electoral Studies* Vol. 12 4, 1993 August, pp. 291–314.

Grunberg, G., 'Recent Developments in French Electoral Sociology', *Electoral Studies* Vol. 7 1, 1988 April, pp. 3–14.

Hadas-Lebel, R., 'La Ve République et la guerre', *Pouvoirs* No. 58 1991 pp. 5–24.

Harrison, M., 'Mitterrand's France in the Atlantic System', *Political Science Quarterly* Vol. 99 2, 1984 Summer, pp. 219–46.

Hassner, P., 'Vers l'Est du nouveau', No. 1 1989 March–April, pp. 108–16.

Hayward, J. and Wright V., 'Presidential Supremacy and the French General Elections of March 1973', *Parliamentary Affairs* Vol 26 3, 1973 Summer, .

Hayward, J., 'Presidential Suicide by Plebiscite: de Gaulle's Exit, April 1969', *Parliamentary Affairs* Vol. 22 4, 1969 Autumn, pp. 289–319.

Heisbourg, F., 'Défence française: la quadrature du circle', *Politique internationale* Vol. 53 1991 Fall, pp. 257–74.

Hoffmann, S., 'La France dans le nouvel ordre européen', *Politique étranger* 1990 Autumn, pp. 503–12.

Hoffmann, S. and I. 'De Gaulle as Political Artist', *Daedalus* Vol 97 1968 pp. 829–97.

Jacobson, H.K., 'The United Nations and decolonisation', *International Organisation* Vol. 16 1, 1962 Winter, pp. 37–56.

Bibliography

Jaumé, L., 'L'Etat Républicain selon de Gaulle', *Commentaire* No. 51 1990 autumn, pp. 523–32 and part II in *Commentaire* No. 52 1990–91 Winter, pp. 749–55.

Keeler, J.S., 'Executive Power and Policy making Patterns in France', *West European Politics* Vol. 16 4, 1993 October, pp. 518–44.

Lambert, J., 'Breakdown at Brussels', *The World Today* Vol. 19 3, 1963 March, pp. 125–34.

de La Serre, F., 'France: the Impact of François Mitterrand', Chapter 1 in C. Hill ed., *The Actors in Europe's Foreign Policy* London: Routledge, 1996.

de La Serre F. and Moreau-Defarges, P., 'France: a penchant for leadership', in C. Hill ed., *European Political Cooperation and National Foreign Policies* London: Unwin, 1983 pp. 56–71.

Leigh, M., 'Linkage Politics. The French Referendum and the Paris: Summit of 1972', *Journal of Common Market Studies* Vol. 14 1975 December, pp. 157–70.

Lellouche, P., 'France and the Euromissiles: The Limits of Immunity', *Foreign Affairs* Vol. 62 2, 1983–84 Winter, pp. 318–34.

Lewis-Beck, M.R., 'Economics and the French Voter', *Public Opinion Quarterly* 1983 Vol 47 pp. 347–60.

Luchaire, F., 'La Constitution après un quart de siècle', *La Revue Administrative* No. 262 1991 July–April, pp. 301–7.

Maus, D., 'La cohabitation: Deux ou trois choses que je sais d'elle', *Revue Politique et parlementaire* No. 995 1991 September–October, pp. 26–30.

Menon, A., 'France and the IGC of 1996', *Journal of European Public Policy* Vol. 3 2, 1996 pp. 231–52.

Moïsi, D., 'French Foreign Policy: The Challenge of Adaptation', *Foreign Affairs* Vol. 67 1, 1988 Fall, pp. 151–64.

Montricher, N., de 'Decentralisation in France', *Governance* Vol. 8 3, 1995 July, pp. 405–18.

Parodi, J.-L., 'Proportionnalisation périodique, cohabitation, atomisation partisane: un triple défi pour le régime semi-présidentiel de la Cinquième République', *Revue française de science politique* Vol. 3–4, 1997 July–August, pp. 292–311.

Parodi, J.-L., 'La France de la cohabitation. Profil de l'année politique 1986–87,', *Pouvoirs* No. 44 1988 pp. 167–78.

Percheron, A., 'Les Français et l'Europe', *Revue française de science politique* Vol. 41 3, 1991 June, pp. 382–406.

Portelli, H., 'Les conquêtes tranquilles du Premier Ministre', *Projet* No. 202 1986 November–December, pp. 49–59.

Portelli, H., 'Union sacrée', *Pouvoirs* No. 58 1991 pp. 25–32.

Revel, J.-F., 'La résurrection d'une voix. Le de Gaulle de Peyrefitte', *Commentaire* No. 69 1995 Spring, pp. 159–61.

Ridley, F.F., 'The Importance of Constitutions', *Parliamentary Affairs* Vol. XIX 2, 1965 March, pp. 312–23.

Rondos, A., 'Mitterrand's African Policies', *Africa Report* Vol. 27 1, 1982 January–February, pp. 46–50.

Rudney, R., 'Mitterrand's New Atlanticism', *Orbis* Vol. 28 1, 1984 Spring, pp. 83–101.

Soutou, G.-H., 'Le Général de Gaulle, le plan Fouchet et l'Europe', *Commentaire* No. 52 1990–91 Winter, pp. 23–30.

Thibaud, P., 'Un temps de Mémoire?', *Le Débat* No. 96 1996 September–October, pp. 166–83.

Weatherford, S. and Weatherford, M.S., 'The Puzzle of Presidential Leadership', *Governance* Vol. 7 2, 1994 April, pp. 146–59.

Wilson, F.L., 'Gaullism without de Gaulle', *Western Political Quartely* Vol 26 3, 1973 September, pp. 485–506.

Yost, D.S., 'France in the New Europe', *Foreign Affairs* Vol. 69 5, 1990–91 Winter, pp. 107–28.

Yost, D.S., 'Radical Change in French Defence Policy?', *Survival* Vol. 28 1, 1986 January–February, pp. 53–68.

Yost, D.S., 'France and West European Defence Identity', *Survival* Vol. 33 4, 1991 July–August, pp. 327–51.

Index

Index

Index

Index

Index

Index

Index

Index

Index

Index

Index

Index

Index

Index